More praise for

naked economics
by Charles Wheelan

"I recommend this book to anyone who wants to gain an understanding of basic economics with little pain and much pleasure."
—Gary Becker, 1992 Nobel Prize winner in Economics

"I devoured *Naked Economics* whole, start to finish. Finally an economist was speaking my language! Finally I could grasp not only the meanings of all those acronyms I only pretended to understand, but how the institutions and concepts for which they stand might—and do—impact my life. Bravo, Charles Wheelan, for doing the impossible: making the study of economics fascinating, comprehensible, and laugh-out-loud funny."
—Deborah Copaken Kogan, author of *Shutterbabe: Adventures in Love and War*

"From simple supply and demand to the much more frightening subject of monetary policy, this book manages to explain our global economy in a way that is (gasp!) actually entertaining."
—*Book Magazine*

"Translates the arcane and often inscrutable jargon of the professional economist into language accessible to the inquiring but frustrated layman. . . . Clear, concise, informative, [and] witty."
—*Chicago Tribune*

"In just a few easy lessons, . . . Wheelan can teach the most innocent reader to think like an economist."
—*Kirkus Reviews*

Look for

naked statistics

STRIPPING THE DREAD FROM THE DATA

charles wheelan

BEST-SELLING AUTHOR OF *NAKED ECONOMICS*

naked economics

Undressing the Dismal Science

fully revised and updated

CHARLES WHEELAN

Foreword by Burton G. Malkiel

W. W. Norton & Company
New York • London

"Mum's the Word" reprinted with permission. Further reproduction
prohibited. © 1998 The Economist Newspaper Group, Inc.
www.economist.com.

"Two Cheers for Sweatshops," Hearts and Heads," and
"I Love D.C." reprinted with permission of the *New York Times*.

For information about permission to reproduce
selections from this book, write to Permissions,
W. W. Norton & Company, Inc.,
500 Fifth Avenue, New York, NY 10110

For information about special discounts for bulk
purchases, please contact W. W. Norton Special Sales at
specialsales@wwnorton.com or 800-233-4830

Manufacturing by Courier Westford
Book design by BTDnyc
Production manager: Julia Druskin

Library of Congress has catalogued an earlier edition as follows:

Wheelan, Charles J.
Naked economics : undressing the dismal science / Charles Wheelan ;
foreword by Burton G. Malkiel. — Fully rev. and updated.
p. cm.
Includes bibliographical references and index.
ISBN 978-0-393-33764-8 (pbk.)
1. Economics. I. Title.
HB171.W54 2010
330—dc22

                                             2009052148

W. W. Norton & Company, Inc.
500 Fifth Avenue, New York, N.Y. 10110
www.wwnorton.com

W. W. Norton & Company Ltd.
Castle House, 75/76 Wells Street, London W1T 3QT

1 2 3 4 5 6 7 8 9 0

For Leah

Contents

Foreword
by Burton G. Malkiel

I t is widely believed that Scotsman Thomas Carlyle labeled economics the "dismal science" well over one hundred years ago because it seemed boring, uninteresting, unclear, and full of "on the one hand, on the other hand." Indeed, Harry Truman is reported to have said that to avoid ambiguity, he wanted to have "one-armed economists." In fact, Carlyle had something very different in mind. What Carlyle reminded us was that scarcity was pervasive—that we have to make choices between competing satisfactions, between jam today and jam tomorrow, and between conflicting values and goals. Above all, the dour Scot emphasized that everything has a cost and nothing can be produced without work and sacrifice.

To be sure, many people do believe that economics and economists are dismal in the popular sense, that is, extraordinarily dull. As one definition goes: "An economist is someone who is good with numbers but does not have the personality to be an accountant." The tarnished image of economists is in large part earned by their tendency to opaque writing, their use of often inscrutable diagrams, and their excessive use of mathematics. Moreover, they often fail to admit what they don't know.

Why is economics the butt of so many jokes, and why do students often become glassy-eyed when confronted with the study of economics as a discipline? The reasons, I think, are that economists generally do not write well and that most economics texts rely far too much on algebraic manipulation and complex diagrams. Moreover, few economists are able to transmit the considerable excitement of economic analysis or to show its relevance to everyday life. This book by Charles Wheelan changes all that. Wheelan has an anti-Midas touch. If he touched gold he would turn it to life.

This is a truly unique book. It contains no equations, no inaccessible jargon, and no inscrutable diagrams. While equations and diagrams may well be behind many of the ideas in economics, Wheelan shows that they can be reduced to plain English. He boils economics down to its essentials. He demonstrates that the term "lucid economist" is not an oxymoron.

In these pages, we see how many of the criticisms of economists are undeserved. Economic analysis is a hard and complex subject—in many cases far more complex than analysis in the physical sciences. Physics can elegantly explain simple contained systems such as the planets revolving around the sun or electrons in orbit around an atom. But even the physical sciences have difficulty understanding phenomena in nature. Weather forecasting is a case in point. Despite complex satellite observations and intricate weather forecasting models, meteorologists often cannot improve on very naive forecasting models such as "The weather tomorrow will be exactly like it is today." To be sure, the inertia model misses all the turning points but retains an excellent overall record. And when forecasters are asked to make longer-run projections on such subjects as global warming, their range of forecasts makes economic forecasts appear precise by comparison.

Economics is more difficult than the physical sciences because we cannot usually run controlled laboratory experiments and because people do not always behave predictably. A whole new branch of behavioral economics has attracted considerable attention by combining the insights of psychologists and economists, but we still are unable to predict individual behavior with any precision. But that we are far from understanding everything does not mean that we understand nothing. We do know that individual behavior is strongly influenced by incentives. We do know that there are many logical regularities, and we have enjoyed a steady accumulation of knowledge. We do know that every sale involves a purchase and that obvious opportunities for profit are rarely overlooked—the basic idea behind the theory that our securities markets are remarkably efficient.

And as inexact as economic science may be, it has a direct impact on our lives and it has a critical role to play in government policymaking. Economists influence all branches of government. The tasks of promoting economic growth and high employment while avoiding inflation have long been recognized as the domain of government economists. Remember Bill Clinton's most successful campaign slogan during the 1992 election? "It's the economy, stupid!" Promoting competition and restraining monopolies (Justice Department), limiting pollution (Environmental Protection Agency), and providing medical care (Health and Human Services) are examples of major activities within different cabinet departments that have crucially important economic components. Indeed, it is hard to think of any political decisions, be they on social, tax and expenditure, international, agricultural, or national security issues, that do not have economic consequences. And however skeptical politicians may be about the ability of economists to solve these problems, the economists' advice is not ignored. Indeed, as John Maynard Keynes once wrote, "Practical men, who believe themselves to be quite exempt from any intellectual influence, are usually the slaves of some defunct economist. Madmen in authority, who hear voices in the air, are distilling their frenzy from some academic scribbler of a few years back."

The influence of economists is also increasingly pervasive in the business and financial communities. Peter Lynch, the former manager of Fidelity's Magellan mutual fund, once opined that if you spent fourteen minutes talking to an economist you would have wasted twelve minutes. Perhaps it is ironic that the investment performance of professional mutual fund managers is now regularly evaluated based on techniques developed by financial economists. Moreover, economists influence countless other business decisions. They project product demand for companies as diverse as General Motors and Procter & Gamble. They are employed in large numbers by consulting firms engaged in business tasks from strategic planning to inventory control. They help investment firms fashion portfolios of securities by analyzing the trade-offs between expected return and risk. They advise chief financial officers of corporations on dividend policy and on the effect of debt on the price of the firm's common stock. In our financial markets, option traders on the floors of the major options exchanges carry hand-held computers programmed with an economic model to tell them the prices at which they should trade put and call options. The fact is that economic analysis is incredibly useful for investors and producers as well as for government policymakers.

Ordinary consumers will also find that economics can illuminate many perplexing everyday issues. Why is it so hard for individuals to buy health insurance? Why do we stop at McDonald's along a highway even though many other establishments may make better hamburgers? Why do so many people apply to "prestige" colleges even though many other institutions offer just as good an education at far lower prices? Have you ever wondered what such common terms as "adverse selection," "public goods," and "the prisoner's dilemma" have to do with everyday life? These are among the subjects treated in this delightful book.

It's often said that if you ask ten economists the same question you will get ten different answers. But I'll wager that if you asked ten economists why there is a shortage of cabs and apartments in New York City, all ten would tell you that limitations on the number of taxi medallions and rent control are what restrict the supply of these goods and services. There are certainly many areas where economists are in virtual unanimous agreement. Economists overwhelmingly agree that free international trade can improve the standard of living of the trading countries and that tariffs and import quotas reduce general welfare. Economists generally agree that rent controls reduce the volume and quality of housing. Economists were virtually unanimous in their forecast that the horrific tragedy of September 11, 2001, would lead to a contraction of economic activity. My own experience in government suggests that there is far less difference in the views of economists (be they conservative Republicans or liberal Democrats) than there is between economists and those who come from different disciplines. Economists of contrasting political views agree among themselves on most issues. A bipartisan majority of economists is quite likely to unite on the opposite side of a bipartisan coalition of politicians.

The reason, I believe, is that economists have a unique way of viewing the world and thinking about how to solve problems. Thinking like an economist involves chains of deductive reasoning in conjunction with simplified models such as supply and demand. It involves identifying trade-offs in the context of constraints. It measures the cost of one choice in terms of the foregone benefits of another. It involves the goal of efficiency—that is, getting the most out of limited resources. It takes a marginalist or incremental approach. It asks how much extra benefit can be achieved by incurring some extra cost. It recognizes that resources have many diverse uses and that substitutions can be made among different resources to achieve desired results. Finally, the economist has a predilection to believe that welfare is increased by allowing individuals to make their own choices and to argue that competitive markets are a particularly efficient mechanism for giving expression to individual choices. And while all economic problems involve normative issues (views about what should be), thinking like an economist involves an analytical approach that usually abstracts from or at least downplays "value" issues.

This gem of a book is both well balanced and extremely comprehensive. It recognizes the benefits of the free market in making our lives better and shows why centrally controlled economies ultimately fail to increase the living standards of their citizens. At the same time it recognizes the crucial role of government in creating the legal framework that makes markets possible and in providing public goods. It also understands the role of government in correcting situations when the free market creates undesirable externalities such as environmental pollution or where private markets will fail to produce some of the goods the country's citizens desire.

Did you ever wonder why mohair farmers earned a subsidy from the federal government for decades? Wheelan explains how politics and economics can lead to such results. Do you really understand why Ben Bernanke is often referred to as the second most powerful person in the United States? Wheelan demystifies the effect of monetary policy on economic activity. Did you ever consider that you never fully understood the final scene from the movie *Trading Places* when the bad guys were wiped out in the commodities futures market? Wheelan makes the theory of supply and demand completely accessible. Have you ever wondered if the people who protest against globalization have a good point and whether either the developed or developing nations would be better off with less economic integration? Wheelan will make the issues crystal-clear. When you read the newspapers about disputes concerning current economic issues, are you often perplexed and dismayed at the cacophony of competing arguments? Wheelan parses the jargon and pierces the politics to lay bare the essential issues. In so doing, he successfully transforms the dismal science into a lively weaving of economics and politics into the fabric of national discourse and policy.

Wheelan has produced a delightfully readable guide to economic literacy. By boiling economics down to its essentials, he makes the reader a more informed citizen who can better understand the major economic issues of the day. He shows that economics can be explained without graphs, charts, and equations. He demonstrates that economic analysis can be intensely interesting. The book should provide a useful supplement for the college and high school basic course on the economy. More important, it can stand on its own as an introduction to the field that will change the views of those people who have rejected the study of economics as incredibly tedious and terminally boring. I have often considered writing a basic introduction to economics myself, but competing projects always intervened. Had I done so, this is the book I would have wanted to write.

BURTON G. MALKIEL
Princeton, New Jersey
January 2010

Introduction

The scene is strikingly familiar. At a large American university, a graduate student stands at the front of a grand lecture hall drawing graphs and equations on a chalkboard. He may speak proficient English; he may not. The material is dry and mathematical. Come exam time, students may be asked to derive a demand curve or differentiate a total cost function. This is Economics 101.

Students are rarely asked, as they might be, why basic economics made the collapse of the Soviet Union inevitable (allocating resources without a price system is overwhelmingly difficult in the long run), what economic benefit smokers provide for nonsmokers (they die earlier, leaving more Social Security and pension benefits for the rest of us), or why mandating more generous maternity leave benefits may actually be detrimental to women (employers may discriminate against young women when hiring).

Some students will stick with the discipline long enough to appreciate "the big picture." The vast majority will not. Indeed, most bright, intellectually curious college students suffer through Econ 101, are happy to pass, and then wave goodbye to the subject forever. Economics is filed away with calculus and chemistry—rigorous subjects that required a lot of memorization and have little to do with anything that will come later in life. And, of course, a lot of bright students avoid the course in the first place. This is a shame on two levels.

First, many intellectually curious people are missing a subject that is provocative, powerful, and highly relevant to almost every aspect of our lives. Economics offers insight into policy problems ranging from organ donation to affirmative action. The discipline is intuitive at times and delightfully counterintuitive at others. It is peppered with great thinkers. Some, such as Adam Smith and Milton Friedman, have captured mainstream attention. But others, such as Gary Becker and George Akerlof, have not gotten the recognition outside of academe that they deserve. Too many people who would gladly curl up with a book on the Civil War or a biography of Samuel Johnson have been scared away from a subject that should be accessible and fascinating.

Second, many of our brightest citizens are economically illiterate. The media are full of references to the powerful Ben Bernanke, who has played a crucial role in the U.S. government response to the global financial crisis. But how many people can explain what exactly he does? Even many of our political leaders could use a dose of Econ 101. Just about every political debate includes an assertion by one or more candidate that outsourcing and globalization are "stealing" American jobs, leaving us poorer and more likely to be unemployed. International trade, like any kind of market-based competition, does create some losers. But the notion that it makes us collectively worse off is wrong. In fact, those kinds of statements are the economic equivalent of warning that the U.S. Navy is at risk of sailing over the edge of the world. In my lifetime, the guy who made the most colorful assertion along these lines was Ross Perot, a quirky third party candidate in 1992 (when Bill Clinton and George H. W. Bush were running as the mainstream candidates); Perot argued emphatically during the presidential debates that the North American Free Trade Agreement would lead to a "giant sucking sound" as jobs left the United States for Mexico. The phrase was memorable; the economics were wrong. It didn't happen.

The Perot campaign was, as he might have put it, "a dog that didn't hunt." But that does not mean that those world leaders who do get themselves elected have a solid grasp of basic economics. The French government in 2000 undertook a program to tackle chronic double-digit unemployment with a policy that was the economic equivalent of fool's gold. The Socialist-led government lowered the maximum workweek from thirty-nine hours to thirty-five hours; the supposed logic was that if all people with jobs work fewer hours, then there will be work left over for the unemployed to do. The policy did have a certain intuitive appeal; then again, so does using leeches to suck toxins out of the body. Sadly, neither leeches nor a shorter workweek will cause anything but harm in the long run.

The French policy was based on the fallacy that there are a fixed number of jobs in the economy, which must therefore be rationed. It's utter nonsense. The American economy has created millions of new Internet-related jobs over the last three decades—jobs that not only didn't exist in 1980, but that no one could have even imagined—all without the government trying to divvy up work hours.

In 2008, the French government under Nicolas Sarkozy passed legislation allowing companies and workers to negotiate away the thirty-five-hour workweek, in large part because the policy did nothing to fix the unemployment problem. No sane economist ever thought it would—which doesn't necessarily mean that politicians (and the people who elect them) were willing to listen to that advice.

Which is not to say that America doesn't have its own economic issues to deal with. Antiglobalization protesters first took to the streets in Seattle in 1999, smashing windows and overturning cars to protest a meeting of the World Trade Organization. Were the protesters right? Will globalization and burgeoning world trade ruin the environment, exploit workers in the developing world, and put a McDonald's on every corner? Or was *New York Times* columnist Thomas Friedman closer to the mark when he called the protesters "a Noah's ark of flat-earth advocates, protectionist trade unions and yuppies looking for their 1960's fix"?[1]

During the 2008 presidential primaries, Barack Obama criticized the North American Free Trade Agreement, which was negotiated during the presidency of fellow Democrat Bill Clinton. Were Obama's comments good economics, or just good politics (since he happened to be running against Bill Clinton's wife)? After Chapter 12, you can decide.

I offer only one promise in this book: There will be no graphs, no charts, and no equations. These tools have their place in economics. Indeed, mathematics can offer a simple, even elegant way of representing the world—not unlike telling someone that it is seventy-two degrees outside rather than having to describe how warm or cool it feels. But at bottom, the most important ideas in economics are intuitive. They derive their power from bringing logic and rigor to bear on everyday problems. Consider a thought exercise proposed by Glenn Loury, a theoretical economist at Boston University: Suppose that ten job applicants are vying for a single position. Nine of the job candidates are white and one is black. The hiring company has an affirmative action policy stipulating that when minority and nonminority candidates are of equal merit, the minority candidate will be hired.

Further suppose that there are two top candidates; one is white, the other is black. True to policy, the firm hires the black candidate. Loury (who is black) makes this subtle but simple point: Only one of the white candidates has suffered from affirmative action; the other eight wouldn't have gotten the job anyway. *Yet all nine white candidates go away angry, feeling that they have been discriminated against.* Loury is not necessarily a foe of affirmative action. He merely adds nuance to a discussion that usually has none. Affirmative action can harm the very race relations that it seeks to heal.

Or consider the periodic campaign to mandate that insurance companies cover the cost of two nights in the hospital for women who have delivered babies, rather than just one. President Bill Clinton found this issue sufficiently important that he vowed in his 1998 State of the Union address to end "drive-by deliveries." But there is a cost to such a plan that should be made explicit. An extra night in the hospital is not medically necessary in most cases, but it is expensive, which is why new parents don't pay for it themselves and insurance companies don't want to pay for it either. If insurance companies are forced to offer this benefit (or any other new benefit mandated by law), then they will recover their extra costs by raising premiums. And when premiums go up, some people on the margin will no longer be able to afford any health insurance at all. So the real policy question is: Are we willing to pass a law that will make many women more comfortable if it means that a much smaller number of men and women will lose coverage for basic care?

The tradeoff underlying that seemingly narrow question has enormous resonance as America debates health care reform. The more generous a health care system is in the benefits it guarantees, the more it is going to cost. That's true regardless of whether the government is operating the system or not. In fact, the most important question related to health care reform often gets far too little attention: Given the proliferation of fabulously expensive medical technology, some of which produces great results and some of which doesn't, how do we design a system that says "yes" to procedures that justify their cost and "no" to those that don't?

Is economics one big advertisement for the Republican Party? Not exactly. Even Milton Friedman, a Nobel laureate in economics and the most articulate spokesman for free markets, would concede that unfettered markets can lead to deeply flawed outcomes. Consider the American lust for the automobile. The problem is not that we like cars; the problem is that we don't have to pay the full cost of driving them. Yes, we buy the car and then pay for maintenance, insurance, and gasoline. But we don't have to pay for some of the other significant costs of our driving: the emissions we leave behind, the congestion we cause, the wear and tear on public roads, the danger we pose to drivers in smaller cars. The effect is a bit like a night on the town with Dad's credit card: We do a lot of things that we wouldn't do if we had to pay the whole bill. We drive huge cars, we avoid public transportation, we move to far-flung suburbs and then commute long distances.

Individuals don't get the bill for this behavior, but society does—in the form of air pollution, global warming, and urban sprawl. The best way to deal with this growing problem is not the stuff that laissez-faire conservatives usually talk about. It is higher taxes on gasoline and cars. Only with those kinds of measures, as we shall explore in Chapter 3, will the cost of climbing behind the wheel of a car (or a hulking SUV) reflect the real social cost of that activity. Similarly, larger subsidies for public transportation would properly reward those commuters who spare the rest of us by not getting into their cars.

Meanwhile, economists have done some of the most substantive work on social issues like discrimination. Have the world's symphony orchestras historically discriminated against women? Harvard economist Claudia Goldin and Princeton economist Cecilia Rouse came up with a novel way of finding out. In the 1950s, American orchestras began to use "blind" auditions, meaning that the aspiring orchestra member would perform behind screens. Judges did not know the identity or gender of the musician trying out. Did women do better under this blind system than they did when judges knew their gender? Yes, decidedly so. Once the auditions became anonymous, women were roughly 50 percent more likely to make it past the first round and several times more likely to make the final cut.[2]

Economics presents us with a powerful, and not necessarily complex, set of analytical tools that can be used to look back and explain why events unfolded the way they did; to look around and make sense of the world; and to look forward so that we can anticipate the effects of major policy changes. Economics is like gravity: Ignore it and you will be in for some rude surprises.

The demise of the investment bank Lehman Brothers, which declared bankruptcy on September 15, 2008, ushered in "the financial crisis," which deserves its frequent description as the worst economic downturn since the Great Depression. How did it happen? How did so many consumers, who are supposed to have a rational understanding of their own well-being, end up crushed by a housing "bubble"? Who were the knuckleheads who loaned them all that money? Why did Wall Street create things like "CDOs" and credit-default swaps, and why did they prove so devastating to the financial system?

Chapter 2 makes the case that most of the reckless behavior that led to the financial crisis was predictable, given the incentives built into the system. Why did mortgage brokers originate so many reckless loans? *Because it wasn't their money!* They were paid on commission by the banks that made the loans. More mortgages meant more commissions, and bigger mortgages meant bigger commissions.

So why were the banks willing to put so much of their own capital at risk (particularly given the incentives of the mortgage brokers who were bringing them customers)? Because banks typically "sell" most of their mortgage loans, meaning that they get a lump sum of cash now from some third-party investor who gets the stream of future mortgage payments in return. (You may now recognize this situation as an adult version of "hot potato"; it doesn't matter how bad a loan is as long as you can pass it on to someone else before the borrower defaults.)

Okay, then who would buy these loans? That's what Chapter 2 explains. I'll give you one clue now: Wall Street gets involved and it doesn't end well.

Having written all that, I must admit that there is some soul searching going on in the economics profession. As obvious as the financial crisis seems after the fact, few economists saw it coming (with some notable exceptions). Virtually none anticipated how severe it might be. In the fall of 2005, several prominent economists wrote in a prestigious journal, "As of the end of 2004, our analysis reveals little evidence of a housing bubble."[3]

Wrong. Actually the article was worse than wrong, because it was written explicitly to refute the signs of a bubble that had become obvious to many laypeople—which is kind of like the fire department showing up at a house with smoke wafting from the roof and declaring, "No, that's not a fire," only to have flames start leaping from the attic twenty minutes later. There was a bubble. And it can be explained best by incorporating psychology into economics, namely the tendency of individuals to believe that whatever is happening now is what's most likely to happen in the future.

Economics is evolving, like every discipline. One of the most interesting and productive areas of inquiry is the field of behavioral economics, which explores how individuals make decisions—sometimes in ways that aren't as rational as economists have traditionally theorized. We humans underestimate some risks (obesity) and overestimate others (flying); we let emotion cloud our judgment; we overreact to both good news and bad news (rising home prices and then falling home prices).

Most of this was obvious to Shakespeare, but it's relatively new to mainstream economics. As *New York Times* columnist David Brooks noted, "Economic behavior can be accurately predicted through elegant models. This view explains a lot, but not the current financial crisis—how so many people could be so stupid, incompetent and self-destructive all at once. The crisis has delivered a blow to classical economics and taken a body of psychological work that was at the edge of public policy thought and brought it to front and center."[4]

Of course, most of the old ideas are still pretty darn important. Federal Reserve chairman Ben Bernanke was a scholar of the Great Depression before leaving academe, a fact that has had implications far beyond the Ivory Tower. Chapter 10 will make the case that Bernanke's creative and aggressive interventions at the Federal Reserve, many of which were inspired by what went wrong in the 1930s, prevented a bad situation from getting much, much worse.

This book walks through some of the most powerful concepts in economics while simplifying the building blocks or skipping them entirely. Each chapter covers subjects that could be made into an entire book. Indeed, there are minor points in every chapter that have launched and sustained entire academic careers. I have glossed over or skipped much of the technical structure that forms the backbone of the discipline. And that is exactly the point: One need not know where to place a load-bearing wall in order to appreciate the genius of Frank Lloyd Wright. This book is not economics for dummies; it is economics for smart people who never studied economics (or have only a vague recollection of doing so). Most of the great ideas in economics are intuitive when the dressings of complexity are peeled away. *That is naked economics.*

Economics should not be accessible only to the experts. The ideas are too important and too interesting. Indeed, naked economics can even be fun.

Acknowledgments

Many waves of people have helped to bring this project to fruition, almost like a relay race with fresh legs pushing me toward the finish line at every stage. In the beginning, Tifanny Richards was a strong believer that there would be a market for an accessible book on economics. Her wonderful encouragement moved this book off the starting line. Tabitha Griffin brought the project to W. W. Norton, something for which I will always be grateful.

Then came the second leg. When Tifanny and Tabitha went on to other opportunities, I was fortunate to end up in excellent hands once again. Tina Bennett is everything that one could hope for in an agent: smart, supportive, and always interested in new ideas. Meanwhile, I was lucky to have Drake McFeely take on the task of editing the book. Who knows how the man can find time to run the company, edit books, and cavort with Nobel Prize winners, but he does and I am a beneficiary of his experience and judgment. Of course, Eve Lazovitz is the one who made Drake's trains run on time for the first edition, albeit with a delicate touch. Jeff Shreve was a kind but stern taskmaster for the second edition. Without their support (and deadlines), this book would still be an unfinished manuscript scrawled on legal pads.

Mary Ellen Moore and Danielle Kutasov offered excellent research assistance, finding the facts, figures, and anecdotes that had eluded me. Three accomplished economists were kind enough to take time from their busy schedules to read the first edition manuscript and make helpful comments: Burton Malkiel, Robert Willis, and Kenneth Rogoff. These three men are giants of the profession, and each had many other things that they might have done with their time. Robert Johnson was kind enough to read the international economics chapter that has been added to the second edition. I appreciate his willingness to share his expertise on the topic.

I owe a debt to my former editors at *The Economist*. John Micklethwait was generous in allowing me to disappear for a stretch while I finished the first edition of this book and was also willing to read and make comments on the finished product. I owe Ann Wroe credit for her clever subtitle. The fact that both John and Ann find time to edit one of the world's great publications while also raising families and writing books of their own continues to be an inspiration.

More recently, the Harris School of Public Policy at the University of Chicago and Dartmouth College have both offered me an intellectual "home" where I have the privilege of teaching great students and working on projects like this one. At the Harris School, former Dean Susan Mayer was a particularly enthusiastic supporter of my ongoing quest to make important academic ideas more accessible to the lay public. At Dartmouth, Bruce Sacerdote has been both a terrific intellectual companion and a great water-ski buddy.

I also owe a different kind of debt. The vast majority of ideas I describe in this book are not my own. Rather, I am a translator whose work derives its value from the brilliance of the original, which in this case is centuries of work done by great thinkers. I hope this book reflects my enormous respect for that work.

Last, I would like to acknowledge those who inspired my interest in the subjects that make up this book. I've made the case that economics is often poorly taught. That is true. But it's also true that the discipline can come alive in the hands of the right person, and I was fortunate to work and study with many of them: Gary Becker, Bob Willis, Ken Rogoff, Robert Willig, Christina Paxson, Duncan Snidal, Alan Krueger, Paul Portney, Sam Peltzman, Don Coursey, Paul Volcker. My hope is that this book will help to transmit their knowledge and enthusiasm to many new readers and students.

naked economics

CHAPTER 1

The Power of Markets:

Who feeds Paris?

n 1989, as the Berlin Wall was toppling, Douglas Ivester, head of Coca-Cola Europe (and later CEO), made a snap decision. He sent his sales force to Berlin and told them to start passing out Coke. Free. In some cases, the Coca-Cola representatives were literally passing bottles of soda through holes in the Wall. He recalls walking around Alexanderplatz in East Berlin at the time of the upheaval, trying to gauge whether there was any recognition of the Coke brand. "Everywhere we went, we asked people what they were drinking, and whether they liked Coca-Cola. But we didn't even have to say the name! We just shaped our hands like the bottle, and people understood. We decided we would move as much Coca-Cola as we could, as fast as we could—even before we knew how we would get paid."[1]

Coca-Cola quickly set up business in East Germany, giving free coolers to merchants who began to stock the "real thing." It was a money-losing proposition in the short run; the East German currency was still worthless—scraps of paper to the rest of the world. But it was a brilliant business decision made faster than any government body could ever hope to act. By 1995, per capita consumption of Coca-Cola in the former East Germany had risen to the level in West Germany, which was already a strong market.

In a sense, it was Adam Smith's invisible hand passing Coca-Cola through the Berlin Wall. Coke representatives weren't undertaking any great humanitarian gesture as they passed beverages to the newly liberated East Germans. Nor were they making a bold statement about the future of communism. They were looking after business—expanding their global market, boosting profits, and making shareholders happy. And that is the punch line of capitalism: The market aligns incentives in such a way that individuals working for their own best interest—passing out Coca-Cola, spending years in graduate school, planting a field of soybeans, designing a radio that will work in the shower—leads to a thriving and ever-improving standard of living for most (though not all) members of society.

Economists sometimes ask, "Who feeds Paris?"—a rhetorical way of drawing attention to the mind-numbing array of things happening every moment of every day to make a modern economy work. Somehow the right amount of fresh tuna makes its way from a fishing fleet in the South Pacific to a restaurant on the Rue de Rivoli. A neighborhood fruit vendor has exactly what his customers want every morning—from coffee to fresh papayas—even though those products may come from ten or fifteen different countries. In short, a complex economy involves billions of transactions every day, the vast majority of which happen without any direct government involvement. And it is not just that things get done; our lives grow steadily better in the process. It is remarkable enough that we can now shop for a television twenty-four hours a day from the comfort of our own homes; it is equally amazing that in 1971 a twenty-five-inch color television set cost an average worker 174 hours of wages. Today, a twenty-five-inch color television set—one that is more dependable, gets more channels, and has better reception—costs the average worker about twenty-three hours of pay.

If you think that a better, cheaper television set is not the best measure of social progress (a reasonable point, I concede), then perhaps you will be moved by the fact that, during the twentieth century, American life expectancy climbed from forty-seven years to seventy-seven, infant mortality plunged by 93 percent, and we wiped out or gained control over diseases such as polio, tuberculosis, typhoid, and whooping cough.[2]

Our market economy deserves a lot of the credit for that progress. There is an old Cold War story about a Soviet official who visits an American pharmacy. The brightly lit aisles are lined with thousands of remedies for every problem from bad breath to toe fungus. "Very impressive," he says. "But how can you make sure that every store stocks all of these items?" The anecdote is interesting because it betrays a total lack of understanding of how a market economy works. In America, there is no central authority that tells stores what items to stock, as there was in the Soviet Union. Stores sell the products that people want to buy, and, in turn, companies produce items that stores want to stock. The Soviet economy failed in large part because government bureaucrats directed everything, from the number of bars of soap produced by a factory in Irktusk to the number of university students studying electrical engineering in Moscow. In the end, the task proved overwhelming.

Of course, those of us accustomed to market economies have an equally poor understanding of communist central planning. I was once part of an Illinois delegation visiting Cuba. Because the visit was licensed by the U.S. government, each member of the delegation was allowed to bring back $100 worth of Cuban merchandise, including cigars. Having been raised in the era of discount stores, we all set out looking for the best price on Cohibas so that we could get the most bang for our $100 allowance. After several fruitless hours, we discovered the whole point of communism: The price of cigars was the same everywhere. There is no competition between stores because there is no profit as we know it. Every store sells cigars—and everything else for that matter—at whatever price Fidel Castro (or his brother Raul) tells them to. And every shopkeeper selling cigars is paid the government wage for selling cigars, which is unrelated to how many cigars he or she sells.

Gary Becker, a University of Chicago economist who won the Nobel Prize in 1992, has noted (borrowing from George Bernard Shaw) that "economy is the art of making the most of life." Economics is the study of how we do that. There is a finite supply of everything worth having: oil, coconut milk, perfect bodies, clean water, people who can fix jammed photocopy machines, etc. How do we allocate these things? Why is it that Bill Gates owns a private jet and you don't? He is rich, you might answer. But why is he rich? Why does he have a larger claim on the world's finite resources than everyone else? At the same time, how is it possible in a country as rich as the United States—a place where Alex Rodriguez can be paid $275 million to play baseball—that one in five children is poor or that some adults are forced to rummage through garbage cans for food? Near my home in Chicago, the Three Dog Bakery sells cakes and pastries *only for dogs.* Wealthy professionals pay $16 for birthday cakes for their pets. Meanwhile, the Chicago Coalition for the Homeless estimates that fifteen thousand people are homeless on any given night in that same city.

These kinds of disparities grow even more pronounced as we look beyond the borders of the United States. Three-quarters of the people in Chad have no access to clean drinking water, let alone pastries for their pets. The World Bank estimates that half of the world's population survives on less than $2 a day. How does it all work—or, in some cases, not work?

Economics starts with one very important assumption: Individuals act to make themselves as well off as possible. To use the jargon of the profession, individuals seek to maximize their own utility, which is a similar concept to happiness, only broader. I derive utility from getting a typhoid immunization and paying taxes. Neither of these things makes me particularly happy, but they do keep me from dying of typhoid or going to jail. That, in the long run, makes me better off. Economists don't particularly care what gives us utility; they simply accept that each of us has his or her own "preferences." I like coffee, old houses, classic films, dogs, bicycling, and many other things. Everyone else in the world has preferences, which may or may not have anything in common with mine.

Indeed, this seemingly simple observation that different individuals have different preferences is sometimes lost on otherwise sophisticated policymakers. For example, rich people have different preferences than poor people do. Similarly, our individual preferences may change over the course of our life cycle as we (we hope) grow wealthier. The phrase "luxury good" actually has a technical meaning to economists; it is a good that we buy in increasing quantities as we grow richer—things like sports cars and French wines. Less obviously, concern for the environment is a luxury good. Wealthy Americans are willing to spend more money to protect the environment *as a fraction of their incomes* than are less wealthy Americans. The same relationship holds true across countries; wealthy nations devote a greater share of their resources to protecting the environment than do poor countries. The reason is simple enough: We care about the fate of the Bengal tiger *because we can*. We have homes and jobs and clean water and birthday cakes for our dogs.

Here is a nettlesome policy question: Is it fair for those of us who live comfortably to impose our preferences on individuals in the developing world? Economists argue that it is not, though we do it all the time. When I read a story in the Sunday *New York Times* about South American villagers cutting down virgin rain forest and destroying rare ecosystems, I nearly knock over my Starbucks latte in surprise and disgust. But I am not they. My children are not starving or at risk of dying from malaria. If they were, and if chopping down a valuable wildlife habitat enabled me to afford to feed my family and buy a mosquito net, then I would sharpen my ax and start chopping. I wouldn't care how many butterflies or spotted weasels I killed. This is not to suggest that the environment in the developing world does not matter. It does. In fact, there are many examples of environmental degradation that will make poor countries even poorer in the long run. Cutting down those forests is bad for the rest of us, too, since deforestation is a major contributor to rising CO_2 emissions. (Economists often argue that rich countries ought to pay poor countries to protect natural resources that have global value.)

Obviously if the developed world were more generous, then Brazilian villagers might not have to decide between destroying the rain forest and buying mosquito nets. For now, the point is more basic: It is simply bad economics to impose our preferences on individuals whose lives are much, much different. This will be an important point later in the book when we turn to globalization and world trade.

Let me make one other important point regarding our individual preferences: Maximizing utility is not synonymous with acting self-ishly. In 1999, the *New York Times* published the obituary of Oseola McCarty, a woman who died at the age of ninety-one after spending her life working as a laundress in Hattiesburg, Mississippi. She had lived alone in a small, sparsely furnished house with a black-and-white television that received only one channel. What made Ms. McCarty exceptional is that she was by no means poor. In fact, four years before her death she gave away $150,000 to the University of Southern Mississippi—a school that she had never attended—to endow a schol-arship for poor students.

Does Oseola McCarty's behavior turn the field of economics on its head? Are Nobel Prizes being recalled to Stockholm? No. She simply derived more utility from saving her money and eventually giving it away than she would have from spending it on a big-screen TV or a fancy apartment.

Okay, but that was just money. How about Wesley Autrey, a fifty-year-old construction worker in New York City. He was waiting for the subway in Upper Manhattan with his two young daughters in January 2007 when a stranger nearby began having convulsions and then fell on the train tracks. If this wasn't bad enough, the Number 1 train was already visible as it approached the station.

Mr. Autrey jumped on the tracks and shielded the man as five train cars rolled over both of them, close enough that the train left a smudge of grease on Mr. Autrey's hat. When the train came to a stop, he yelled from underneath, "We're O.K. down here, but I've got two daughters up there. Let them know their father's O.K."[3] This was all to help a complete stranger.

We all routinely make altruistic decisions, albeit usually on a smaller scale. We may pay a few cents extra for dolphin-safe tuna, or send money to a favorite charity, or volunteer to serve in the armed forces. All of these things can give us utility; none would be considered selfish. Americans give more than $200 billion to assorted charities every year. We hold doors open for strangers. We practice remarkable acts of bravery and generosity. None of this is incompatible with the basic assumption that individuals seek to make themselves as well off as possible, however they happen to define that. Nor does this assumption imply that we always make perfect—or even good—decisions. We don't. But each of us does try to make the best possible decision given whatever information is available at the time.

So, after only a few pages, we have an answer to a profound, age-old philosophical question: Why did the chicken cross the road? Because it maximized his utility.

Bear in mind that maximizing utility is no simple proposition. Life is complex and uncertain. There are an infinite number of things that we could be doing at any time. Indeed, every decision that we make involves some kind of trade-off. We may trade off utility now against utility in the future. For example, you may derive some satisfaction from whacking your boss on the head with a canoe paddle at the annual company picnic. But that momentary burst of utility would presumably be more than offset by the disutility of spending many years in a federal prison. (But those are just my preferences.) More seriously, many of our important decisions involve balancing the value of consumption now against consumption in the future. We may spend years in graduate school eating ramen noodles because it dramatically boosts our standard of living later in life. Or, conversely, we may use a credit card to purchase a big-screen television today even though the interest on that credit card debt will lessen the amount that we can consume in the future.

Similarly, we balance work and leisure. Grinding away ninety hours a week as an investment banker will generate a lot of income, but it will also leave less time to enjoy the goods that can be purchased with that income. My younger brother began his career as a management consultant with a salary that had at least one more digit than mine has now. On the other hand, he worked long and sometimes inflexible hours. One fall we both excitedly signed up for an evening film class taught by Roger Ebert. My brother proceeded to miss *every single class for thirteen weeks.*

However large our paychecks, we can spend them on a staggering array of goods and services. When you bought this book, you implicitly decided not to spend that money somewhere else. (Even if you shoplifted the book, you could have stuffed a Stephen King novel in your jacket instead, which is flattering in its own kind of way.) Meanwhile, time is one of our most scarce resources. At the moment, you are reading instead of working, playing with the dog, applying to law school, shopping for groceries, or having sex. Life is about trade-offs, and so is economics.

In short, getting out of bed in the morning and making breakfast involves more complex decisions than the average game of chess. (Will that fried egg kill me in twenty-eight years?) How do we manage? The answer is that each of us implicitly weighs the costs and benefits of everything he or she does. An economist would say that we attempt to maximize utility given the resources at our disposal; my dad would say that we try to get the most bang for our buck. Bear in mind that the things that give us utility do not have to be material goods. If you are comparing two jobs—teaching junior high school math or marketing Camel cigarettes—the latter job would almost certainly pay more while the former job would offer greater "psychic benefits," which is a fancy way of saying that at the end of the day you would feel better about what you do. That is a perfectly legitimate benefit to be compared against the cost of a smaller paycheck. In the end, some people choose to teach math and some people choose to market cigarettes.

Similarly, the concept of cost is far richer (pardon the pun) than the dollars and cents you hand over at the cash register. The real cost of something is what you must give up in order to get it, which is almost always more than just cash. There is nothing "free" about concert tickets if you have to stand in line in the rain for six hours to get them. Taking the bus for $1.50 may not be cheaper than taking a taxi for $7 if you are running late for a meeting with a peevish client who will pull a $50,000 account if you keep her waiting. Shopping at a discount store saves money but it usually costs time. I am a writer; I get paid based on what I produce. I could drive ninety miles to shop at an outlet in Kenosha, Wisconsin, to save $50 on a new pair of dress shoes. Or I could walk into Nordstrom on Michigan Avenue and buy the shoes while I am out for lunch. I generally choose the latter; the total cost is $225, fifteen minutes of my time, and some hectoring from my mother, who will invariably ask, "Why didn't you drive to Kenosha?"

Every aspect of human behavior reacts to cost in some way. When the cost of something falls, it becomes more attractive to us. You can learn that by deriving a demand curve, or you can learn it by shopping the day after Christmas, when people snap up things that they weren't willing to buy for a higher price several days earlier. Conversely, when the cost of something goes up, we use less of it. This is true of everything in life, even cigarettes and crack cocaine. Economists have calculated that a 10 percent decrease in the street price of cocaine eventually causes the number of adult cocaine users to grow by about 10 percent. Similarly, researchers estimated that the first proposed settlement between the tobacco industry and the states (rejected by the U.S. Senate in 1998) would have raised the price of a pack of cigarettes by 34 percent. In turn, that increase would have reduced the number of teenage smokers by a quarter, leading to 1.3 million fewer smoking-related premature deaths among the generation of Americans seventeen or younger at the time.[4] Of course, society has already raised the cost of smoking in ways that have nothing to do with the price of a pack of cigarettes. Standing outside an office building when it is seventeen degrees outside is now part of the cost of smoking at work.

This broad view of cost can explain some very important social phenomena, one of which is the plummeting birth rate in the developed world. Having a child is more expensive than it was fifty years ago. This is not because it is more expensive to feed and clothe another little urchin around the house. If anything, those kinds of costs have gone down, because we have become far more productive at making basic consumer goods like food and clothing. Rather, the primary cost of raising a child today is the cost of the earnings forgone when a parent, still usually the mother, quits or cuts back on work to look after the child at home. Because women have better professional opportunities than ever before, it has grown more costly for them to leave the workforce. My neighbor was a neurologist until her second child was born, at which point she decided to stay home. *It's expensive to quit being a neurologist.*

Meanwhile, most of the economic benefits of having a large family have disappeared in the developed world. Young children no longer help out on the farm or provide extra income for the family (though they can be taught at a young age to fetch a beer from the refrigerator). We no longer need to have many children in order to ensure that some of them live through childhood or that we have enough dependents to provide for us in retirement. Even the most dour of economists would concede that we derive great pleasure from having children. The point is that it is now more expensive to have eleven of them than it used to be. The data speak to that point: The average American woman had 3.77 children in 1905; she now has 2.07—a 45 percent drop.[5]

There is a second powerful assumption underpinning all of economics: Firms—which can be anything from one guy selling hot dogs to a multinational corporation—attempt to maximize profits (the revenue earned by selling stuff minus the cost of producing it). In short, firms try to make as much money as possible. Hence, we have an answer to another of life's burning questions: Why did the entrepreneur cross the road? Because he could make more money on the other side.

Firms take inputs—land, steel, knowledge, baseball stadiums, etc.—and combine them in a way that adds value. That process can be as simple as selling cheap umbrellas on a busy corner in New York City when it starts to rain (where do those guys come from?) or as complex as assembling Boeing's 787 Dreamliner (a passenger jet that required 800,000 hours on Cray supercomputers just to design). A profitable firm is like a chef who brings home $30 worth of groceries and creates an $80 meal. She has used her talents to create something that is worth far more than the cost of the inputs. That is not always an easy thing to do. Firms must decide what to produce, how and where to produce it, how much to produce, and at what price to sell what they produce—all in the face of the same kinds of uncertainties that consumers deal with.

How? These are massively complex decisions. One powerful feature of a market economy is that it directs resources to their most productive use. Why doesn't Brad Pitt sell automobile insurance? Because it would be an enormous waste of his unique talents. Yes, he is a charismatic guy who could probably sell more insurance policies than the average salesman. But he is also one of a handful of people in the world who can "open" a movie, meaning that millions of people around the world will go to see a film just because Brad Pitt is in it. That is money in the bank in the risky Hollywood movie business, so studios are willing to pay handsomely to put Brad Pitt in a starring role—about $30 million a film. Insurance agencies would also be willing to pay for the Pitt charisma—but more like $30,000. Brad Pitt will go where he is paid the most. And he will be paid the most in Hollywood because that is where he can add the most value.

Prices are like giant neon billboards that flash important information. At the beginning of the chapter, we asked how a restaurant on the Rue de Rivoli in Paris has just the right amount of tuna on most nights. It is all about prices. When patrons start ordering more of the sashimi appetizer, the restaurateur places a larger order with his fish wholesaler. If tuna is growing more popular at other restaurants, too, then the wholesale price will go up, meaning that fishermen some-where in the Pacific will get paid more for their tuna catch than they used to. Some fishermen, recognizing that tuna now commands a premium over other kinds of fish, will start fishing for tuna instead of salmon. Meanwhile, some tuna fishermen will keep their boats in the water longer or switch to more expensive fishing methods that can now be justified by the higher price their catch will fetch. These guys don't care about upscale diners in Paris. They care about the wholesale price of fish.

Money talks. Why are the pharmaceutical companies scouring the rain forests looking for plants with rare healing properties? Because the blockbuster drugs they may uncover earn staggering amounts of money. Other kinds of entrepreneurial activity take place on a smaller scale but are equally impressive in their own way. For several summers I coached a Little League baseball team near Cabrini Green, which is one of Chicago's rougher neighborhoods. One of our team customs was to go out periodically for pizza, and one of our favorite spots was Chester's, a small shack at the corner of Division and Sedgwick that was a testimony to the resiliency and resourcefulness of entrepre-neurs. (It has since been demolished to make way for a new park as part of an aggressive development of Cabrini Green.) Chester's made decent pizza and was always busy. Thus, it was basically an armed robbery waiting to happen. But that did not deter the management at Chester's. They merely installed the same kind of bulletproof glass that one would find at the drive-up window of a bank. The custom-ers placed their money on a small carousel, which was then rotated through a gap in the bulletproof glass. The pizza came out the other direction on the same carousel.

Profit opportunities attract firms like sharks to blood, even when bulletproof glass is required. We look for bold new ways to make money (creating the first reality TV show); failing that, we look to get into a business that is making huge profits for someone else (thereby creating the next twenty increasingly pathetic reality TV shows). All the while, we are using prices to gauge what consumers want. Of course, not every market is easy to enter. When LeBron James signed a three-year $60 million contract with the Cleveland Cavaliers, I thought to myself, "I need to play basketball for the Cleveland Cavaliers." I would have gladly played for $58 million, or, if pressed, for $58,000. Several things precluded me from entering that market, however: (1) I'm five-ten; (2) I'm slow; and (3) when shooting under pressure, I have a tendency to miss the backboard. Why is LeBron James paid $20 million a year? Because nobody else can play like him. His unique talents create a barrier to entry for the rest of us. LeBron James is also the beneficiary of what University of Chicago labor economist Sherwin Rosen dubbed the "superstar" phenomenon. Small differences in talent tend to become magnified into huge differentials in pay as a market becomes very large, such as the audience for professional basketball. One need only be slightly better than the competition in order to gain a large (and profitable) share of that market.

In fact, LeBron's salary is chump change compared to what talk-show host Rush Limbaugh is now paid. He recently signed an eight-year $400 million contract with Clear Channel Communications, the company that syndicates his radio program around the country. Is Rush that much better than other political windbags willing to offer their opinions? He doesn't have to be. He need only be a tiny bit more interesting than the next best radio option at that time of day in order to attract a huge audience—20 million listeners daily. Nobody tunes into their second-favorite radio station, so it's winner-take-all when it comes to listeners and the advertisers willing to pay big bucks to reach them.

Many markets have barriers that prevent new firms from entering, no matter how profitable making widgets may be. Sometimes there are physical or natural barriers. Truffles cost $500 a pound because they cannot be cultivated; they grow only in the wild and must be dug up by truffle-hunting pigs or dogs. Sometimes there are legal barriers to entry. Don't try to sell sildenafil citrate on a street corner or you may end up in jail. This is not a drug that you snort or shoot up, nor is it illegal. It happens to be Viagra, and Pfizer holds the patent, which is a legal monopoly granted by the U.S. government. Economists may quibble over how long a patent should last or what kinds of innovations should be patentable, but most would agree that the entry barrier created by a patent is an important incentive for firms to make the kinds of investments that lead to new products. The political process creates entry barriers for dubious reasons, too. When the U.S. auto industry was facing intense competition from Japanese automakers in the 1980s, the American car companies had two basic options: (1) They could create better, cheaper, more fuel-efficient cars that consumers might want to buy; or (2) they could invest heavily in lobbyists who would persuade Congress to enact tariffs and quotas that would keep Japanese cars out of the market.

Some entry barriers are more subtle. The airline industry is far less competitive than it appears to be. You and some college friends could start a new airline relatively easily; the problem is that you wouldn't be able to land your planes anywhere. There are a limited number of gate spaces available at most airports, and they tend to be controlled by the big guys. At Chicago's O'Hare Airport, one of the world's biggest and busiest airports, American and United control some 80 percent of all the gates.[6] Or consider a different kind of entry barrier that has become highly relevant in the Internet age: network effects. The basic idea of a network effect is that the value of some goods rises with the number of other people using them. I don't think Microsoft Word is particularly impressive software, but I own it anyway because I spend my days e-mailing documents to people who do like Word (or at least they use it). It would be very difficult to introduce a rival word-processing package—no matter how good the features or how low the price—as long as most of the world is using Word.

Meanwhile, firms are not just choosing what goods or services to produce but also how to produce them. I will never forget stepping off a plane in Kathmandu; the first thing I saw was a team of men squatting on their haunches as they cut the airport grass by hand with sickles. Labor is cheap in Nepal; lawn mowers are very expensive. The opposite is true in the United States, which is why we don't see many teams of laborers using sickles. It is also why we have ATMs and self-service gas stations and those terribly annoying phone trees ("If you are now frustrated to the point of violence, please press the pound key"). All are cases where firms have automated jobs that used to be done by living beings. After all, one way to raise profits is by lowering the cost of production. That may mean laying off twenty thousand workers or building a plant in Vietnam instead of Colorado.

Firms, like consumers, face a staggering array of complex choices. Again, the guiding principle is relatively simple: What is going to make the firm the most money in the long run?

All of which brings us to the point where producers meet consumers. How much are you going to pay for that doggie in the window? Introductory economics has a very simple answer: the market price. This is that whole supply and demand thing. The price will settle at the point where the number of dogs for sale exactly matches the number of dogs that consumers want to buy. If there are more potential pet owners than dogs available, then the price of dogs will go up. Some consumers will then decide to buy ferrets instead, and some pet shops will be induced by the prospect of higher profits to offer more dogs for sale. Eventually the supply of dogs will match the demand. Remarkably, some markets actually work this way. If I choose to sell a hundred shares of Microsoft on the NASDAQ, I have no choice but to accept the "market price," which is simply the price at which the number of Microsoft shares for sale on the exchange exactly equals the number of shares that buyers would like to purchase.

Most markets do not look quite so much like the textbooks. There is not a "market price" for Gap sweatshirts that changes by the minute depending on the supply and demand of reasonably priced outerwear. Instead, the Gap, like most other firms, has some degree of market power, which means very simply that the Gap has some control over what it can charge. The Gap could sell sweatshirts for $9.99, eking out a razor-thin profit on each. Or it could sell far fewer sweatshirts for $29.99, but make a hefty profit on each. If you were in the mood to do calculus at the moment, or I had any interest in writing about it, then we would find the profit-maximizing price right now. I'm pretty sure I had to do it on a final exam once. The basic point is that the Gap will attempt to pick a price that leads to the quantity of sales that earn the company the most money. The marketing executives may err either way: They may underprice the items, in which case they will sell out; or they may overprice the items, in which case they will have a warehouse full of sweatshirts.

Actually, there is another option. A firm can attempt to sell the same item to different people at different prices. (The fancy name is "price discrimination.") The next time you are on an airplane, try this experiment: Ask the person next to you how much he or she paid for the ticket. It's probably not what you paid; it may not even be close. You are sitting on the same plane, traveling to the same destination, eating the same peanuts—yet the prices you and your row mate paid for your tickets may not even have the same number of digits.

The basic challenge for the airline industry is to separate business travelers, who are willing to pay a great deal for a ticket, from pleasure travelers, who are on tighter budgets. If an airline sells every ticket at the same price, the company will leave money on the table no matter what price it chooses. A business traveler may be willing to pay $1,800 to fly round trip from Chicago to San Francisco; someone flying to cousin Irv's wedding will shell out no more than $250. If the airline charges the high fare, it will lose all of its pleasure travelers. If it charges the low fare, it will lose all the profits that business travelers would have been willing to pay. What to do? Learn to distinguish business travelers from pleasure travelers and then charge each of them a different fare.

The airlines are pretty good at this. Why will your fare drop sharply if you stay over a Saturday night? Because Saturday night is when you are going to be dancing at cousin Irv's wedding. Pleasure travelers usually spend the weekend at their destination, while business travelers almost never do. Buying the ticket two weeks ahead of time will be much, much cheaper than buying it eleven minutes before the flight leaves. Vacationers plan ahead while business travelers tend to buy tickets at the last minute. Airlines are the most obvious example of price discrimination, but look around and you will start to see it everywhere. Al Gore complained during the 2000 presidential campaign that his mother and his dog were taking the same arthritis medication but that his mother paid much more for her prescription. Never mind that he made up the story after reading about the pricing disparity between humans and canines. The example is still perfect. There is nothing surprising about the fact that the same medicine will be sold to dogs and people at different prices. It's airline seats all over again. People will pay more for their own medicine than they will for their pet's. So the profit-maximizing strategy is to charge one price for patients with two legs and another price for patients with four.

Price discrimination will become even more prevalent as technology enables firms to gather more information about their customers. It is now possible, for example, to charge different prices to customers ordering on-line rather than over the phone. Or, a firm can charge different prices to different on-line customers depending on the pattern of their past purchases. The logic behind firms like Priceline (a website where consumers bid for travel services) is that every customer could conceivably pay a different price for an airline ticket or hotel room. In an article entitled "How Technology Tailors Price Tags," the *Wall Street Journal* noted, "Grocery stores appear to be the model of one price for all. But even today, they post one price, charge another to shoppers willing to clip coupons and a third to those with frequent-shopper cards that allow stores to collect detailed data on buying habits."[7]

What can we infer from all of this? Consumers try to make themselves as well off as possible and firms try to maximize profits. Those are seemingly simple concepts, yet they can tell us a tremendous amount about how the world works.

The market economy is a powerful force for making our lives better. The only way firms can make profits is by delivering goods that we want to buy. They create new products—everything from thermal coffee mugs to lifesaving antibiotics. Or they take an existing product and make it cheaper or better. This kind of competition is fabulously good for consumers. In 1900, a three-minute phone call from New York to Chicago cost $5.45, the equivalent of about $140 today. Now the same call is essentially free if you have a mobile phone with unlimited minutes. Profit inspires some of our greatest work, even in areas like higher education, the arts, and medicine. How many world leaders fly to North Korea when they need open-heart surgery?

At the same time, the market is amoral. Not immoral, simply amoral. The market rewards scarcity, which has no inherent relation to value. Diamonds are worth thousands of dollars a carat while water (if you are bold enough to drink it out of the tap) is nearly free. If there were no diamonds on the planet, we would be inconvenienced; if all the water disappeared, we would be dead. The market does not provide goods that we need; it provides goods that *we want to buy*. This is a crucial distinction. Our medical system does not provide health insurance for the poor. Why? Because they can't pay for it. Our most talented doctors do provide breast enhancements and face-lifts for Hollywood stars. Why? Because they can pay for it. Meanwhile, firms can make a lot of money doing nasty things. Why do European crime syndicates kidnap young girls in Eastern Europe and sell them into prostitution in wealthier countries? Because it's profitable.

In fact, criminals are some of the most innovative folks around. Drug traffickers can make huge profits by transporting cocaine from where it is produced (in the jungles of South America) to where it is consumed (in the cities and towns across the United States). This is illegal, of course; U.S. authorities devote a great amount of resources to interdicting the supply of such drugs headed toward potential consumers. As with any other market, drug runners who find clever ways of eluding the authorities are rewarded with huge profits.

Customs officials are pretty good at sniffing out (literally in many cases) large caches of drugs moving across the border, so drug traffickers figured out that it was easier to skip the border crossings and move their contraband across the sea and into the United States using small boats. When the U.S. Coast Guard began tracking fishing boats, drug traffickers invested in "go fast" boats that could outrun the authorities. And when U.S. law enforcement adopted radar and helicopters to hunt down the speedboats, the drug runners innovated yet again, creating the trafficking equivalent of Velcro or the iPhone: homemade submarines. In 2006, the Coast Guard stumbled across a forty-nine-foot submarine—handmade in the jungles of Colombia—that was invisible to radar and equipped to carry four men and three tons of cocaine. In 2000, Colombian police raided a warehouse and discovered a one-hundred-foot submarine under construction that would have been able to carry two hundred tons of cocaine. Coast Guard Rear Admiral Joseph Nimmich told the *New York Times*, "Like any business, if you're losing more and more of your product, you try to find a different way."[8]

The market is like evolution; it is an extraordinarily powerful force that derives its strength from rewarding the swift, the strong, and the smart. That said, it would be wise to remember that two of the most beautifully adapted species on the planet are the rat and the cockroach.

Our system uses prices to allocate scarce resources. Since there is a finite amount of everything worth having, the most basic function of any economic system is to decide who gets what. Who gets tickets to the Super Bowl? The people who are willing to pay the most. Who had the best seats for the Supreme Soviet Bowl in the old USSR (assuming some such event existed)? The individuals chosen by the Communist Party. Prices had nothing to do with it. If a Moscow butcher received a new shipment of pork, he slapped on the official state price for pork. And if that price was low enough that he had more customers than pork chops, he did not raise the price to earn some extra cash. He merely sold the chops to the first people in line. Those at the end of the line were out of luck. Capitalism and communism both ration goods. We do it with prices; the Soviets did it by waiting in line. (Of course, the communists had many black markets; it is quite likely that the butcher sold extra pork chops illegally out the back door of his shop.)

Because we use price to allocate goods, most markets are self-correcting. Periodically the oil ministers from the OPEC nations will meet in an exotic locale and agree to limit the global production of oil. Several things happen shortly thereafter: (1) Oil and gas prices start to go up; and (2) politicians begin falling all over themselves with ideas, mostly bad, for intervening in the oil market. But high prices are like a fever; they are both a symptom and a potential cure. While politicians are puffing away on the House floor, some other crucial things start to happen. We drive less. We get one heating bill and decide to insulate the attic. We go to the Ford showroom and walk past the Expeditions to the Escorts.

When gas prices approached $4 a gallon in 2008, the rapid response of American consumers surprised even economists. Americans began buying smaller cars (SUV sales plunged while subcompact sales rose). We drove fewer total miles (the first monthly drop in 30 years). We climbed on public buses and trains, often for the first time; transit ridership was higher in 2008 than at any time since the creation of the interstate highway system five decades earlier.[9]

Not all such behavioral changes were healthy. Many consumers switched from cars to motorcycles, which are more fuel efficient but also more dangerous. After falling steadily for years, the number of U.S. motorcycle deaths began to rise in the mid-1990s, just as gas prices began to climb. A study in the *American Journal of Public Health* estimated that every $1 increase in the price of gasoline is associated with an additional 1,500 motorcycle deaths annually.[10]

High oil prices cause things to start happening on the supply side, too. Oil producers outside of OPEC start pumping more oil to take advantage of the high price; indeed, the OPEC countries usually begin cheating on their own production quotas. Domestic oil companies begin pumping oil from wells that were not economical when the price of petroleum was low. Meanwhile, a lot of very smart people begin working more seriously on finding and commercializing alternative sources of energy. The price of oil and gasoline begins to drift down as supply rises and demand falls.

If we fix prices in a market system, private firms will find some other way to compete. Consumers often look back nostalgically at the "early days" of airplane travel, when the food was good, the seats were bigger, and people dressed up when they traveled. This is not just nostalgia speaking; the quality of coach air travel has fallen sharply. But the price of air travel has fallen even faster. Prior to 1978, airline fares were fixed by the government. Every flight from Denver to Chicago cost the same, but American and United were still competing for customers. They used quality to distinguish themselves. When the industry was deregulated, price became the primary margin for competition, presumably because that is what consumers care more about. Since then, everything related to being in or near an airplane has become less pleasant, but the average fare, adjusted for inflation, has fallen by nearly half.

In 1995, I was traveling across South Africa, and I was struck by the remarkable service at the gas stations along the way. The attendants, dressed in sharp uniforms, often with bow ties, would scurry out to fill the tank, check the oil, and wipe the windshield. The bathrooms were spotless—a far cry from some of the scary things I've seen driving across the USA. Was there some special service station mentality in South Africa? No. The price of gasoline was fixed by the government. So service stations, which were still private firms, resorted to bow ties and clean bathrooms to attract customers.

Every market transaction makes all parties better off. Firms are acting in their own best interests, and so are consumers. This is a simple idea that has enormous power. Consider an inflammatory example: The problem with Asian sweatshops is that there are not enough of them. Adult workers take jobs in these unpleasant, low-wage manufacturing facilities voluntarily. (I am not writing about forced labor or child labor, both of which are different cases.) So one of two things must be true. Either (1) workers take unpleasant jobs in sweatshops because it is the best employment option they have; or (2) Asian sweatshop workers are persons of weak intellect who have many more attractive job offers but choose to work in sweatshops instead.

Most arguments against globalization implicitly assume number two. The protesters smashing windows in Seattle were trying to make the case that workers in the developing world would be better off if we curtailed international trade, thereby closing down the sweatshops that churn out shoes and handbags for those of us in the developed world. But how exactly does that make workers in poor countries better off? It does not create any new opportunities. The only way it could possibly improve social welfare is if fired sweatshop workers take new, better jobs—opportunities they presumably ignored when they went to work in a sweatshop. When was the last time a plant closing in the United States was hailed as good news for its workers?

Sweatshops are nasty places by Western standards. And yes, one might argue that Nike should pay its foreign workers better wages out of sheer altruism. But they are a symptom of poverty, not a cause. Nike pays a typical worker in one of its Vietnamese factories roughly $600 a year. That is a pathetic amount of money. It also happens to be twice an average Vietnamese worker's annual income.[11] Indeed, sweatshops played an important role in the development of countries like South Korea and Taiwan, as we will explore in Chapter 12.

Given that economics is built upon the assumption that humans act consistently in ways that make themselves better off, one might reasonably ask: Are we really that rational? Not always, it turns out. One of the fiercest assaults on the notion of "strict rationality" comes from a seemingly silly observation. Economist Richard Thaler hosted a dinner party years ago at which he served a bowl of cashews before the meal. He noticed that his guests were wolfing down the nuts at such a pace that they would likely spoil their appetite for dinner. So Thaler took the bowl of nuts away, at which point his guests thanked him.[12]

Believe it or not, this little vignette exposes a fault in the basic tenets of microeconomics: In theory, it should never be possible to make rational individuals better off by denying them some option. People who don't want to eat too many cashews should just stop eating cashews. But they don't. And that finding turns out to have implications far beyond salted nuts. For example, if humans lack the self-discipline to do things that they know will make themselves better off in the long run (e.g., lose weight, stop smoking, or save for retirement), then society could conceivably make them better off by helping (or coercing) them to do things they otherwise would not or could not do—the public policy equivalent of taking the cashew bowl away.

The field of behavioral economics has evolved as a marriage between psychology and economics that offers sophisticated insight into how humans really make decisions. Daniel Kahneman, a professor in both psychology and public affairs at Princeton, was awarded the Nobel Prize in Economics in 2002 for his studies of decision making under uncertainty, and, in particular, "how human decisions may systematically depart from those predicted by standard economic theory."[13]

Kahneman and others have advanced the concept of "bounded rationality," which suggests that most of us make decisions using intuition or rules of thumb, kind of like looking at the sky to determine if it will rain, rather than spending hours poring over weather forecasts. Most of the time, this works just fine. Sometimes it doesn't. The behavioral economists study ways in which these rules of thumb may lead us to do things that diminish our utility in the long run.

For example, individuals don't always have a particularly refined sense of risk and probability. This point was brought home to me recently as I admired a large Harley Davidson motorcycle parked on a sidewalk in New Hampshire (a state that does not require motorcycle helmets). The owner ambled up and said, "Do you want to buy it?" I replied that motorcycles are a little too dangerous for me, to which he exclaimed, "You're willing to fly on a plane, aren't you!"

In fact, riding a motorcycle is 2,000 times more dangerous than flying for every kilometer traveled. That's not an entirely fair comparison since motorcycle trips tend to be much shorter. Still, any given motorcycle journey, regardless of length, is 14 times more likely to end in death than any trip by plane. Conventional economics makes clear that some people will ride motorcycles (with or without helmets) because the utility they get from going fast on a two wheeler outweighs the risks they incur in the process. That's perfectly rational. But if the person making that decision doesn't understand the true risk involved, then it may not be a rational trade-off after all.

Behaviorial economics has developed a catalog of these kinds of potential errors, many of which are an obvious part of everyday life. Many of us don't have all the self-control that we would like. Eighty percent of American smokers say they want to quit; most of them don't. (Reports from inside the White House suggested that President Obama was still trying to kick the habit even after moving into the

Oval Office.) Some very prominent economists, including one Nobel Prize winner, have argued for decades that there is such a thing as "rational addiction," meaning that individuals will take into account the likelihood of addiction and all its future costs when buying that first pack of Camels. MIT economist Jonathan Gruber, who has studied smoking behavior extensively, thinks that is nonsense. He argues that consumers don't rationally weigh the benefits of smoking enjoyment against future health risks and other costs, as the standard economic model assumes. Gruber writes, "The model is predicated on a description of the smoking decision that is at odds with laboratory evidence, the behavior of smokers, econometric [statistical] analysis, and common sense."[14]

We may also lack the basic knowledge necessary to make sensible decisions in some situations. Annamaria Lusardi of Dartmouth College and Olivia Mitchell of the Wharton School at the University of Pennsylvania surveyed a large sample of Americans over the age of fifty to gauge their financial literacy. Only a third could do simple interest rate calculations; most did not understand the concept of investment diversification. (If you don't know what that means either, you will after reading Chapter 7.) Based on her research, Professor Lusardi has concluded that "financial illiteracy" is widespread.[15]

These are not merely esoteric fun facts that pipe-smoking academics like to kick around in the faculty lounge. Bad decisions can have bad outcomes—for all of us. The global financial crisis arguably has its roots in irrational behavior. One of our behavioral "rules of thumb" as humans is to see patterns in what is really randomness; as a result, we assume that whatever is happening now will continue to happen in the future, even when data, probability, or basic analysis suggest the contrary. A coin that comes up heads four times in a row is "lucky"; a basketball player who has hit three shots in a row has a "hot hand."

A team of cognitive psychologists made one of the enduring contributions to this field by disproving the "hot hand" in basketball using NBA data and by conducting experiments with the Cornell varsity men's and women's basketball teams. (This is the rare academic paper that includes interviews with the Philadelphia 76ers.) Ninety-one percent of basketball fans believe that a player has "a better chance of making a shot after having just made his last two or three shots than he does after having just missed his last two or three shots." In fact, there is no evidence that a player's chances of making a shot are greater after making a previous shot—not with field goals for the 76ers, not with free throws for the Boston Celtics, and not when Cornell players shot baskets as part of a controlled experiment.[16]

Basketball fans are surprised by that—just as many homeowners were surprised in 2006 when real estate prices stopped going up. Lots of people had borrowed a lot of money on the assumption that what goes up must keep going up; the result has been a wave of foreclosures with devastating ripple effects throughout the global economy—which is a heck of a lot more significant than eating too many cashews. Chapter 3 discusses what, if anything, public policy ought to do about our irrational tendencies.

As John F. Kennedy famously remarked, "Life is not fair." Neither is capitalism in some important respects. Is it a good system?

I will argue that a market economy is to economics what democracy is to government: a decent, if flawed, choice among many bad alternatives. Markets are consistent with our views of individual liberty. We may disagree over whether or not the government should compel us to wear motorcycle helmets, but most of us agree that the state should not tell us where to live, what to do for a living, or how to spend our money. True, there is no way to rationalize spending money on a birthday cake for my dog when the same money could have vaccinated several African children. But any system that forces me to spend money on vaccines instead of doggy birthday cakes can only be held together by oppression. The communist governments of the twentieth century controlled their economies by controlling their citizens' lives. They often wrecked both in the process. During the twentieth century, communist governments killed some 100 million of their own people in peacetime, either by repression or by famine.

Markets are consistent with human nature and therefore wildly successful at motivating us to reach our potential. I am writing this book because I love to write. I am writing this book because I believe that economics will be interesting to lay readers. And I am writing this book because I really want a summer home in New Hampshire. We work harder when we benefit directly from our work, and that hard work often yields significant social gains.

Last and most important, we can and should use government to modify markets in all kinds of ways. The economic battle of the twentieth century was between capitalism and communism. Capitalism won. Even my leftist brother-in-law does not believe in collective farming or government-owned steel mills (though he did once say that he would like to see a health care system modeled after the U.S. Post Office). On the other hand, reasonable people can disagree sharply over when and how the government should involve itself in a market economy or what kind of safety net we should offer to those whom capitalism treats badly. The economic battles of the twenty-first century will be over how unfettered our markets should be.

CHAPTER 2

Incentives Matter:

Why you might be able to save your face by cutting off your nose (if you are a black rhinoceros)

The black rhinoceros is one of the most endangered species on the planet. Some 4,000 of them roam southern Africa, down from about 65,000 in 1970. This is an ecological disaster in the making. It is also a situation in which basic economics can tell us why the species is in such trouble—and perhaps even what we can do about it.

Why do people kill black rhinos? For the same reason they sell drugs or cheat on their taxes. Because they can make a lot of money relative to the risk of getting caught. In many Asian countries, the horn of the black rhino is believed to be a powerful aphrodisiac and fever reducer. It is also used to make the handles on traditional Yemenese daggers. As a result, a single rhino horn can fetch $30,000 on the black market—a princely sum in countries where per capita income is around $1,000 a year and falling. In other words, the black rhino is worth far more dead than alive to the people of impoverished southern Africa.

Sadly, this is a market that does not naturally correct itself. Unlike automobiles or personal computers, firms can't produce new black rhinos as they see the supply dwindling. Indeed, quite the opposite force is at work; as the black rhino becomes more and more imperiled, the black market price for rhino horn rises, providing even more incentive for poachers to hunt down the remaining animals. This vicious circle is compounded by another aspect of the situation that is common to many environmental challenges: Most black rhinos are communal property rather than private property. That may sound wonderful. In fact, it creates more conservation problems than it solves. Imagine that all of the black rhinos were in the hands of a single avaricious rancher who had no qualms about making rhino horns into Yemenese daggers. This rancher has not a single environmental bone in his body. Indeed, he is so mean and selfish that sometimes he kicks his dog just because it gives him utility. Would this ogre of a rhino rancher have let his herd fall from 65,000 to 4,000 in thirty years? Never. He would have bred and protected the animals so that he would always have a large supply of horns to ship off to market—much as cattle ranchers manage their herds. This has nothing to do with altruism; it has everything to do with maximizing the value of a scarce resource.

Communal resources, on the other hand, present some unique problems. First, the villagers who live in close proximity to these majestic animals usually derive no benefit from having them around. To the contrary, large animals like rhinos and elephants can cause massive damage to crops. To put yourself in the shoes of local villagers, imagine that the people of Africa suddenly took a keen interest in the future of the North American brown rat and that a crucial piece of the conservation strategy involved letting these creatures live and breed in your house. Further imagine that a poacher came along and offered you cash to show him where the rats were nesting in your basement. Hmm. True, millions of people around the world derive utility from conserving species like the black rhino or the mountain gorilla. But that can actually be part of the problem; it is easy to be a "free rider" and let someone else, or some other organization, do the work. Last year, how much time and money did you contribute to preserving endangered species?

Tour and safari operators, who do make a lot of money by bringing wealthy tourists to see rare wildlife, face a similar "free rider" problem. If one tour company invests heavily in conservation, other tour companies that have made no such investment still enjoy all the benefits of the rhinos that have been saved. So the firm that spends money on conservation actually suffers a cost disadvantage in the market. Their tours will have to be more expensive (or they will have to accept a lower profit margin) in order to recoup their conservation investment. Obviously there is a role for government here. But the governments in sub-Saharan Africa are low on resources at best and corrupt and dysfunctional at worst. The one party who has a clear and powerful incentive is the poacher, who makes a king's ransom by hunting down the remaining rhinos, killing them, and then sawing off their horns.

This is pretty depressing stuff. But economics also offers at least some insight into how the black rhino and other endangered species can be saved. An effective conservation strategy must properly align the incentives of the people who live in or near the black rhino's natural habitat. Translation: Give local people some reason to want the animals alive rather than dead. This is the premise of the budding eco-tourism industry. If tourists are willing to pay great amounts of money to spot and photograph black rhinos, and, more important, *if local citizens somehow share the profits from this tourism*, then the local population has a large incentive to keep such animals alive. This has worked in places like Costa Rica, a country that has protected its rain forests and other ecological features by setting aside more than 25 percent of the country as national parks. Tourism currently generates over $1 billion in annual revenue, accounting for 11 percent of the national income.[1]

Sadly, this process is working in reverse at the moment with the mountain gorilla, another seriously endangered species (made famous by Dian Fossey, author of *Gorillas in the Mist*). It is estimated that only 620 mountain gorillas are left in the dense jungles of East Africa. But the countries that make up this region—Uganda, Rwanda, Burundi, and Congo—are embroiled in a series of civil wars that have devastated the tourism trade. In the past, local inhabitants have preserved the gorillas' habitat not because they have any great respect for the mountain gorilla, but because they can make more money from tourists than they can by chopping down the forests that make up the gorillas' habitat. That has changed as the violence in the region grinds on. One local man told the *New York Times*, "[The gorillas] are important when they bring in tourists. If not, they are not. If the tourists don't come, we will try our luck in the forest. Before this, we were good timber cutters."[2]

Meanwhile, conservation officials are experimenting with another idea that is about as basic as economics can be. Black rhinos are killed because their horns fetch a princely sum. If there is no horn, then presumably there is no reason to poach the animals. Thus, some conservation officials have begun to capture black rhinos, saw off their horns, and then release the animals back into the wild. The rhinos are left mildly disadvantaged relative to some of their predators, but they are less likely to be hunted down by their most deadly enemy, man. Has it worked? The evidence is mixed. In some cases, poachers have continued to kill dehorned rhinos, for a number of possible reasons. Killing the animals without horns saves the poachers from wasting time tracking the same animal again. Also, there is some money to be made from removing and selling even the stump of the horn. And, sadly, dead rhinos, even without horns, make the species more endangered, which drives up the value of existing horn stocks.

All of this ignores the demand side of the equation. Should we allow trade in products made from endangered species? Most would say no. Making rhino-horn daggers illegal in countries like the United States lowers the overall demand, which diminishes the incentive for poachers to hunt down the animals. At the same time, there is a credible dissenting view. Some conservation officials argue that selling a limited amount of rhino horn (or ivory, in the case of elephants) that has been legally stockpiled would have two beneficial effects. First, it would raise money to help strapped governments pay for antipoaching efforts. Second, it would lower the market price for these illicit items and therefore diminish the incentive to poach the animals.

As with any complex policy issue, there is no right answer, but there are some ways of approaching the problem that are more fruitful than others. The point is that protecting the black rhino is at least as much about economics as it is about science. We know how the black rhino breeds, what it eats, where it lives. What we need to figure out is how to stop human beings from shooting them. That requires an understanding of how humans behave, not black rhinos.

Incentives matter. When we are paid on commission, we work harder; if the price of gasoline goes up, we drive less; if my three-year-old daughter learns that she will get an Oreo if she cries while I'm talking on the phone, then she will cry while I am talking on the phone. This was one of Adam Smith's insights in *The Wealth of Nations:* "It is not from the benevolence of the butcher, the brewer, or the baker that we expect our dinner, but from their regard to their own interest." Bill Gates did not drop out of Harvard to join the Peace Corps; he dropped out to found Microsoft, which made him one of the richest men on the planet and launched the personal computer revolution in the process—making all of us better off, too. Self-interest makes the world go around, a point that seems so obvious as to be silly. Yet it is routinely ignored. The old slogan "From each according to his abilities, to each according to his needs" made a wonderful folk song; as an economic system, it has led to everything from inefficiency to mass starvation. In any system that does not rely on markets, personal incentives are usually divorced from productivity. Firms and workers are not rewarded for innovation and hard work, nor are they punished for sloth and inefficiency.

How bad can it get? Economists reckon that by the time the Berlin Wall crumbled, some East German car factories were actually destroying value. Because the manufacturing process was so inefficient and the end product was so shoddy, the plants were producing cars worth less than the inputs used to make them. Basically, they took perfectly good steel and ruined it! These kinds of inefficiencies can also exist in nominally capitalist countries where large sectors of the economy are owned and operated by the state, such as India. By 1991, the Hindustan Fertilizer Corporation had been up and running for twelve years.[3] Every day, twelve hundred employees reported to work with the avowed goal of producing fertilizer. There was just one small complication: The plant had never actually produced any salable fertilizer. None. Government bureaucrats ran the plant using public funds; the machinery that was installed never worked properly. Nevertheless, twelve hundred work-ers came to work every day and the government continued to pay their salaries. The entire enterprise was an industrial charade. It limped along because there was no mechanism to force it to shut down. When gov-ernment is bankrolling the business, there is no need to produce some-thing and then sell it for more than it cost to make.

These examples seem funny in their own way, but they aren't. Right now, the North Korean economy is in such shambles that the country cannot feed itself, nor does it produce anything valu-able enough to trade to the outside world in exchange for significant quantities of food. The nation is on the brink of famine, according to diplomats, United Nations officials, and other observers. This mass starvation would be a tragic repeat of the 1990s, when famine killed something on the order of a million people and left 60 percent of North Korean children malnourished. Journalists described starving people eating grass and scouring railroad tracks for bits of coal or food that may have fallen from passing trains.

In the United States, there is a great deal of hand-wringing about two energy-related issues: our dependence on foreign oil and the environmental impact of CO_2 emissions. To economists, the fix for these interrelated issues is as close to a no-brainer as we ever get: Make carbon-based energy more expensive. If it costs more, we will use less—and therefore pollute less, too. I have powerful childhood memories of my father, who has no great affection for the environ-ment but could squeeze a nickel out of a stone, stalking around the house closing the closet doors and telling us that he was not paying to air-condition our closets.

Meanwhile, American public education operates a lot more like North Korea than Silicon Valley. I will not wade into the school voucher debate, but I will discuss one striking phenomenon related to incentives in education that I have written about for *The Economist*.[4] The pay of American teachers is not linked in any way to performance; teachers' unions have consistently opposed any kind of merit pay. Instead, salaries in nearly every public school district in the country are determined by a rigid formula based on experience and years of schooling, factors that researchers have found to be generally unrelated to performance in the classroom. This uniform pay scale creates a set of incentives that economists refer to as adverse selection. Since the most talented teachers are also likely to be good at other professions, they have a strong incentive to leave education for jobs in which pay is more closely linked to productivity. For the least talented, the incentives are just the opposite.

The theory is interesting; the data are amazing. When test scores are used as a proxy for ability, the brightest individuals shun the teaching profession at every juncture. The brightest students are the least likely to choose education as a college major. Among students who do major in education, those with higher test scores are less likely to become teachers. And among individuals who enter teaching, those with the highest test scores are the most likely to leave the profession early. None of this proves that America's teachers are being paid enough. Many of them are not, especially those gifted individuals who stay in the profession because they love it. But the general problem remains: Any system that pays all teachers the same provides a strong incentive for the most talented among them to look for work elsewhere.

Human beings are complex creatures who are going to do whatever it takes to make themselves as well off as possible. Sometimes it is easy to predict how that will unfold; sometimes it is enormously complex. Economists often speak of "perverse incentives," which are the inadvertent incentives that can be created when we set out to do something completely different. In policy circles, this is sometimes called the "law of unintended consequences." Consider a well-intentioned proposal to require that all infants and small children be restrained in car seats while flying on commercial airlines. During the

Clinton administration, FAA administrator Jane Garvey told a safety conference that her agency was committed to "ensuring that children are accorded the same level of safety in aircraft as are adults." James Hall, chairman of the National Transportation Safety Board at the time, lamented that luggage had to be stowed for takeoff while "the most precious cargo on that aircraft, infants and toddlers, were left unrestrained."[5] Garvey and Hall cited several cases in which infants might have survived crashes had they been restrained. Thus, requiring car seats for children on planes would prevent injuries and save lives.

Or would it? Using a car seat requires that a family buy an extra seat on the plane, which dramatically increases the cost of flying. Airlines no longer offer significant children's discounts; a seat is a seat, and it is likely to cost at least several hundred dollars. As a result, some families will choose to drive rather than fly. Yet driving—even with a car seat—is dramatically more dangerous than flying. As a result, requiring car seats on planes might result in more injuries and deaths to children (and adults), not fewer.

Consider another example in which good intentions led to a bad outcome because the incentives were not fully anticipated. Mexico City is one of the most polluted cities in the world; the foul air trapped over the city by the surrounding mountains and volcanoes has been described by the *New York Times* as "a grayish-yellow pudding of pollutants."[6] Beginning in 1989, the government launched a program to fight this pollution, much of which is caused by auto and truck emissions. A new law required that all cars stay off the streets one day a week on a rotating basis (e.g., cars with certain license plate numbers could not be driven on Tuesday). The logic of the plan was straightforward: Fewer cars on the road would lead to less air pollution.

So what really happened? As would be expected, many people did not like the inconvenience of having their driving days limited. They reacted in a way that analysts might have predicted but did not. Families who could afford a second car bought one, or simply kept their old car when buying a new one, so that they would always have one car that could be driven on any given day. This proved to be worse for emissions than no policy at all, since the proportion of old cars on the road went up, and old cars are dirtier than new cars. The net effect of the policy change was to put more polluting cars on the road, not fewer. Subsequent studies found that overall gas consumption had increased and air quality did not improve at all. The policy was later dropped in favor of a mandatory emissions test.[7]

Good policy uses incentives to some positive end. London has dealt with its traffic congestion problems by applying the logic of the market: It raised the cost of driving during the hours of peak demand. Beginning in 2003, the city of London began charging a £5 ($8) congestion fee for all drivers entering an eight-square-mile section of the central city between 7:00 a.m. and 6:30 p.m.[8] In 2005, the congestion charge was raised to £8 ($13), and in 2007, the size of the zone for which the fee must be paid was expanded. Drivers are responsible for paying the charge by phone, Internet, or in selected retail shops. Video cameras were installed in some 700 locations to scan license plates and match the data against records of motorists who have paid the charge. Motorists caught driving in central London without paying the fee are fined £80 ($130).

The plan was designed to take advantage of one of the most basic features of markets: Raising prices reduces demand. Raising the cost of driving discourages some drivers and improves the flow of traffic. Experts also predicted an increase in the use of public transit, both because it is a cheap alternative to driving, but also because buses would be able to move more quickly through central London. (Faster trips lower the opportunity cost of taking public transit.) Within a month, the results were striking. Traffic fell 20 percent (settling after several years at 15 percent lower). Average speed in the congestion zone doubled; bus delays were cut in half; and the number of bus passengers climbed 14 percent. The only unpleasant surprise was that the program had such a significant deterrent effect on car traffic that revenues from the fee were lower than expected.[9] Retailers have also complained that the fee discourages shoppers from visiting central London.

Good policy uses incentives to channel behavior toward some desired outcome. Bad policy either ignores incentives, or fails to anticipate how rational individuals might change their behavior to avoid being penalized.

The wonder of the private sector, of course, is that incentives magically align themselves in a way that makes everyone better off. Right? Well, not exactly. From top to bottom, corporate America is a cesspool of competing and misaligned incentives. Have you ever seen some variation of the sign near the cash register at a fast-food restaurant that says, "Your meal is free if you don't get a receipt. Please see a manager"? Does Burger King have a passionate interest in providing a receipt so that your family bookkeeping will be complete? Of course not. Burger King does not want its employees stealing. And the only way employees can steal without getting caught is by performing transactions without recording them on the cash register—selling you a burger and fries without issuing a receipt and then pocketing the cash. This is what economists call a principal-agent problem. The principal (Burger King) employs an agent (the cashier) who has an incentive to do a lot of things that are not necessarily in the best interest of the firm. Burger King can either spend a lot of time and money monitoring its employees for theft, or it can provide an incentive for you to do it for them. That little sign by the cash register is an ingenious management tool.

Principal-agent problems are as much a problem at the top of corporate America as they are at the bottom, in large part because the agents who run America's large corporations (CEOs and other top executives) are not necessarily the principals who own those companies (the shareholders). I own shares in Starbucks, but I don't even know the CEO's name. How can I be sure that he (she?) is acting in my best interest? Indeed, there is ample evidence to suggest that corporate managers are no different from Burger King cashiers—they have some incentives that are not always in the best interest of the firm. They may steal from the cash register figuratively by showering themselves with private jets and country club memberships. Or they may make strategic decisions from which they benefit but shareholders do not. For example, a shocking two-thirds of all corporate mergers do not add value to the merged firms and a third of them leave shareholders worse off. Why would very smart CEOs engage so often in behavior that seems to make little financial sense?

One partial answer, economists have argued, is that CEOs benefit from mergers even when shareholders are left with losses. A CEO draws a lot of attention to himself by engineering a complex corporate transaction. He is left running a bigger company, which is almost always more prestigious, even if the new entity is less profitable than the merged companies were when they were on their own. Big companies have big offices, big salaries, and big airplanes. On the other hand, some mergers and takeovers make perfect strategic sense. As an uninformed shareholder with a large financial stake in the company, how do I tell the difference? If I don't even know the name of the CEO of Starbucks, how can I be sure that she (he?) is not spending the bulk of her day chasing attractive secretaries around her office? Hell, this is harder than being a manager at Burger King.

For a time, clever economists believed that stock options were the answer. They were supposed to be the CEO equivalent of the sign near the cash register asking if you received your receipt. Most American CEOs and other important executives receive a large share of their compensation in the form of stock options. These options enable the recipient to purchase the company's stock in the future at some predetermined price, say $10. If the company is highly profitable and the stock does well, climbing to say $57, then those stock options are very valuable. (It is good to be able to buy something for $10 when it is selling on the open market for $57.) On the other hand, if the company's stock falls to $7, the options are worthless. There is no point in buying something for $10 when you can buy it on the open market for $3 less. The point of this compensation scheme is to align the incentives of the CEO with the interests of the shareholders. If the share price goes up, the CEO gets rich—but the shareholders do well, too.

It turns out that wily CEOs can find ways to abuse the options game (just as cashiers can find new ways to steal from the register). Before the first edition of this book came out, I asked Paul Volcker, former chairman of the Federal Reserve, to give it a read since he had been a professor of mine. Volcker read the book. He liked the book. But he said that I should not have written admiringly about stock options as a tool for aligning the interests of shareholders and management because they are "an instrument of the devil."

Paul Volcker was right. I was wrong. The potential problem with options is that executives can do things to goose the firm's stock in the short run that are bad or disastrous for the company in the long run—after the CEO has sold tens of thousands of options for an astronomical profit. Michael Jensen, a Harvard Business School professor who has spent his career on issues related to management incentives, is even harsher than Paul Volcker. He describes options as "managerial heroin," because they create an incentive for managers to seek short-term highs while doing enormous long-term damage.[10] Studies have found that companies with large options grants are more likely to engage in accounting fraud and more likely to default on their debt.[11]

Meanwhile, CEOs (with or without options) have their own monitoring headaches. Investment banks like Lehman Brothers and Bear Stearns were literally destroyed by employees who took huge risks at the firm's expense. This is a crucial link in the chain of causality for the financial crisis; Wall Street is where a bad problem became disastrous. Banks across the country could afford to feed the real estate bubble with reckless loans because they could quickly bundle these loans together, or "securitize" them, and sell them off to investors. (A bank takes your mortgage, bundles it together with my mortgage and lots of others, and then sells the package off to some party willing to pay cash now in exchange for a future stream of income—our monthly mortgage payments.) This is not inherently a bad thing when done responsibly; the bank gets its capital back right away, which can then be used to make new loans. However, if you take the word "responsibly" out of that sentence, it does become a bad thing.

Simon Johnson, former chief economist for the International Monetary Fund, wrote an excellent postmortem of the financial crisis for *The Atlantic* in 2009. He notes, "Major commercial and investment banks—and the hedge funds that ran alongside them—were the big beneficiaries of the twin housing and equity-market bubbles of this decade, their profits fed by an ever-increasing volume of transactions founded on a relatively small base of actual physical assets. Each time a loan was sold, packaged, securitized, and resold, banks took their transaction fees, and the hedge funds buying those securities reaped ever-larger fees as their holdings grew."[12]

Each transaction carries some embedded risk. The problem is that the bankers making huge commissions on the buying and selling of what would later become known as "toxic assets" do not bear the full risk of those products; their firms do. Heads they win, tails the firm loses. In the case of Lehman Brothers, that's a pretty accurate description of what happened. Yes, the Lehman employees lost their jobs, but those most responsible for the collapse of the firm don't have to give back the huge bonuses they made in the good years.

One other culpable party deserves mention, and again misaligned incentives was a key problem. The credit rating agencies—Standard & Poor's, Moody's, and others—are supposed to be the independent authorities that evaluate the risk of these newfangled products. Many of the "toxic assets" now at the heart of the financial meltdown were given stellar credit ratings. Part of this was pure incompetence. It didn't help, however, that the credit rating agencies are paid by the firms selling the bonds or securities being rated. That's a little like a used car salesman paying an appraiser to stand around the lot and provide helpful advice to customers. "Hey Bob, why don't you come over here and tell the customer whether he is getting a good deal or not." How useful do you think that would be?

These corporate incentive problems remain unresolved as far as I can tell, both for senior executives in public companies and for other employees taking risks with their firm's capital. There is a fundamental tension that is tough to resolve. On the one hand, firms need to reward innovation, risk, insight, hard work, and so on. These are good things for the firm, and employees who do them well should be paid handsomely—even astronomically in some cases. On the other hand, the employees doing fancy things (like designing new financial products) will always have more information about what they are really up to than their superiors will; and their superiors will have more information than the shareholders. The challenge is to reward good outcomes without creating incentives for employees to game the system in ways that damage the company in the long run.

One need not be a corporate titan to deal with principal-agent problems. There are plenty of situations in which we must hire someone whose incentives are similar but not identical to our own—and the distinction between "similar" and "identical" can make all the difference. Take real estate agents, a particular breed of scoundrel who purport to have your best interest at stake but may not, regardless of whether you are buying or selling a property. Let's look at the buy side first. The agent graciously shows you lots of houses and eventually you find one that is just right. So far, so good. Now it is time to bargain with the seller over the purchase price, often with your agent as your chief adviser. Yet your real estate agent will be paid a percentage of the eventual purchase price. The more you are willing to pay, the more your agent makes and the less time the whole process will take.

There are problems on the sell side, too, though they are more subtle. The better price you get for your house, the more money your agent will make. That is a good thing. But the incentives are still not perfectly aligned. Suppose you are selling a house in the $300,000 range. Your agent can list the house for $280,000 and sell it in about twenty minutes. Or she could list it for $320,000 and wait for a buyer who really loves the place. The benefit to you of pricing the house high is huge: $40,000. Your real estate agent may see things differently. Listing high would mean many weeks of showing the house, holding open houses, and baking cookies to make the place smell good. Lots of work, in other words. Assuming a 3 percent commission, your agent can make $8,400 for doing virtually nothing or $9,600 for doing many weeks of work. Which would you choose? On the buy side or the sell side, your agent's most powerful incentive is to get a deal done, whether it is at a price favorable to you or not.

Economics teaches us how to get the incentives right. As Gordon Gekko told us in the movie *Wall Street*, greed is good, so make sure that you have it working on your side. Yet Mr. Gekko was not entirely correct. Greed can be bad—even for people who are entirely selfish. Indeed, some of the most interesting problems in economics involve situations in which rational individuals acting in their own best interest do things that make themselves worse off. Yet their behavior is entirely logical.

The classic example is the prisoner's dilemma, a somewhat contrived but highly powerful model of human behavior. The basic idea is that two men have been arrested on suspicion of murder. They are immediately separated so that they can be interrogated without communicating with one another. The case against them is not terribly strong, and the police are looking for a confession. Indeed, the authorities are willing to offer a deal if one of the men rats out the other as the trigger man.

If neither man confesses, the police will charge them both with illegal possession of a weapon, which carries a five-year jail sentence. If both of them confess, then each will receive a twenty-five-year murder sentence. If one man rats out the other, then the snitch will receive a light three-year sentence as an accomplice and his partner will get life in prison. What happens?

The men are best off collectively if they keep their mouths shut. But that's not what they do. Each of them starts thinking. Prisoner A figures that if his partner keeps his mouth shut, then he can get the light three-year sentence by ratting him out. Then it dawns on him: His partner is almost certainly thinking the same thing—in which case he had better confess to avoid having the whole crime pinned on himself. Indeed, his best strategy is to confess regardless of what his partner does: It either gets him the three-year sentence (if his partner stays quiet) or saves him from getting life in prison (if his partner talks).

Of course, Prisoner B has the same incentives. They both confess, and they both get twenty-five years in prison when they might have served only five. Yet neither prisoner has done anything irrational.

The amazing thing about this model is that it offers great insight into real-world situations in which unfettered self-interest leads to poor outcomes. It is particularly applicable to the way in which renewable natural resources, such as fisheries, are exploited when many individuals are drawing from a common resource. For example, if Atlantic swordfish are harvested wisely, such as by limiting the number of fish caught each season, then the swordfish population will remain stable or even grow, providing a living for fishermen indefinitely. But no one "owns" the world's swordfish stocks, making it difficult to police who catches what. As a result, independent fishing boats start to act a lot like our prisoners under interrogation. They can either limit their catch in the name of conservation, or they can take as many fish as possible. What happens?

Exactly what the prisoner's dilemma predicts: The fishermen do not trust each other well enough to coordinate an outcome that would make them all better off. Rhode Island fisherman John Sorlien told the *New York Times* in a story on dwindling fish stocks, "Right now, my only incentive is to go out and kill as many fish as I can. I have no incentive to conserve the fishery, because any fish I leave is just going to be picked up by the next guy."[13] So the world's stocks of tuna, cod, swordfish, and lobster are fished away. Meanwhile, politicians often make the situation worse by bailing out struggling fishermen with assorted subsidies. This merely keeps boats in the water when some fishermen might otherwise quit.

Sometimes individuals need to be saved from themselves. One nice example of this is the lobstering community of Port Lincoln on Australia's southern coast. In the 1960s, the community set a limit on the number of traps that could be set and then sold licenses for those traps. Since then, any newcomer could enter the business only by buying a license from another lobsterman. This limit on the overall catch has allowed the lobster population to thrive. Ironically, Port Lincoln lobstermen catch more than their American colleagues while working less. Meanwhile, a license purchased in 1984 for $2,000 now fetches about $35,000. As Aussie lobsterman Daryl Spencer told the *Times*, "Why hurt the fishery? It's my retirement fund. No one's going to pay me $35,000 a pot if there are no lobsters left. If I rape and pillage the fishery now, in ten years my licenses won't be worth anything." Mr. Spencer is not smarter or more altruistic than his fishing colleagues around the world; he just has different incentives. Oddly, some environmental groups oppose these kinds of licensed quotas because they "privatize" a public resource. They also fear that the licenses will be bought up by large corporations, driving small fishermen out of business.

So far, the evidence strongly suggests that creating private property rights—giving individual fishermen the right to a certain catch, including the option of selling that right—is the most effective tool in the face of collapsing commercial fisheries. A 2008 study of the world's commercial fisheries published in *Science* found that individual transferable quotas can stop or even reverse the collapse of fishing stocks. Fisheries managed with transferable quotas were half as likely to collapse as fisheries that use traditional methods.[14]

Two other points regarding incentives are worth noting. First, a market economy inspires hard work and progress not just because it rewards winners, but because it crushes losers. The 1990s were a great time to be involved in the Internet. They were bad years to be in the electric typewriter business. Implicit in Adam Smith's invisible hand is the idea of "creative destruction," a term coined by the Austrian economist Joseph Schumpeter. Markets do not suffer fools gladly. Take Wal-Mart, a remarkably efficient retailer that often leaves carnage in its wake. Americans flock to Wal-Mart because the store offers an amazing range of products cheaper than they can be purchased anywhere else. This is a good thing. Being able to buy goods cheaper is essentially the same thing as having more income. At the same time, Wal-Mart is the ultimate nightmare for Al's Glass and Hardware in Pekin, Illinois—and for mom-and-pop shops everywhere else. The pattern is well established: Wal-Mart opens a giant store just outside of town; several years later, the small shops on Main Street are closed and boarded up.

Capitalism can be a brutal, cruel process. We look back and speak admiringly of technological breakthroughs like the steam engine, the spinning wheel, and the telephone. But those advances made it a bad time to be, respectively, a blacksmith, a seamstress, or a telegraph operator. Creative destruction is not just something that might happen in a market economy. It is something that *must* happen. At the beginning of the twentieth century, half of all Americans worked in farming or ranching.[15] Now that figure is about one in a hundred and still falling. (Iowa is still losing roughly fifteen hundred farmers a year.) Note that two important things have *not* happened: (1) We have not starved to death; and (2) we do not have a 49 percent unemployment rate. Instead, American farmers have become so productive that we need far fewer of them to feed ourselves. The individuals who would have been farming ninety years ago are now fixing our cars, designing computer games, playing professional football, etc. Just imagine our collective loss of utility if Steve Jobs, Steven Spielberg, and Oprah Winfrey were corn farmers.

Creative destruction is a tremendous positive force in the long run. The bad news is that people don't pay their bills in the long run. The folks at the mortgage company can be real sticklers about getting that check every month. When a plant closes or an industry is wiped out by competition, it can be years or even an entire generation before the affected workers and communities recover. Anyone who has ever driven through New England has seen the abandoned or underutilized mills that are monuments to the days when America still manufactured things like textiles and shoes. Or one can drive through Gary, Indiana, where miles of rusting steel plants are a reminder that the city was not always most famous for having more murders per capita than any other city in the United States.

Competition means losers, which goes a long way toward explaining why we embrace it heartily in theory and then often fight it bitterly in practice. A college classmate of mine worked for a congressman from Michigan shortly after our graduation. My friend was not allowed to drive his Japanese car to work, lest it be spotted in one of the Michigan congressman's reserved parking spaces. That congressman will almost certainly tell you that he is a capitalist. Of course he believes in markets—unless a Japanese company happens to make a better, cheaper car, in which case the staff member who bought that vehicle should be forced to take the train to work. (I would argue that the American automakers would have been much stronger in the long run if they had faced this international competition head-on instead of looking for political protection from the first wave of Japanese imports in the 1970s and 1980s.) This is nothing new; competition is always best when it involves other people. During the Industrial Revolution, weavers in rural England demonstrated, petitioned Parliament, and even burned down textile mills in an effort to fend off mechanization. Would we be better off now if they had succeeded and we still made all of our clothes by hand?

If you make a better mousetrap, the world will beat a path to your door; if you make the old mousetrap, it is time to start firing people. This helps to explain our ambivalence to international trade and globalization, to ruthless retailers like Wal-Mart, and even to some kinds of technology and automation. Competition also creates some interesting policy trade-offs. Government inevitably faces pressure to help firms and industries under siege from competition and to protect the affected workers. Yet many of the things that minimize the pain inflicted by competition—bailing out firms or making it hard to lay off workers—slow down or stop the process of creative destruction. To quote my junior high school football coach: "No pain, no gain."

One other matter related to incentives vastly complicates public policy: It is not easy to transfer money from the rich to the poor. Congress can pass the laws, but wealthy taxpayers do not stand idly by. They change their behavior in ways that avoid as much taxation as possible—moving money around, making investments that shelter income, or, in extreme cases, moving to another jurisdiction. When Bjorn Borg dominated the tennis world during my childhood, the Swedish government taxed his earnings at an extremely high rate. Borg did not lobby the Swedish government for lower taxes or write passionate op-eds about the role of taxes in the economy. He merely transferred his residence to Monaco, where the tax burden is much lower.

At least he was still playing tennis. Taxes provide a powerful incentive to avoid or reduce the activity that is taxed. In America, where much of our revenue comes from the income tax, high taxes discourage . . . income? Will people really stop or start working based on tax rates? Yes—especially when the worker involved is the family's second earner. Virginia Postrel, a columnist on economics for the *New York Times*, has declared that tax rates are a feminist issue. Because of the "marriage tax," second earners in families with high household incomes, who are more likely to be women, pay an average of 50 cents in taxes for every dollar they earn, which profoundly affects the decision to work or stay home. "By disproportionately punishing married women's work, the tax system distorts women's personal choices. And by discouraging valuable work, it lowers our overall standard of living," she writes. She offers some interesting evidence. As a result of the 1986 tax reform, marginal tax rates for women in the highest income brackets fell more sharply than tax rates for women with lower incomes, meaning that they saw a much sharper drop in the amount that the government takes from every paycheck. Did they respond differently from women who did not get the same large tax break? Yes, their participation in the work force jumped three times as much.[16]

On the corporate side, high taxes can have a similar effect. High taxes lower a firm's return on investment, thereby providing less incentive to invest in plants, research, and other activities that lead to economic growth. Once again we are faced with an unpleasant trade-off: Raising taxes to provide generous benefits to disadvantaged Americans can simultaneously discourage the kinds of productive investments that might make them better off.

If tax rates get high enough, individuals and firms may slip into the "underground economy" where they opt to break the law and avoid taxes entirely. Scandinavian countries, which offer generous government programs funded by high marginal tax rates, have seen large growth in the size of their black market economies. Experts estimate that the underground economy in Norway grew from 1.5 percent of gross national product in 1960 to 18 percent by the mid-1990s. Cheating the tax man can be a vicious circle. As more individuals and firms slip into the underground economy, tax rates must go up for everyone else in order to provide the same level of government revenue. Higher taxes in turn cause more flight to the underground economy—and so on.[17]

The challenge of transferring money from rich to poor is not just on the taxation side. Government benefits create perverse incentives, too. Generous unemployment benefits diminish the incentive to find work. Welfare policy, prior to reform in 1996, offered cash payments only to unemployed single women with children, which implicitly punished poor women who were married or employed—two things that the government generally does not try to discourage.

This is not to suggest that all government benefits go to poor people. They don't. The largest federal entitlement programs are Social Security and Medicare, which go to all Americans, even the very rich. By providing guaranteed benefits in old age, both programs may discourage personal savings. Indeed, this is the subject of a long-simmering debate. Some economists argue that government old-age benefits cause us to save less (thereby lowering the national savings rate) because we need to set aside less money for retirement. Others argue that Social Security and Medicare do not reduce our personal savings; they merely allow us to pass along more money to our children and grandchildren. Empirical studies have not found a clear answer one way or the other. This is not merely an esoteric squabble among academics. As we shall explore later in the book, a low savings rate can limit the pool of capital available to make the kinds of investments that allow us to improve our standard of living.

None of this should be interpreted as a blanket argument against taxes or government programs. Rather, economists spend much more time than politicians thinking about what kind of taxes we should collect and how we should structure government benefits. For example, both a gasoline tax and an income tax generate revenue. Yet they create profoundly different incentives. The income tax will discourage some people from working, which is a bad thing. The gasoline tax will discourage some people from driving, which can be a good thing. Indeed, "green taxes" collect revenue by taxing activities that are detrimental to the environment and "sin taxes" do the same thing for the likes of cigarettes, alcohol, and gambling.

In general, economists tend to favor taxes that are broad, simple, and fair. A simple tax is easily understood and collected; a fair tax implies only that two similar individuals, such as two people with the same income, will pay similar taxes; a broad tax means that revenue is raised by imposing a small tax on a very large group rather than imposing a large tax on a very small group. A broad tax is harder to evade because fewer activities are exempted, and, since the tax rate is lower, there is less incentive to evade it anyway. We should not, for example, impose a large tax on the sale of red sports cars. The tax could be avoided, easily and legally, by buying another color—*in which case everybody is made worse off.* The government collects no revenue and sports car enthusiasts do not get to drive their favorite color car.

This phenomenon, whereby taxes make individuals worse off without making anyone else better off, is referred to as "deadweight loss."

It would be preferable to tax all sports cars, or even all cars, because more revenue could be raised with a much smaller tax. Then again, a gasoline tax collects revenue from drivers, just as a tax on new cars does, but it also provides an incentive to conserve fuel. Those who drive more pay more. So now we're raising a great deal of revenue with a tiny tax and doing a little something for the environment, too. Many economists would go yet one step further: We should tax the use of all kinds of carbon-based fuels, such as coal, oil, and gasoline. Such a tax would raise revenue from a broad base while creating an incentive to conserve nonrenewable resources and curtail the CO_2 emissions that cause global warming.

Sadly, this thought process does not lead us to the optimal tax. We have merely swapped one problem for another. A tax on red sports cars would be paid only by the rich. A carbon tax would be paid by rich and poor alike, but it would probably cost the poor a larger fraction of their income. Taxes that fall more heavily on the poor than the rich, so-called regressive taxes, often offend our sense of justice. (Progressive taxes, such as the income tax, fall more heavily on the rich than the poor.) Here, as elsewhere, economics does not give us a "right answer"—only an analytical framework for thinking about important questions. Indeed the most efficient tax of all—one that is perfectly broad, simple, and fair (in the narrow, tax-related sense of the word)—is a lump-sum tax, which is imposed uniformly on every individual in a jurisdiction. Former British Prime Minister Margaret Thatcher actually tried it in 1989 with the community charge, or "poll tax." What happened? Britons rioted in the streets at the prospect of every adult paying the same tax for local community services regardless of income or property wealth (though there were some reductions for students, the poor, and the unemployed). Obviously good economics is not always good politics.

Meanwhile, not all benefits are created equal either. One of the biggest poverty-fighting tools in recent years has been the earned income tax credit (EITC), an idea that economists have pushed for decades because it creates a far better set of incentives than traditional social welfare programs. Most social programs offer benefits to individuals who are not working. The EITC does just the opposite; it uses the income tax system to subsidize low-wage workers so that their total income is raised above the poverty line. A worker who earns $11,000 and is supporting a family of four might get an additional $8,000 through the EITC and matching state programs. The idea was to "make work pay." Indeed, the system provides a powerful incentive for individuals to get into the labor force, where it is hoped they can learn skills and advance to higher-paying jobs. Of course, the program has an obvious problem, too. Unlike welfare, the EITC does not help individuals who cannot find work at all; in reality, those are the folks who are likely to be most desperate.

When I applied to graduate school many years ago, I wrote an essay expressing my puzzlement at how a country that could put a man on the moon could still have people sleeping on the streets. Part of that problem is political will; we could take a lot of people off the streets tomorrow if we made it a national priority. But I have also come to realize that NASA had it easy. Rockets conform to the unchanging laws of physics. We know where the moon will be at a given time; we know precisely how fast a spacecraft will enter or exit the earth's orbit. If we get the equations right, the rocket will land where it is supposed to—always. Human beings are more complex than that. A recovering drug addict does not behave as predictably as a rocket in orbit. We don't have a formula for persuading a sixteen-year-old not to drop out of school. But we do have a powerful tool: We know that people seek to make themselves better off, however they may define that. Our best hope for improving the human condition is to understand why we act the way we do and then plan accordingly. Programs, organizations, and systems work better when they get the incentives right. It is like rowing downstream.

CHAPTER 3

Government and the Economy:

Government is your friend (and a round of applause for all those lawyers)

The first car I ever owned was a Honda Civic. I loved the car, but I sold it with a lot of good miles left in it. Why? Two reasons: (1) It didn't have a cup holder; and (2) my wife was pregnant, and I had become fearful that our whole family would get flattened by a Chevy Suburban. I could have gotten beyond the cup holder problem. But putting a car seat in a vehicle that weighed a quarter as much as the average SUV was not an option. So we bought a Ford Explorer and became part of the problem for all of those people still driving Honda Civics.*

The point is this: My decision to buy and drive an SUV affects everyone else on the road, yet none of those people has a say in my decision. I do not have to compensate all the owners of Honda Civics for the fact that I am putting their lives slightly more at risk. Nor do I have to compensate asthmatic children who will be made worse off by the exhaust I generate as I cruise around the city getting nine miles to the gallon. And I have never mailed off a check to people living on small Pacific islands who may someday find their entire countries underwater because my CO_2 emissions are melting the polar ice caps. Yet these are real costs associated with driving a less fuel-efficient car.

---

* When our Ford Explorer rolled over at 65 mph on an interstate three years later, we bought a Volvo.

My decision to buy a Ford Explorer causes what economists refer to as an externality, which means that the private costs of my behavior are different from the social costs. When my wife and I went to the Bert Weinman Ford Dealership and the salesman, Angel, asked, "What is it going to take for me to put you in this car?," we tallied up the costs of driving an Explorer rather than a Civic: more gas, more expensive insurance, higher car payments. There was nothing on our tally sheet about asthmatic children, melting polar ice caps, or pregnant women driving Mini Coopers. Are these costs associated with driving an Explorer? Yes. Do we have to pay them? No. Therefore, they did not figure into our decision (other than as a vague sense of guilt as we contemplated telling our environmentally conscious relatives who live in Boulder, Colorado, and flush the toilet only once a day in order to conserve water).

When an externality—the gap between the private cost and the social cost of some behavior—is large, individuals have an incentive to do things that make them better off at the expense of others. The market, left alone, will do nothing to fix this problem. In fact, the market "fails" in the sense that it encourages individuals and firms to cut corners in ways that make society worse off as a result. If this concept were really as dry as most economics textbooks make it seem, then a movie like *Michael Clayton* would not have made millions at the box office. After all, that film is about a simple externality: A large agribusiness company stands accused of producing a pesticide that is seeping into local water supplies and poisoning families. *There is no market solution in this case; the market is the problem.* The polluting company maximizes profits by selling a product that causes cancer in innocent victims. Farmers who are unaware of (or indifferent to) the pollution will actually reward the company by buying more of its product, which will be cheaper or more effective than what can be produced by competitors that invest in making their products nontoxic. The only redress in this film example (like *Erin Brockovich* and *A Civil Action* before it) was through a nonmarket, government-supported mechanism: the courts. And, of course, George

Clooney looks good making sure justice is done (as Julia Roberts and John Travolta did before him).

Consider a more banal example, but one that raises the ire of most city dwellers: people who don't pick up after their dogs. In a perfect world, we would all carry pooper scoopers because we derive utility from behaving responsibly. But we don't live in a perfect world. From the narrow perspective of some individual dog walkers, it's easier ("less costly" in economist speak) to ignore Fido's unsightly pile and walk blithely on. (For those who think this is a trivial example, an average of 650 people a year break bones or are hospitalized in Paris after slipping in dog waste, according to the *New York Times*.)[1] The pooper-scooper decision can be modeled like any other economic decision; a dog owner weighs the costs and benefits of behaving responsibly and then scoops or does not scoop. But who speaks for the woman running to catch the bus the next morning who makes one misstep and is suddenly having a very bad day? No one, which is why most cities have laws requiring pet owners to pick up after their animals.

Thankfully there is a broader point: One crucial role for government in a market economy is dealing with externalities—those cases in which individuals or firms engage in private behavior that has broader social consequences. I noted in Chapter 1 that all market transactions are voluntary exchanges that make the involved parties better off. That's still true, but note the word "involved" that has left me some wiggle room. The problem is that all of the individuals *affected* by a market transaction may not be sitting at the table when the deal is struck. My former neighbor Stuart, with whom we shared an adjoining wall, was an avid bongo drum player. I'm sure that both he and the music shop owner were both pleased when he purchased a new set of bongos. (Based on the noise involved, he may even have purchased some kind of high-tech amplifier.) *But I was not happy about that transaction.*

Externalities are at the root of all kinds of policy issues, from the mundane to those that literally threaten the planet:

- *The Economist* has suggested somewhat peevishly that families traveling with small children on airplanes should be required to fly at the back of the plane so that other passengers might enjoy a "child-free zone." An editorial in the magazine noted, "Children, just like cigarettes or mobile phones, clearly impose a negative externality on people who are near them. Anybody who has suffered a 12-hour flight with a bawling baby in the row immediately ahead or a bored youngster viciously kicking their seat from behind, will grasp this as quickly as they would love to grasp the youngster's neck. Here is a clear case of market failure: parents do not bear the full costs (indeed young babies travel free), so they are too ready to take their noisy brats with them. Where is the invisible hand when it is needed to administer a good smack?"[2]

- Mobile phone use is under stricter scrutiny, both in public places, such as restaurants and commuter trains, where the behavior is fabulously annoying, but also in vehicles, where it has been linked to a higher rate of accidents. Texting is the second-most dangerous thing you can do while driving a car, next to driving drunk.

- In Chicago, Mayor Richard Daley attempted to impose a 1-cent tax on every $2 of take-out food purchases, arguing that the "litter tax" would reimburse the city for the costs of picking up litter, much of which consists of discarded fast-food containers. The mayor's economics were sound—litter is a classic externality—but a judge ruled the ordinance unconstitutional because it was "vague and lacking in uniformity" in the way it dealt with different kinds of fast-food containers. Now there is talk at the federal level of a junk food tax (or a soda tax) to deal with a different kind of food-related externality: obesity. The health care costs associated with obesity are now roughly as high as those related to smoking. Society picks up at least some of the tab for those bills through the costs of government health programs and higher insurance premiums—giving me a reason to care whether you have a Big Mac for lunch or not.

- Global warming is one of the most difficult international challenges in large part because firms that emit large amounts of greenhouse gases pay only a small share of the cost of those emissions. Indeed, even the countries in which they reside do not bear the full cost of the pollution. A steel plant in Pennsylvania emits CO_2 that may one day cause a flood in Bangladesh. (Meanwhile, acid rain caused by U.S. emissions is already killing Canadian forests.) The same thing is true in all kinds of factories around the world. Any solution to global warming will have to raise the cost of emitting greenhouse gases in a way that is binding upon all of the earth's polluters—not the easiest of tasks.

It is worth noting that there can be positive externalities as well; an individual's behavior can have a positive impact on society for which he or she is not fully compensated. I once had an office window that looked out across the Chicago River at the Wrigley Building and the Tribune Tower, two of the most beautiful buildings in a city renowned for its architecture. On a clear day, the view of the skyline, and of these two buildings in particular, was positively inspiring. But I spent five years in that office without paying for the utility that I derived from this wonderful architecture. I didn't mail a check to the Tribune Company every time I glanced out the window. Or, in the realm of economic development, a business may invest in a downtrodden neighborhood in a way that attracts other kinds of investment. Yet this business is not compensated for anchoring what may become an economic revitalization, which is why local governments often offer subsidies for such investment.

Some activities have both positive and negative externalities. Cigarettes kill people who smoke them; that is old news. Responsible adults are free to smoke or not smoke as they choose. But cigarette smoke can also harm those who happen to be lingering nearby, which

is why most office buildings consider smoking to be slightly less acceptable than running through the halls naked. Meanwhile, all fifty states
filed suit against the tobacco industry (and subsequently accepted
large settlements) on the grounds that smokers generate extra health
care costs that must be borne by state governments. In other words,
my taxes go to remove part of some smoker's lung. (Private insurance
companies do not have this problem; they simply recoup the extra cost
of insuring smokers by charging them higher premiums.)

At the same time, smokers do provide a benefit to the rest of us.
They die young. According to the American Lung Association, the
average smoker dies seven years earlier than the average nonsmoker,
which means that smokers pay into Social Security and private pension
funds for all of their working lives but then don't stick around very
long to collect the benefits. Nonsmokers, on average, get more back
relative to what they paid in. The good folks at Philip Morris have
even quantified this benefit for us. In 2001, they released a report on
the Czech Republic (just as parliament was considering raising cigarette
taxes) showing that premature deaths from smoking save the Czech
government roughly $28 million a year in pension and old-age housing
benefits. The net benefit of smoking to the government, including taxes
and subtracting public health costs, was reckoned to be $148 million.[3]

How does a market economy deal with externalities? Sometimes
the government regulates the affected activity. The federal government issues thousands of pages of regulations every year on everything
from groundwater contamination to poultry inspection. The states have
their own regulatory structures; California, for example, has a strict set
of emissions standards for automobiles. Local governments have zon-
ing laws that forbid private property owners from impinging on their
neighbors by constructing buildings that may be unsafe, inappropriate
for the neighborhood, or simply ugly. The island of Nantucket allows
only a few select colors of exterior paint lest irresponsible property
owners use neon colors that would destroy the quaint character of the
island. I live in a historic neighborhood in which every external change

to our homes—from the color of new windows to the size of a flower box—must be approved by an architecture committee.

There is another approach to dealing with externalities that tends to be favored in some cases by economists: taxing the offending behavior rather than banning it. I've conceded that my Ford Explorer was a menace to society. As Cornell economist Robert Frank noted in an op-ed for the *New York Times*, we are locked in an SUV arms race. "Any family can only choose the size of its own vehicle. It cannot dictate what others buy. Any family that unilaterally bought a smaller vehicle might thus put itself at risk by unilaterally disarming," he wrote.[4] Should the Hummer be banned? Should Detroit be ordered to manufacture safer, more fuel-efficient cars?

Economists, including Mr. Frank, would argue not. The primary problem with SUVs—and all vehicles, for that matter—is that they are too cheap to drive. The private cost of driving a Hummer to the grocery store is obviously far lower than the social cost. *So raise the private cost.* As Mr. Frank writes, "The only practical remedy, given the undeniable fact that driving bulky, polluting vehicles causes damage to others, is to give ourselves an incentive to take this damage into account when deciding what vehicles to buy." If the real cost to society of having an Explorer on the road is 75 cents a mile instead of the 50 cents a mile that it costs the vehicle's owner to operate the vehicle, then tack on a tax that equates the two. This might be accomplished with a gas tax, or an emissions tax, or a weight tax, or some combination thereof. The result will make driving a Hummer to the grocery store a lot less attractive.

But now we have entered strange terrain. Is it appropriate to allow some drivers to pay for the privilege of driving a vehicle so bulky that it might run over a Mini Cooper without even spilling the sixty-four-ounce drink in the monster cup holder? Yes, for the same reason that most of us eat ice cream even though it causes heart disease. We weigh the health costs of Starbucks Almond Fudge against that divine, creamy taste and decide to have a pint every once in a while. We don't quit ice cream entirely, nor do we have it with every meal. Economics tells us that the environment requires the same kinds of trade-offs as everything else in life. We should raise the cost of driving an SUV (or any vehicle) to reflect its true social cost and then let individual drivers decide if it still makes sense to commute forty-five miles to work in a Chevy Tahoe.

Taxing a behavior that generates a negative externality creates a lot of good incentives. First, it limits the behavior. If the cost of driving a Ford Explorer goes to 75 cents a mile, then there will be fewer Explorers on the road. As important, those people who are still driving them—and paying the full social freight—will be those who value driving an SUV the most, perhaps because they actually haul things or drive off-road. Second, a gas-guzzler tax raises revenue, which a ban on certain kinds of vehicles does not. That revenue might be used to pay for some of the costs of global warming (such as research into alternative energy sources, or at least building a dike around some of those Pacific island nations). Or it might be used to reduce some other tax, such as the income or payroll tax, that discourages behavior we would rather encourage.

Third, a tax that falls most heavily on hulking, fuel-hungry vehicles will encourage Detroit to build more fuel-efficient cars, albeit with a carrot rather than a stick. If Washington arbitrarily bans vehicles that get less than eighteen miles per gallon without raising the cost of driving those vehicles, then Detroit will produce a lot of vehicles that get—no big surprise here—about eighteen miles a gallon. Not twenty, not twenty-eight, not sixty using new solar technology. On the other hand, if consumers are going to be stuck with a tax based on fuel consumption and/or the mass of the vehicle, then they will have very different preferences when they step into the showroom. The automakers will respond quickly, and other products like the Hummer will be sent where they belong, to some kind of museum for mutant industrial products.

Is taxing externalities a perfect solution? No, far from it. The auto example alone has a number of problems, the most obvious of which is getting the size of the tax right. Scientists are not yet in complete agreement on how quickly global warming is happening, let alone what the costs might be, or, many steps beyond that, what the real cost of driving a Hummer for a mile might be. Is the right tax $0.75, $2.21, $3.07? You will never get a group of scientists to agree on that, let alone the Congress of the United States. There is an equity problem, too. I have stipulated correctly that if we raise the cost of driving gas guzzlers, then those who value them most will continue to drive them. But our measure of how much we value something is how much we are willing to pay for it—and the rich can always pay more for something than everyone else. If the cost of driving an Explorer goes to $9 a gallon, then the people driving them might be hauling wine and cheese to beach parties on Nantucket while a contractor in Chicago who needs a pickup truck to haul lumber and bricks can no longer afford it. Who really "values" their vehicle more? (Clever politicians might get around the equity issue by using a tax on gas guzzlers to offset a tax that falls most heavily on the middle class, such as the payroll tax, in which case our Chicago contractor would pay more for his truck but less to the IRS.) And last, the process of finding and taxing externalities can get out of control. Every activity generates an externality at some level. Any thoughtful policy analyst knows that some individuals who wear spandex in public should be taxed, if not jailed. I live in Chicago, where hordes of pasty people, having spent the winter indoors on the couch, flock outside in skimpy clothing on the first day in which the temperature rises above fifty degrees. This can be a scary experience for those forced to witness it and is certainly something that young children should never have to experience. Still, a tax on spandex is probably not practical.

I've wandered from my original, more important point. Anyone who tells you that markets left to their own devices will always lead to socially beneficial outcomes is talking utter nonsense. Markets alone fail to make us better off when there is a large gap between the private cost of some activity and the social cost. Reasonable people can and should debate what the appropriate remedy might be. Often it will involve government.

Of course, sometimes it may not. The parties involved in an externality have an incentive to come to a private agreement on their own. This was the insight of Ronald Coase, a University of Chicago economist who won the Nobel Prize in 1991. If the circumstances are right, one party to an externality can pay the other party to change their behavior. When my neighbor Stuart started playing his bongos, I could have paid him to stop, or to take up a less annoying instrument. If my disutility from his noise is greater than his utility from playing, I could theoretically write him a check to put the bongos away and leave us both better off. Some contrived numbers will actually help to make the point. If Stuart gets $50 of utility from banging away, and I feel the noise does $100 an hour of damage to my psyche, then we're both better off if I write him a check for $75 to take up knitting. He gets cash that does him more good than the bongos; I pay for silence, which is worth more to me than the $75 it costs.

But wait a minute: If Stuart is the guy making the noise, why should I have to pay him to stop? Maybe I don't. One of Coase's key insights is that private parties can only resolve an externality on their own if the relevant property rights are clearly defined—meaning that we know which party has the right to do what. (As we'll explore later in the chapter, property rights often involve things far more complicated than just property.) Does Stuart have the right to make whatever noise he wants? Or do I have the right to work in relative quiet? Presumably the statutes for the city of Chicago answer that question. (The answer may depend on time of day, giving him the right to make noise up until some specified hour and giving me the right to silence during the nighttime hours.)

If I have the right to work in peace, then any payment would have to go the opposite direction. Stuart would have to pay me to start banging away. But he wouldn't do that in this case, because it's not worth it to him. As a temperamental writer, the silence is worth $100 to me, so Stuart would have to pay me at least that much to endure the noise. Playing the bongos is only worth $50 to him. He's not going to write a check for $100 to do something that provides only $50 of utility. So I get my silence for free.

This explains Coase's second important insight: The private parties will always come to the same efficient solution (the one that makes the best use of the resources involved) regardless of which party starts out with the property right. The only difference is who ends up paying whom. In this case, the disputed resource is our common wall and the sound waves that move back and forth across it. The most efficient use of that resource is to keep it quiet, since I value my peaceful writing more than Stuart values his bongo playing. If Stuart has the right to make noise, I'll pay him to stop—and I get to write in peace. If I have the right to silence, Stuart won't be willing to pay enough for me to accede to his bongos—and I get to write in peace.

Remarkably, this kind of thing actually happens in real life. My favorite example is the Ohio power company that neighbors claimed was emitting "a bizarre blue plume" that was causing damage to property and health. The Clean Air Act gave the town's 221 residents the right to sue the utility to stop the pollution. So the American Electric Power company had a decision to make: (1) Stop polluting; or (2) pay the entire town to move somewhere else.[5]

The New York Times reported on the answer: "Utility Buys Town It Choked, Lock, Stock and Blue Plume." The company paid the residents roughly three times what their houses were worth in exchange for a signed agreement never to sue for pollution-related damages. For $20 million, the utility's problems packed up and went away— literally. Presumably this made financial sense. The New York Times reported that this settlement was believed to be the first deal by a company to dissolve an entire town. "It will help the company avoid the considerable expense and public-relations mess of individual lawsuits, legal and environmental experts said."

Coase made one final point: The transactions costs related to striking this kind of deal—everything from the time it takes to find everyone involved to the legal costs of making an agreement—must be reasonably low for the private parties to work out an externality on their own. Stuart and I can haggle over the fence in the backyard. The American Electric Power company can manage to strike a deal with 221 homeowners. But private parties are not going to work out a challenge like CO_2 emissions on their own. Every time I get into my car and turn on the engine, I make all of the six billion inhabitants of the planet slightly worse off. It takes a long time to write checks to six billion people, particularly when you are already late for work. (And it's arguable that some people in cold climates will benefit from climate change, so maybe they should pay me.) The property rights related to greenhouse gases are still ambiguous, too. Do I have the right to emit unlimited CO_2? Or does someone living in a Pacific island nation have the right to stop me from doing something that might submerge their entire country? This is one conflict that governments have to tackle.

But let's back up for a moment. Government does not just fix the rough edges of capitalism; it makes markets possible in the first place. You will get a lot of approving nods at a cocktail party by asserting that if government would simply get out of the way, then markets would deliver prosperity around the globe. Indeed, entire political campaigns are built around this issue. Anyone who has ever waited in line at the Department of Motor Vehicles, applied for a building permit, or tried to pay the nanny tax would agree. There is just one problem with that cocktail party sentiment: It's wrong. Good government makes a market economy possible. Period. And bad government, or no government, dashes capitalism against the rocks, which is one reason that billions of people live in dire poverty around the globe.

To begin with, government sets the rules. Countries without functioning governments are not oases of free market prosperity. They are places in which it is expensive and difficult to conduct even the simplest business. Nigeria has one of the world's largest reserves of oil and natural gas, yet firms trying to do business there face a problem known locally as BYOI—bring your own infrastructure.[6] Angola is rich with oil and diamonds, but the wealth has financed more than a decade of civil war, not economic prosperity. In 1999, Angola's rulers spent $900 million in oil revenues to purchase weapons. Never mind that one child in three dies before the age of five and life expectancy is a shocking forty-two years.[7] These are not countries in which the market economy has failed; they are countries in which the government has failed to develop and sustain the institutions necessary to support a market economy. A report issued by the United Nations Development Program placed much of the blame for world poverty on bad government. Without good governance, reliance on trickle-down economic development and a host of other strategies will not work, the report concluded.[8]

The reality is that nobody ever likes the umpire, but you can't play the World Series without one. So what are the rules for a functional market economy? First, the government defines and protects property rights. You own things: your home, your car, your dog, your golf clubs. Within reasonable limits, you can do with that property as you wish. You can sell it, or rent it, or pledge it as collateral. Most important, you can make investments in your property having full confidence that the returns from that investment will also belong to you. Imagine a world in which you spend all summer tending to your corn crop and then your neighbor drives by in his combine, waves cheerily, and proceeds to harvest the whole crop for himself. Does that sound contrived? Not if you're a musician—because that is pretty much what Napster did by allowing individuals to download music without paying any compensation to the musicians who created it or to the record companies that owned the copyrights. The music industry successfully sued Napster for facilitating piracy.

Property rights are not just about houses, cars, and things you can stack in a closet. Some of the most important property rights involve ownership of ideas, artwork, formulas, inventions, and even surgical procedures. This book is as good an example as any. I write the text. My agent sells it to a publisher, who contracts to have the book printed and distributed. The book is sold in private stores, where private security guards are hired to handle the massive, potentially unruly crowds trying to get a signed copy. At every juncture, only private parties are involved. These would appear to be straightforward market transactions; government could only get in the way. Indeed, I might curse the government for taxing my income, taxing the sale of the book, even taxing the salary that I pay the nanny to look after my children while I write.

In fact, the whole transaction is made possible by one thing: copyright law, which is a crucial form of property right for those of us who write for a living. The United States government guarantees that after I invest my time in producing a manuscript, no company can steal the text and publish it without compensating me. Any professor who photocopies it to use it in a class must pay the publisher a royalty first. Indeed, the government enforces similar rights for Microsoft software, and a related property right, a patent, for the pharmaceutical company that invented Viagra. The case of patents is an interesting one that is often mischaracterized. The ingredients in Viagra cost pennies a pill, but because Pfizer has a patent on Viagra that gives it a monopoly on the right to sell the product for twenty years, the company sells each pill for as much as $7. This huge markup, which is also common with new HIV/AIDS drugs and other lifesaving products, is often described as some kind of social injustice perpetrated by rapacious companies—the "big drug companies" that are periodically demonized during presidential campaigns. What would happen if other companies were allowed to sell Viagra, or if Pfizer were forced to sell the drug more cheaply? The price would fall to the point where it was much closer to the cost of production. Indeed, when a drug comes off patent—the point at which generic substitutes become legal—the price usually falls by 80 or 90 percent.

So why do we allow Pfizer to fleece Viagra users? Because if Viagra did not get patent protection, then Pfizer never would have made the large investments that were necessary to invent the drug in the first place. The real cost of breakthrough drugs is the research and development—scouring the world's rain forests for exotic tree barks with medicinal properties—not making the pills once the formula is discovered. The same is true with drugs for any other illness, no matter how serious or even life-threatening.* The average cost of bringing a new drug to market is somewhere in the area of $600 million. And for every successful drug, there are many expensive research forays that end in failure. Is there a way to provide affordable drugs to low-income Americans—or poor individuals elsewhere in the world—without destroying the incentive to invent those drugs? Yes; the government could buy out the patent when a new drug is invented. The government would pay a firm up front a sum equal to what the firm would have earned over the course of its twenty-year patent. After that, the government would own the property right and could charge whatever price for the drugs it deemed appropriate. It's an expensive solution that comes with some problems of its own. For example, which drug patents would the government buy? Is arthritis serious enough to justify using public funds to make a new drug more affordable? How about asthma? Still, this kind of plan is at least consistent with the economic reality: Individuals and firms will make investments only when they are guaranteed to reap what they sow, literally or figuratively.

I once stumbled on a curious example of how ambiguous property rights can stifle economic development. I was working on a long story on American Indians for *The Economist*. Having spent time on a handful of reservations, I noticed that there was very little private housing stock.

---

* I cannot fully explain why the pharmaceutical companies were so resistant to providing low-cost HIV/AIDS drugs to Africa. These countries will never be able to pay the high prices charged in the developed world, so the companies would not be forgoing profits by selling the drugs cheaply. In places like South Africa, it's either cheap drugs or no drugs. This would appear to be a perfect opportunity for price discrimination: Make the drugs cheap in Cape Town and expensive in New York. True, price discrimination could create an opportunity for a black market; drugs sold cheaply in Africa could be resold illegally at high prices in New York. But that seems a manageable problem relative to the huge public relations cost of denying important drugs to large swathes of the world's population.

Tribal members lived either in houses that had been financed by the federal government or in trailers. Why? One principal reason is that it is difficult, if not impossible, to get a conventional home mortgage on an Indian reservation because the land is owned communally. A tribal member may be given a piece of land to use, but he or she does not own it; the Indian Nation does. What that means to a commercial bank is that a mortgage that has fallen delinquent cannot be foreclosed. If a bank is denied that unpleasant but necessary option, then the lender is left without any effective collateral on its loan. A trailer, on the other hand, is different. If you fall delinquent on your payments, the company can show up one day and haul it off the reservation. But trailers, unlike conventional housing, do not support local building trades. They are assembled thousands of miles away in a factory and then transported to the reservation. That process does not provide jobs for roofers, and masons, and drywallers, and electricians—and jobs are what America's Indian reservations need more than anything else.

Government lowers the cost of doing business in the private sector in all kinds of ways: by providing uniform rules and regulations, such as contract law; by rooting out fraud; by circulating a sound currency. Government builds and maintains infrastructure—roads, bridges, ports, and dams—that makes private commerce less costly. E-commerce may be a modern wonder, but let's not lose sight of the fact that after you order khakis from Gap.com, they are dispatched from a distribution center in a truck barreling along an interstate. In the 1950s and 1960s, new roads, including the interstate highway system, accounted for a significant fraction of new capital created in the United States. And that investment in infrastructure is associated with large increases in productivity in industries that are vehicle-intensive.[9]

Effective regulation and oversight make markets more credible. Because of the diligence of the Securities and Exchange Commission (SEC), one can buy shares in a new company listed on the NASDAQ with a reasonable degree of certainty that neither the company nor the traders on the stock exchange are engaging in fraud. In short, government is responsible for the rule of law. (Failure of the rule of law is one reason why nepotism, clans, and other family-centered behavior are so common in developing countries; in the absence of binding contractual agreements, business deals can be guaranteed only by some kind of personal relationship.) Jerry Jordan, former president of the Federal Reserve Bank of Cleveland, once mused on something that is obvious but too often taken for granted: Our sophisticated institutions, both public and private, make it possible to undertake complex transactions with total strangers. He noted:

> It seems remarkable, when you think about it, that we often take substantial amounts of money to our bank and hand it over to people we have never met before. Or that securities traders can send millions of dollars to people they don't know in countries they have never been in. Yet this occurs all the time. We trust that the infrastructure is set in place that allows us not to worry that the person at the bank who takes our money doesn't just pocket it. Or that when we use credit cards to buy a new CD or tennis racquet over the Internet, from a business that is located in some other state or country, we are confident we will get our merchandise, and they are confident they will get paid.[10]

Shakespeare may have advised us to get rid of all the lawyers, but he was a playwright, not an economist. The reality is that we all complain about lawyers until we have been wronged, at which point we run out and hire the best one we can find. Government enforces the rules in a reasonably fair and efficient manner. Is it perfect? No. But rather than singing the praises of the American justice system, let me simply provide a counterexample from India. Abdul Waheed filed a lawsuit against his neighbor, a milk merchant named Mohammad Nanhe, who had built several drains at the edge of his property that emptied into Mr. Waheed's front yard. Mr. Waheed did not like the water draining onto his property, in part because he had hoped to add a third room to his cement house and he was worried that the drains would create a seepage problem. So he sued. The case came to trial in June 2000 in Moradabad, a city near New Delhi.[11]

There is one major complication with this civil dispute: The case had been filed thirty-nine years earlier; Mr. Waheed was dead and so was Mr. Nanhe. (Their relatives inherited the case.) By one calculation, if no new cases were filed in India, it would still take 324 years to clear all the existing cases from the docket. These are not just civil cases. In late 1999, a seventy-five-year-old man was released from a Calcutta jail after waiting thirty-seven years to be tried on murder charges. He was released because the witnesses and investigating officer were all dead. (A judge had declared him mentally incompetent to stand trial in 1963 but the action was somehow lost.) *Bear in mind that by developing world standards, India has relatively good government institutions.* In Somalia, these kinds of disputes are not resolved in the courts.

All the while, government enforces antitrust laws that forbid companies from conspiring together in ways that erase the benefits of competition. Having three airlines that secretly collude when setting fares is no better than having one slovenly monopoly. The bottom line is that all these institutions form the tracks on which capitalism runs. Thomas Friedman, foreign affairs columnist for the *New York Times*, once made this point in a column. "Do you know how much your average Russian would give for a week of [the U.S. Department of Justice] busting Russia's oligarchs and monopolists?" he queried.[12] He pointed out that with many of the world's economies plagued by endemic corruption, particularly in the developing world, he has found that foreigners often envy us for . . . hold on to your latte here . . . our Washington bureaucrats; "that is, our institutions, our courts, our bureaucracy, our military, and our regulatory agencies—the SEC, the Federal Reserve, the FAA, the FDA, the FBI, the EPA, the IRS, the INS, the U.S. Patent Office and the Federal Emergency Management Agency."

The government has another crucial role: It provides a wide array of goods, so-called "public goods," that make us better off but would not otherwise be provided by the private sector. Suppose I decide to buy an antimissile system to protect myself from missiles lobbed by rogue nations. (It would be similar to the DirecTV satellite dish, only a lot more expensive.) I ask my neighbor Etienne if he would like to share the cost of this system; he says no, knowing full well that my missile defense will shield his house from any missiles that North Korea may send our way. Etienne, and most of my other neighbors, have a powerful incentive to be "free riders" on my system. At the same time, I do not want to pay the full cost of the system myself. In the end, we get no missile defense system even though it might have made us all better off.

Public goods have two salient characteristics. First, the cost of offering the good to additional users—even thousands or millions of people—is very low or even zero. Think of that missile defense system; if I pay to knock terrorist missiles out of the sky, the millions of people who live relatively close to me in the Chicago metropolitan area get that benefit free. The same is true of a radio signal or a lighthouse or a large park; once it is operational for one person, it can serve thousands more at no extra cost. Second, it is very hard, if not impossible, to exclude persons who have not paid for the good from using it. How exactly do you tell a ship's captain that he can't use a lighthouse? Do you make him close his eyes as he sails by? ("Attention USS *Britannica:* You are peeking!") I once had a professor at Princeton who began his lecture on public goods by saying, "Okay, who are the suckers who actually contribute to public radio?"

Free riders can cripple enterprises. Author Stephen King once attempted an experiment in which he offered his new novel directly to readers via the Internet. The plan was that he would offer monthly installments for readers to download in exchange for a $1 payment based on the honor system. He warned that the story would fold if fewer than 75 percent of readers made the voluntary payment. "If you pay, the story rolls. If you don't, it folds," he wrote on the website. The outcome was sadly predictable to economists who have studied these kinds of problems. The story folded. At the time "The Plant" went into hibernation, only 46 percent of readers had paid to download the last chapter offered.

That is the basic problem if public goods are left to private enterprise. Firms cannot force consumers to pay for these kinds of goods, no matter how much utility they may derive from them or how often they use them. (Remember the lighthouse.) And any system of voluntary payments falls prey to the free riders. Think about the following:

- Basic research. We have already discussed the powerful incentives that profits create for pharmaceutical companies and the like. But not all important scientific discoveries have immediate commercial applications. Exploring the universe or understanding how human cells divide or seeking subatomic particles may be many steps removed from launching a communications satellite or developing a drug that shrinks tumors or finding a cleaner source of energy. As important, this kind of research must be shared freely with other scientists in order to maximize its value. In other words, you won't get rich—or even cover your costs in most cases—by generating knowledge that may someday significantly advance the human condition. Most of America's basic research is done either directly by the government at places like NASA and the National Institutes for Health or at research universities, which are nonprofit institutions that receive federal funding.

- Law enforcement. There is no shortage of private security firms— "rent-a-cops" as we used to call them in college as they aggressively sought out twenty-year-old beer drinkers. But there is a limit to what they can or will do. They will only defend your property against some kind of trespass. They will not proactively seek out criminals who might someday break into your house; they will not track Mexican drug kingpins or stop felons from entering the country or solve other crimes so that the perpetrator does not eventually attack you. All of these things would make you and your property safer in the long run, but they have inherent free rider problems. If I pay for this kind of security, everyone else in the country benefits at no cost. Everywhere in the world, most kinds of law enforcement are undertaken by government.

- Parks and open space. Chicago's lakefront is the city's greatest asset. For some thirty miles along Lake Michigan, there are parks and beaches owned by the city and protected from private development. If this is the best use of the land, which I firmly believe it is, then why wouldn't a private landowner use it for the same purposes? After all, we've just stipulated that private ownership of an asset ensures that it will be put to its most productive use. If I owned thirty miles of lakefront, why couldn't I charge bicyclists and roller bladers and picnickers in order to make a healthy profit on my investment? Two reasons: First, it would be a logistical nightmare to patrol such a large area and charge admission. More important, many of the people who value an open lakefront don't actually use it. They may enjoy the view from the window of a high-rise apartment or as they drive along Lake Shore Drive. A private developer would never collect anything from these people and would therefore undervalue the open space. This is true for many of America's natural resources. You have probably never been to Prince William Sound in Alaska and may never go there. Yet you almost certainly cared when the huge oil tanker *Exxon Valdez* ran aground and despoiled the area. Government can make us collectively better off by protecting these kinds of resources.

Obviously not all collective endeavors require the hand of government. Wikipedia is a pretty handy resource, even for those who don't make voluntary contributions to keep it up and running. Every school, church, and neighborhood has a group of eager beavers who do more than their fair share to provide important public benefits, to the great benefit of a much larger group of free riders. Those examples notwithstanding, there are compelling reasons to believe that society would underinvest in things that would make us better off without some kind of mechanism to force cooperation. As much as I love the spirit of Wikipedia, I'm comfortable leaving counterterrorism in the hands of the FBI—the government institution we've created (and pay for with taxes) to act on our behalf.

Government redistributes wealth. We collect taxes from some citizens and provide benefits to others. Contrary to popular opinion, most government benefits do not go to the poor; they go to the middle class in the form of Medicare and Social Security. Still, government has the legal authority to play Robin Hood; other governments around the world, such as the European countries, do so quite actively. What does economics have to say about this? Not much, unfortunately. The most important questions related to income distribution require philosophical or ideological answers, not economic ones. Consider the following question: Which would be a better state of the world, one in which every person in America earned $25,000—enough to cover the basic necessities—or the status quo, in which some Americans are wildly rich, some are desperately poor, and the average income is somewhere around $48,000? The latter describes a bigger economic pie; the former would be a smaller pie more evenly divided.

Economics does not provide the tools for answering philosophical questions related to income distribution. For example, economists cannot prove that taking a dollar forcibly from Steve Jobs and giving it to a starving child would improve overall social welfare. Most people intuitively believe that to be so, but it is theoretically possible that Steve Jobs would lose more utility from having the dollar taken from him than the starving child would gain. This is an extreme example of a more general problem: We measure our well-being in terms of utility, which is a theoretical concept, not a measurement tool that can be quantified, compared among individuals, or aggregated for the nation. We cannot say, for example, that Candidate A's tax plan would generate 120 units of utility for the nation while Candidate B's tax plan would generate only 111.

Consider the following question posed by Amartya Sen, winner of the 1998 Nobel Prize in Economics.[13] Three men have come to you looking for work. You have only one job to offer; the work cannot be divided among the three of them and they are all equally qualified. One of your goals is to make the world a better place by hiring the man who needs the job the most.

The first man is the poorest of the three. If improving human welfare is your primary aim, then presumably he should get the job. Or maybe not. The second man is not the poorest, but he is the unhappiest because he has only recently become poor and he is not accustomed to the deprivation. Offering him the job will cause the greatest gain in happiness.

The third man is neither the poorest nor the unhappiest. But he has a chronic health problem, borne stoically for his whole life, that can be cured with the wages from the job. Thus, giving him the job would have the most profound effect on an individual's quality of life.

Who should get the job? As would be expected of a Nobel Prize winner, Mr. Sen has many interesting things to say about this dilemma. But the bottom line is that there is no right answer. The same thing is true—contrary to what politicians on both sides of the political spectrum will tell you—with issues related to the redistribution of wealth in a modern economy. Will a tax increase that funds a better safety net for the poor but lowers overall economic growth make the country better off? That is a matter of opinion, not economic expertise. (Note that every presidential administration is able to find very qualified economists to support its ideological positions.) Liberals (in the American sense of the word) often ignore the fact that a growing pie, even if unequally divided, will almost always make even the small pieces larger. The developing world needs economic growth (to which international trade contributes heavily) to make the poor better off. Period. One historical reality is that government policies that ostensibly serve the poor can be ineffective or even counterproductive if they hobble the broader economy.

Meanwhile, conservatives often blithely assume that we should all rush out into the street and cheer for any policy that makes the economy grow faster, neglecting the fact that there are perfectly legitimate intellectual grounds for supporting other policies, such as protecting the environment or redistributing income, that may diminish the overall size of the pie. Indeed, some evidence suggests that our sense of well-being is determined at least as much by our relative wealth as it is by our absolute level of wealth. In other words, we derive utility not just from having a big television but from having a television that is as big as or bigger than the neighbors.'

Then there is one of the most controversial questions of all: Should government protect people from themselves? Should society expend resources to stop you from doing stupid things that don't affect the rest of us? Or is that your business? The most important thing to realize is that the answer to this question is philosophical; the best economics can do is frame the range of defensible views. At one end of the continuum is the belief that individuals are rational (or at least more rational than government), meaning that individual citizens are the best judge of what is good for them, not the rest of us. If you like to sniff glue and then roll backward down the basement steps, good for you. Just make sure that you pay all your own health care costs and don't drive a car after you've been into the glue.

The behavioral economists have provided plenty of ammunition for the opposite end of the continuum, where reasonable people argue that society can and should stop people from doing things that are likely to turn out badly. We have good evidence that human decision making is prone to certain kinds of errors, such as underestimating risk or planning poorly for the future. As a practical matter, those mistakes often do spill over to affect the rest of us, as we saw in the real estate collapse and the accompanying mortgage mess.

And there is a range of views in between (e.g., you're allowed to sniff glue and roll down the steps but only while wearing a helmet). One intriguing and practical middle ground is the notion of "libertarian paternalism," which was advanced in an influential book called

Nudge by Richard Thaler, a professor of behavioral science and economics at the University of Chicago, and Cass Sunstein, a Harvard Law School professor now serving in the Obama administration. The idea behind benign paternalism is that individuals do make systematic errors of judgment, but society should not force you to change your behavior (that's the libertarian part); instead, we should merely point you in the right direction (that's the paternalism part).

One of Thaler and Sunstein's key insights is that our decisions are often a product of inertia. If our employer automatically signs us up for some kind of insurance coverage, then we'll stick with that, even if six other plans are offered. Conversely, we may not sign up for any plan at all if it requires some proactive behavior on our part—reading a benefits manual, filling out a form, going to a stupid human resources seminar, or doing anything else that involves time and effort. Thaler and Sunstein propose that inertia (and other decision-making foibles) can be used to some advantage. If policymakers are concerned about some individual behavior, such as inadequate retirement savings, then the libertarian paternalistic option is to make the default option one that automatically puts a decent amount of money from every paycheck into a retirement account. That's the "nudge." Anyone is free to choose another option at any time. But a shockingly high proportion of people will stay wherever you put them in the first place.

This idea has profound implications when it comes to something like organ donation. Spain, France, Norway, Israel, and many other countries have "opt-out" (or presumed consent) laws when it comes to organ donation. You are an organ donor unless you indicate otherwise, which you are free to do. (In contrast, the United States has an "opt-in" system, meaning that you are not an organ donor unless you sign up to be one.) Inertia matters, even when it comes to something as serious as organ donation. Economists have found that presumed consent laws have a significant positive effect on organ donation, controlling for relevant country characteristics such as religion and health expenditures. Spain has the highest rate of cadaveric organ donations

in the world—50 percent higher than the United States.[14] True liber-
tarians (as opposed to the paternalistic kind) reject presumed consent
laws, because they imply that the government "owns" your internal
organs until you make some effort to get them back.

Good government matters. The more sophisticated our economy
becomes, the more sophisticated our government institutions need to
be. The Internet is a perfect example. The private sector is the engine
of growth for the web economy, but it is the government that roots out
fraud, makes on-line transactions legally binding, sorts out property
rights (such as domain names), settles disputes, and deals with issues
that we have not even thought about yet.

   One sad irony of September 11 was that one simple-minded view
of government—that "taxpayers know better what to do with their
money than the government does"—was exposed for its hollowness.
Individual taxpayers cannot gather intelligence, track down a fugi-
tive in the mountains of Afghanistan, do research on bioterrorism,
or protect planes and airports. It is true that if the government takes
money out of my paycheck, then there are things that would have
given me utility that I can no longer buy. But it is also true that there
are things that would make me better off that I cannot buy for myself.
I cannot build a missile defense system, or protect endangered species,
or stop global warming, or install traffic lights, or regulate the New
York Stock Exchange, or negotiate lower trade barriers with China.
Government enables us to work collectively to do those things.

CHAPTER 4

Government and the Economy II:

The army was lucky to get that screwdriver for $500

By now you are probably ready to extol the virtues of bureaucracy at your next dinner party. Not so fast. If government were so wonderful, then the most government-intensive countries in the world—places like North Korea and Cuba—would be economic powerhouses. They're not. Government is good at doing some things and tragically bad at doing others. Government can deal with significant externalities—or it can regulate an economy to the point of ruin. Government can provide essential public goods—or it can squander enormous tax revenues on ineffective programs and pet projects. Government can transfer money from the wealthy to the disadvantaged—or it can transfer money from common folk to the politically well-connected. In short, government can be used to create the foundations for a vibrant market economy or to stifle highly productive behavior. The wisdom, of course, lies in telling the difference.

There is an old joke, one of Ronald Reagan's favorites, that goes something like this:

A Soviet woman is trying to buy a Lada, one of the cheap automobiles made in the former Soviet Union. The dealer tells her that there is a shortage of these cars, despite their reputation for shoddy quality. Still, the woman insists on placing an order. The dealer gets out a large, dusty ledger and adds the woman's name to the long wait-ing list. "Come back two years from now on March 17th," he says.

The woman consults her calendar. "Morning or afternoon?" she asks.

"What difference does it make?" the surly dealer replies. "That's two years from now!"

"The plumber is coming that day," she says.

If the USSR taught us anything, it is that monopoly stifles any need to be innovative or responsive to customers. And government is one very large monopoly. Why is the clerk at the Department of Motor Vehicles plodding and surly? Because she can be. *What would your business look like if your customers, by law, could not go anywhere else?* It would certainly make me think twice about working late, or, for that matter, working at all on warm summer days when the Cubs were playing at home.

Government operations are often described as inefficient. In fact, they operate exactly as we would expect given their incentives. Think about the Department of Motor Vehicles, which has a monopoly on the right to grant driver's licenses. What is the point of being friendly, staying open longer, making customers comfortable, adding clerks to shorten lines, keeping the office clean, or interrupting a personal call when a customer comes to the window? *None of these things will pro-duce even one more customer!* Every single person who needs a driver's license already comes to the DMV and will continue to come no matter how unpleasant the experience. There are limits, of course. If service becomes bad enough, then voters may take action against the politicians in charge. But that is an indirect, cumbersome process. Compare that to your options in the private sector. If a rat scampered across the counter at your favorite Chinese take-out restaurant, you would (presumably) just stop ordering there. End of problem. The restaurant will get rid of the rats or go out of business. Meanwhile, if you stop going to the Department of Motor Vehicles, you may end up in jail.

This contrast was illustrated to me quite sharply when a check I was expecting from Fidelity, the mutual fund company, failed to show up in the mail. (I needed the money to pay back my mother, who can be a fierce creditor.) Day after day went by—no check. Meanwhile, my mother was "checking in" with increasing frequency. One of two parties was guilty, Fidelity or the U.S. Postal Service, and I was getting progressively more angry. Finally I called Fidelity to demand proof that the check had been mailed. I was prepared to move all of my (relatively meager) assets to Vanguard, Putnam, or some other mutual fund company (or at least make the threat). Instead, I spoke with a very friendly customer assistant who explained that the check had been mailed two weeks earlier but apologized profusely for my inconvenience anyway. She canceled the check and issued another one in a matter of seconds. Then she apologized some more for a problem that, it was now apparent, her company did not cause.

The culprit was the post office. So I got even angrier and then . . . I did nothing. What exactly was I supposed to do? The local postmaster does not accept complaints by phone. I did not want to waste time writing a letter (which might never arrive anyway). Nor would it help to complain to our letter carrier, who has never been consumed by the quality of his service. Roughly once a month he gets "off" by a house and delivers every family's mail to the house one door to the west. The point, carefully disguised in this diatribe, is that the U.S. Postal Service has a monopoly on the delivery of first-class mail. And it shows.

There are two broader lessons to be learned from this. First, government should not be the sole provider of a good or service unless there is a compelling reason to believe that the private sector will fail in that role. This exclusion leaves plenty for government to do in areas ranging from public health to national defense. Having just lambasted the Department of Motor Vehicles, I must admit that issuing driver's licenses is probably a function that should remain in the hands of government. Private firms issuing driver's licenses might not compete only on price and quality of service; they would have a powerful incentive to attract customers by issuing licenses to drivers who don't deserve them.

Still, that leaves a lot of things that government should not be doing. Delivering mail is one of them. A century ago the government may have had legitimate reasons for being in the mail business. The U.S. Postal Service indirectly assisted underdeveloped regions of the country by guaranteeing mail delivery at a subsidized rate (since delivering mail to remote areas is more expensive than delivering to a metropolitan area but the stamp costs the same). The technology was different, too. In 1820, it was unlikely that more than one private firm would have made the massive investment necessary to build a system that could deliver mail anywhere in the country. (A private monopoly is no better—and perhaps worse—than a government monopoly.) Times have changed. FedEx and UPS have proved that private firms are perfectly capable of building worldwide delivery infrastructures.

Is there a huge economic cost associated with mediocre mail service? Probably not. But imagine the U.S. Postal Service controlling other important sectors of the economy. Elsewhere in the world, the government runs steel mills, coal mines, banks, hotels, airlines. All the benefits that competition can bring to these businesses are lost, and citizens are made worse off as a result. (Food for thought: One of the largest government monopolies remaining in the United States is public education.)

There is a second more subtle point. Even if government has an important role to play in the economy, such as building roads and bridges, it does not follow that government must actually do the work. Government employees do not have to be the ones pouring cement. Rather, government can plan and finance a new highway and then solicit bids from private contractors to do the work. If the bidding process is honest and competitive (big "ifs" in many cases), then the project will go to the firm that can do the best work at the lowest cost. In short, a public good is delivered in a way that harnesses all the benefits of the market.

This distinction is sometimes lost on American taxpayers, a point that Barack Obama made during one of his town hall meetings on health care reform. He said, "I got a letter the other day from a woman. She said, 'I don't want government-run health care. I don't want socialized medicine. And don't touch my Medicare.'" The irony, of course, is that Medicare *is* government-run health care; the program allows Americans over age 65 to seek care from their private doctors, who are then reimbursed by the federal government.Even the Central Intelligence Agency has taken this lesson to heart. The CIA needs to be on the cutting edge of technology, yet it cannot provide the same incentives to innovate as the private sector can. Someone who makes a breakthrough discovery at the CIA will not find himself or herself worth hundreds of millions of dollars six months later, as might happen at a Silicon Valley startup. So the CIA decided to use the private sector for its own ends by using money appropriated by Congress to open its own venture capital firm, named In-Q-It (in a sly reference to Q, the technology guru who develops gadgets for James Bond).[1] An In-Q-It executive explained that the purpose of the venture was to "move information technology to the agency more quickly than traditional Government procurement processes allow." Like any other venture capital firm, In-Q-It will make investments in small firms with promising new technologies. In-Q-It and the firms it bankrolls will make money—perhaps a lot of money—if these technologies turn out to have valuable commercial applications. At the same time, the CIA will retain the right to use any new technology with potential intelligence-gathering applications. A Silicon Valley entrepreneur funded by In-Q-It may develop a better way to encrypt data on the Internet— something that e-commerce firms would snap up. Meanwhile, the CIA would end up with a better way to safeguard information sent to Washington by covert operatives around the world.

In the private sector, markets tell us where to devote our resources. While sitting in the center-field seats at a Chicago White Sox game, I spotted a vendor walking through the stands wearing what was prominently advertised as the Margarita Space Pak. This piece of technology enabled the vendor to make frozen margaritas on the spot; somehow he mixed the drinks in his backpack-like device and then poured them through a hose into plastic cups. The ostensible social benefit of this breakthrough technology was that baseball fans could now enjoy margaritas, rather than just beer, without leaving their seats. I suspect that some of our country's top engineering minds—a scarce resource—devoted their time and effort to creating the Margarita Space Pak, which means that they were *not* spending their time searching for a cheaper, cleaner source of energy or a better way to deliver nutrients to malnourished children in Africa. Does the world need the Margarita Space Pak? No. Could the engineering minds that created it have been put to some more socially useful purpose? Yes. But—this is an important point—*that's my opinion and I don't run the world.*

When government controls some element of the economy, scarce resources are allocated by autocrats or bureaucrats or politicians rather than by the market. In the former Soviet Union, massive steel plants churned out tons of steel, but the average citizen couldn't buy soap or decent cigarettes. In hindsight, it should not have been a surprise that the USSR was the first to send a rocket into orbit (and equally obvious that it would not invent the Margarita Space Pak). The government could simply mandate that resources be spent on the space program, even if people would rather have had fresh vegetables or tube socks. Some of these resource allocation decisions were tragic. For example, Soviet central planners did not consider birth control to be an economic priority. The Soviet government could have made contraceptives available to all; any country that can build intercontinental ballistic missiles has the know-how to make a birth control pill, or at least a condom. But contraception simply was not where central planners chose to channel the country's resources, leaving abortion as the only form of family planning. In the years of communism, there were roughly two abortions for every single live birth. Since the collapse of the Soviet Union, Western contraceptives have become widely available and the abortion rate has fallen by half.

Even in democratic countries, the political process can devote resources to some pretty strange places. I once interviewed a technology expert about the government's plans at the time to build a high-speed particle accelerator (a good example of basic research). The accelerator would bring jobs and federal money to the location that landed the project. This was in the early 1990s, and the two leading sites were northern Illinois and somewhere in Texas. According to the fellow I was speaking with, Illinois was the more attractive site because it already had a particle accelerator and a major federal laboratory. Much of the scientific infrastructure was in place and would not have to be duplicated. Despite that, the project was sited in Texas. "Why?" I asked. This guy looked at me as if I were some kind of idiot. "Because George [H. W.] Bush was president," he answered, as if there could be no more obvious reason to put a giant particle accelerator in Texas. In the end, the government spent roughly $1 billion on the project and then abandoned it.

The private sector allocates resources where they will earn the highest return. In contrast, the government allocates resources wherever the political process sends them. (Consider a front-page headline in the *Wall Street Journal:* "Industries That Backed Bush Are Now Seeking Return on Investment.")[2]

Is that because Republicans are particularly prone to this kind of money-grubbing political influence? Perhaps. But that wouldn't explain this more recent *New York Times* headline: "In Washington, One Bank Chief Still Holds Sway." The story began, "Jamie Dimon, the head of JPMorgan Chase, will hold a meeting of his board here in the nation's capital for the first time on Monday, with a special guest expected: the White House chief of staff, Rahm Emanuel. Mr. Emanuel's appearance would underscore the pull of Mr. Dimon, who amid the disgrace of his industry has emerged as President Obama's favorite banker, and in turn, the envy of his Wall Street rivals. It also reflects a good return on what Mr. Dimon has labeled his company's 'seventh line of business'—government relations."[3]

There is nothing inherently wrong with this. Politics is a necessary but imperfect process, and everyone has a right to seek influence. Military bases get built or closed in a way that reflects the makeup of the Senate Armed Services Committee as much as or more than the military needs of the country. A private army is not an option, so this is the best we can reasonably expect. But the less the economy is left to politics, the better. Powerful politicians should not be deciding, for example, who gets bank credit and who does not. Yet that is exactly what happens in autocratic nations like China and in democratic countries like Indonesia where politicians play "crony capitalism." Projects that have the potential to be highly profitable do not get financing while dubious undertakings sponsored by the president's brother-in-law are lavished with government funds. Consumers lose in two ways. First, their tax money is squandered when projects that never should have been funded in the first place go bust (or when the whole banking system needs to be bailed out because it is full of rotten, politically motivated loans). Second, the economy does not develop as quickly or efficiently as it might because credit (a finite resource) is channeled away from worthwhile projects: car plants don't get built; students don't get loans; entrepreneurs don't get funding. As a result, resources are squandered and the economy does not perform anywhere near its potential.

Government need not run steel mills or parcel out bank loans to meddle in the economy. The more subtle and pervasive kind of government involvement is regulation. Markets work because resources flow to where they are valued most. Government regulation inherently interferes with that process. In the world painted by economics textbooks, entrepreneurs cross the road to earn higher profits. In the real world, government officials stand by the road and demand a toll, if they don't block the crossing entirely. The entrepreneurial firm may have to obtain a license to cross the road, or have its vehicle emissions tested by the Department of Transportation as it crosses the road, or prove to the INS that the workers crossing the road are U.S. citizens. Some of these regulations may make us better off. It's good to have government officials blocking the road when the "entrepreneur" is carrying seven kilos of cocaine. But every single regulation carries a cost, too.

Milton Friedman, who was a delightful writer and an articulate spokesman for a less intrusive government (and a far more subtle thinker than many of the writers who haunt the op-ed pages these days purporting to have inherited his mantle), makes this point in *Capitalism and Freedom* by recounting an exchange between an economist and a representative of the American Bar Association at a large meeting of lawyers.[4] The economist was arguing before the group that admission to the bar should be less restrictive. Allowing more lawyers to practice, including those who might not be the sharpest knives in the drawer, would lower the cost of legal services, he argued. After all, some legal procedures, such as basic wills and real estate closings, do not require the services of a brilliant Constitutional scholar. He argued by analogy that it would be absurd for the government to require that all automobiles be Cadillacs. At that point, a lawyer in the audience rose and said, "The country cannot afford anything but Cadillac lawyers!"

In fact, demanding only "Cadillac lawyers" completely misses all that economics seeks to teach us about trade-offs (for reasons that have nothing to do with the fact that General Motors is a basket case). In a world with only Cadillacs, most people would not be able to afford any transportation at all. Sometimes there is nothing wrong with allowing people to drive Toyota Corollas.

For a striking international example of the effects of regulation on the economy, consider the civil unrest in 2000 in Delhi, India.[5] Delhi is one of the most polluted cities in the world. After the Supreme Court of India made a major decision regarding industrial pollution, thousands of Delhi residents took to the streets in violent protest. "Mobs torched buses, threw stones, and blocked major roads," the

New York Times reported. Here is the twist: *The protesters were supporting the polluters.* The Supreme Court held the city of Delhi in contempt for failing to close some ninety thousand small factories that pollute the area. Those factories employed roughly a million people who would be thrown out of work. The headline on the story nicely encapsulated the trade-off: "A Cruel Choice in New Delhi: Jobs vs. a Safer Environment."

How about DDT, one of the nastier chemicals mankind has unleashed on the environment? DDT is a "persistent organic pollutant" that works its way into and up the food chain, wreaking havoc along the way. Should this noxious pesticide be banned from the planet? *The Economist* has made a convincing argument that it should not.[6] Much of the developing world is ravaged by malaria; some 300 million people suffer from the disease every year and more than a million die. (Of course, malaria is not a disease that we are particularly sensitive to in the developed world, since it was eradicated in North America and Europe fifty years ago. Tanzanian researcher Wen Kilama once famously pointed out that if seven Boeing 747s, mostly filled with children, crashed into Mt. Kilimanjaro *every day*, then the world would take notice. That is the scale on which malaria kills its victims.)[7]

Harvard economist Jeffrey Sachs has estimated that sub-Saharan Africa would be almost a third richer today if malaria had been eradicated in 1965. Now, back to DDT, which is the most cost-effective way of controlling the mosquitoes that spread the disease. The next best alternative is not only less effective but also four times as expensive. Do the health benefits of DDT justify its environmental costs?

Yes, argue some groups—like the Sierra Club, the Endangered Wildlife Trust, Environmental Defense Fund, and the World Health Organization. Yes, you read those names correctly. They have all embraced DDT as a "useful poison" for fighting malaria in poor countries. When the United Nations convened representatives from 120 countries in South Africa in 2000 to ban "persistent organic pollutants," the delegates agreed to exempt DDT in situations where it is being used to fight malaria.[8]

Meanwhile, not all regulations are created equal. The relevant question is not always whether or not government should involve itself in the economy; the more important issue may be how the subsequent regulation is structured. University of Chicago economist and Nobel laureate Gary Becker spends his summers on Cape Cod, where he is a fond consumer of striped bass.[9] Because the stocks of this fish are dwindling, the government has imposed a limit on the total commercial catch of striped bass allowed every season. Mr. Becker has no problem with that; he would like to be able to eat striped bass ten years from now, too.

Instead, he raised the issue in a column for *Business Week* about how the government chose to limit the total catch. At the time he was writing, the government had imposed an aggregate quota on the quantity of striped bass that could be harvested every season. Mr. Becker wrote, "Unfortunately, this is a very poor way to control fishing because it encourages each fishing boat to catch as much as it can early in the season, before other boats bring in enough fish to reach the aggregate quota that applies to all of them." Everybody loses: The fishermen get low prices for their fish when they sell into a glut early in the season; then, after the aggregate quota is reached early in the season, consumers are unable to get any striped bass at all. Several years later, Massachusetts did change its system so that the striped bass quota is divided among individual fishermen; the total catch is still limited but individual fishermen can fulfill their quota anytime during the season.

The key to thinking like an economist is recognizing the trade-offs inherent to fiddling with markets. Regulation can disrupt the movement of capital and labor, raise the cost of goods and services, inhibit innovation, and otherwise shackle the economy (such as by letting mosquitoes escape alive). *And that is just the regulation inspired by good intentions.* At worst, regulation can become a powerful tool for self-interest as firms work the political system to their own benefit. After all, if you can't beat your competitors, then why not have the government hobble them for you? University of Chicago economist George Stigler won the Nobel Prize in Economics in 1982 for his trenchant observation and supporting evidence that firms and professional associations often seek regulation as a way of advancing their own interests.

Consider a regulatory campaign that took place in my home state of Illinois. The state legislature was being pressured to enact more stringent licensing requirements for manicurists. Was this a grassroots lobbying campaign being waged by the victims of pedicures gone terribly awry? (One can just imagine them limping in pain up the capital steps.) Not exactly. The lobbying was being done by the Illinois Cosmetology Association on behalf of established spas and salons that would rather not compete with a slew of immigrant upstarts. The number of nail salons grew 23 percent in just one year in the late 1990s, with discount salons offering manicures for as little as $6, compared to $25 in a full-service salon. Stricter licensing requirements—which almost always exempt existing service providers—would have limited this fierce competition by making it more expensive to open a new salon.

Milton Friedman has pointed out that the same thing happened on a wider scale in the 1930s. After Hitler came to power in 1933, large numbers of professionals fled Germany and Austria for the United States. In response, many professions erected barriers such as "good citizenship" requirements and language exams that had a tenuous connection to the quality of service provided. Friedman pointed out that the number of foreign-trained physicians licensed to practice in the United States in the five years after 1933 was the same as in the five years before—which would have been highly unlikely if licensing requirements existed only to screen out incompetent doctors but quite likely if the licensing requirements were used to ration the number of foreign doctors allowed into the profession.

By global standards, the United States has a relatively lightly regulated economy (though try making that argument at a Chamber of Commerce meeting). Indeed, one sad irony of the developing world is that governments fail in their most basic tasks, such as defining property rights and enforcing the law, while piling on other kinds of heavy-handed regulation. In theory, this kind of regulation could protect consumers from fraud, improve public health, or safeguard the environment. On the other hand, economists have asked whether this kind of regulation is less of a "helping hand" for society and more of a "grabbing hand" for corrupt bureaucrats whose opportunities to extort bribes rise along with the number of government permits and licenses required for any endeavor.

A group of economists studied the "helping hand" versus "grabbing hand" question by examining the procedures, costs, and expected delays associated with starting up a new business in seventy-five different countries.[10] The range was extraordinary. Registering and licensing a business in Canada requires a mere two procedures compared to twenty in Bolivia. The time required to open a new business legally ranges from two days, again in Canada, to six months in Mozambique. The cost of jumping through these assorted government hoops ranges from 0.4 percent of per capita GDP in New Zealand to 260 percent of per capita GDP in Bolivia. The study found that in poor countries like Vietnam, Mozambique, Egypt, and Bolivia an entrepreneur has to give up an amount equal to one to two times his annual salary (not counting bribes and the opportunity cost of his time) just to get a new business licensed.

So are consumers safer and healthier in countries like Mozambique than they are in Canada or New Zealand? No. The authors find that compliance with international quality standards is lower in countries with more regulation. Nor does this government red tape appear to reduce pollution or raise health levels. Meanwhile, excessive regulation pushes entrepreneurs into the underground economy, where there is no regulation at all. It is hardest to open a new business in countries where corruption is highest, suggesting that excessive regulation is a potential source of income for the bureaucrats who enforce it.

India has over a billion people, many of whom are desperately poor. Education has clearly played a role in moving the nation's economy forward and lifting millions of citizens out of poverty. Higher education in particular has contributed to the creation and expansion of a vibrant information technology sector; however, a recent shortage of skilled workers has been a drag on economic growth. So it's no great economic conundrum as to why a pharmaceutical college in Mumbai would seek to use empty space in its eight-story building to double student enrollment.

The problem is that this action turned the college administration into criminals. It's true—the Indian government imposes strict regulations on its technical colleges that protect against something as reckless and potentially dangerous as using empty space to educate more students. Specifically, the law stipulates that a technical college must provide 168 square feet of building space for each student (to ensure adequate space for learning). That formula precludes the Principal K. M. Kundnani College of Pharmacy from teaching more than 300 students—regardless of the fact that all the lecture halls on the top floor of the building are padlocked for lack of use.

According to the *Wall Street Journal,* "The rules also stipulate the exact size for libraries and administrative offices, the ratio of professors to assistant professors and lecturers, quotas for student enrollment and the number of computer terminals, books and journals that must be on site."[11]

Thankfully, governments sometimes roll back these kinds of regulation. In November 2008, the European Union acted boldly to legalize . . . ugly fruits and vegetables. Prior to that time, supermarkets across Europe were forbidden from selling "overly curved, extra knobbly or oddly shaped" produce. This was a true act of political courage by European Union authorities, given that representatives from sixteen of the twenty-seven member nations tried to block the deregulation while it was being considered by the EU Agricultural Management Committee.[12]

I wish I were making this stuff up.

Let's step out of our cynical mode for a moment and return to the idea that government has the capacity to do many good things. Even then, when government is doing the things that it is theoretically supposed to do, government spending must be financed by levying taxes, and taxes exert a cost on the economy. This "fiscal drag," as Burton Malkiel has called it, stems from two things. First, taxes take money out of our pockets, which necessarily diminishes our purchasing power and therefore our utility. True, the government can create jobs by spending billions of dollars on jet fighters, but we are paying for those jets with money from our paychecks, which means that we buy fewer televisions, we give less to charity, we take fewer vacations. Thus, government is not necessarily creating jobs; it may be simply moving them around, or, on net, destroying them. This effect of taxation is less obvious than the new defense plant at which happy workers churn out shiny airplanes. (When we turn to macroeconomics later in the book, we will examine the Keynesian premise that government can increase economic growth by stoking the economy during economic downturns.)

Second, and more subtly, taxation causes individuals to change their behavior in ways that make the economy worse off without necessarily providing any revenue for the government. Think about the income tax, which can be as high as 50 cents for every dollar earned by the time all the relevant state and federal taxes are tallied up. Some individuals who would prefer to work if they were taking home every dollar they earn may decide to leave the labor force when the marginal tax rate is 50 percent. *Everybody loses in this situation.* Someone whose preference is to work quits his or her job (or does not start working in the first place), yet the government raises no revenue.

As we noted in Chapter 2, economists refer to this kind of inefficiency associated with taxation as "deadweight loss." It makes you worse off without making anyone else better off. Imagine that a burglar breaks into your home and steals assorted personal possessions; in his haste, he makes off with wads of cash but also a treasured family photo album. There is no deadweight loss associated with the cash he has stolen; every dollar purloined from you makes him better off by a dollar. (Perversely, it is simply a transfer of wealth in the eyes of our amoral economists.) On the other hand, the stolen photo album is pure deadweight loss. It means nothing to the thief, who tosses it in a Dumpster when he realizes what he has taken. Yet it is a tremendous loss to you. Any kind of taxation that discourages productive behavior causes some deadweight loss.

Taxes can discourage investment, too. An entrepreneur who is considering making a risky investment may do so when the expected return is $100 million but not when the expected return, diminished by taxation, is only $60 million. An individual may pursue a graduate degree that will raise her income by 10 percent. But that same investment, which is costly in terms of tuition and time, may not be worthwhile if her *after-tax* income—what she actually sees after all those deductions on the paycheck—only goes up 5 percent. (On the day my younger brother got his first paycheck, he came home, opened the envelope, and then yelled, "Who the hell is FICA?") Or consider a family that has a spare $1,000 and is deciding between buying a big-screen television and squirreling the money away in an investment fund. These two options have profoundly differently impacts on the economy in the long run. Choosing the investment makes capital available to firms that build plants, conduct research, train workers. These investments are the macro equivalents of a college education; they make us more productive in the long run and therefore richer. Buying the television, on the other hand, is current consumption. It makes us happy today but does nothing to make us richer tomorrow.

Yes, money spent on a television keeps workers employed at the television factory. But if the same money were invested, it would create jobs somewhere else, say for scientists in a laboratory or workers on a construction site, while also making us richer in the long run. Think about the college example. Sending students to college creates jobs for professors. Using the same money to buy fancy sports cars for high school graduates would create jobs for auto workers. The crucial difference between these scenarios is that a college education makes a young person more productive for the rest of his or her life; a sports car does not. Thus, college tuition is an investment; buying a sports car is consumption (though buying a car for work or business might be considered an investment).

So back to our family with a spare $1,000. What will they choose to do with it? Their decision will depend on the after-tax return the family can expect to earn by investing the money rather than spending it. The higher the tax, such as a capital gains tax, the lower the return on the investment—and therefore the more attractive the television becomes.

Taxation discourages both work and investment. Many economists argue that cutting taxes and rolling back regulation unleashes productive forces in the economy. This is true. The most ardent "supply-siders" argue further that tax cuts can actually raise the amount of revenue collected by the government because we all will work harder, earn higher incomes, and end up paying more in taxes even though tax rates have fallen. This is the idea behind the Laffer curve, which provided the intellectual underpinnings for the large Reagan-era tax cuts. Economist Arthur Laffer theorized in 1974 that high tax rates discourage so much work and investment that cutting taxes will earn the government more revenue, not less. (He first sketched a graph of this idea on a restaurant napkin while having dinner with a group of journalists and politicians. In one of life's delicious ironies, it was Dick Cheney's napkin.)[13] At some level of taxation, this relationship must be true. If the personal income tax is 95 percent, for example, then no one is going to do a whole lot of work beyond what is necessary to subsist. Cutting the tax rate to 50 percent would almost certainly boost government revenues.

But would the same relationship hold true in the United States, where tax rates were much lower to begin with? Both the Reagan tax cuts and the George W. Bush tax cuts provided an answer: no.

These large tax cuts did not boost government revenues (relative to what they would have been in the absence of the tax cut);* they led to large budget deficits. In the case of the Reagan tax cuts, Mr. Laffer's conjecture did appear to hold true for the wealthiest Americans, who ended up sending more money to the Treasury after their tax rates were cut. Of course, this may be mere coincidence. As we shall explore in Chapter 6, highly skilled workers saw their wages rise sharply over the last several decades as the economy increasingly demanded more brains than brawn. Thus, the wealthiest Americans may have paid more in taxes because their incomes went up sharply, not because they were working harder in response to lower tax rates.

In the United States, where tax rates are low relative to the rest of the world, supply-side economics is a chimera: In all but unique circumstances, we cannot cut taxes *and* have more money to spend on government programs—a point that conservative economists readily concede. Bruce Bartlett, an official in both the Reagan and the George H. W. Bush administrations, has publicly lamented that the term "supply-side economics" has morphed from an important and defensible idea—that lower marginal tax rates stimulate economic activity—into the "implausible" notion "that *all* tax cuts raise revenue."[14] When Senator John McCain told the *National Review* in 2007 that tax cuts "as we all know, increase revenues," Harvard economist

---

* There is a subtle but important analytical point here. Those who argue that tax cuts increase government revenues often point out, correctly, that government revenues are higher after a major tax cut than before. But this is not the appropriate comparison to make. The question we should ask is whether government revenues after the tax cut are higher than they would have been if there had not been a tax cut. The reason this distinction matters is that inflation and economic growth push government revenues higher year after year even when the tax rate is unchanged. So it's entirely plausible that revenues would have climbed 5 percent without the tax cut; if they climb 2 percent with the tax cut, government revenues are indeed higher than the year before—but lower than they would have been without the tax cut. If spending growth is not curtailed to match this new revenue reality, then budget deficits will result, which is usually what happens.

Greg Mankiw (who served as chairman of the Council of Economic Advisers for George W. Bush) posed the logical follow-up question on his blog: "If you think tax cuts increase revenue, why advocate spending restraint? Can't we pay for new spending programs with more tax cuts?"[15] If I sound rather emphatic in making this point, I am. The problem with the tax-cuts-increase-revenue fallacy is that it confuses the debate over our public finances by giving the illusion that we can get something for nothing. You should recognize by now that this is not usually the case in economics. There are a lot of good things about tax cuts. They leave more money in our pockets. They stimulate hard work and risk-taking. In fact, the increased economic activity caused by lower tax rates usually does help to make up for *some* of the lost revenue. One dollar in tax cuts may only cost the government eighty cents in lost revenue (or fifty cents in extreme cases), as government is taking a smaller slice of a bigger pie.

Think about a simple numerical example. Suppose the tax rate is 50 percent and the tax base is $100 million. Tax revenues would be $50 million. Now suppose that the tax rate is cut to 40 percent. Some people work extra hours now that they get to keep more of their earnings; a few spouses take second jobs. Assume that the tax base grows to $110 million. Government revenue is now 40 percent of that bigger economy, or $44 million. Government has lost revenue by taking a smaller percentage of preexisting economic activity, but some of that loss is offset by taking a percentage of the new economic activity. If there had been no economic response to the tax cut, the 10 percentage point cut in the tax rate would have cost the government $10 million in lost revenue; instead, only $6 million is forgone. (In the case of a tax increase, the same phenomenon is likely in reverse: The increase in new revenues will be offset in part by some shrinking of the economic pie.) Tax experts typically take these behavioral responses into account when projecting the effects of a tax cut or a tax increase.

In all but the most extraordinary of circumstances, there is no free lunch. Lower tax rates mean less total government revenue—and therefore fewer resources to fight wars, balance the budget, catch terrorists, educate children, or do anything else governments typically do. That's the tradeoff. The bastardization of supply-side economics has taken an important intellectual debate—whether we should pay more in taxes to get more in government services, or pay less and get less—and transformed it into an intellectually dishonest premise: that we can pay less and get more. I wish that were true, just as I wish that I could get rich by working less or lose weight by eating more. So far, it hasn't happened.

Having said all that, the proponents of smaller government have a point. Lower taxes can lead to more investment, which causes a faster long-term rate of economic growth. It is facile to dismiss this as a bad idea or a policy that strictly favors the rich. A growing pie is important—perhaps even most important—for those with the smallest slices. When the economy grows slowly or sinks into recession, it is steelworkers and busboys who are laid off, not brain surgeons and university professors. In 2009, in the midst of the recession induced by the financial crisis, the American poverty rate was more than 13 percent—the highest rate in more than a decade.

Conversely, the 1990s were pretty good for those at the bottom of the economic ladder. Rebecca Blank, a University of Michigan economist and member of the Council of Economic Advisers in the Clinton administration, looked back on the remarkable economic expansion of the 1990s and noted:

> I believe that the first and most important lesson for anti-poverty warriors from the 1990s is that sustained economic growth is a wonderful thing. To the extent that policies can help maintain strong employment growth, low unemployment, and expanding wages among workers, these policies may matter as much or more than the dollars spent on targeted programs for the poor. If there are no job opportunities, or if wages are falling, it is much more expensive—both in terms of

dollars spent and political capital—for government programs alone to lift people out of poverty.[16]

So, for two chapters now I have danced around the obvious "Goldilocks" question: Is the role that government plays in the United States economy too big, too small, or just about right? I can finally offer a simple, straightforward, and unequivocal answer: It depends on whom you ask. There are smart and thoughtful economists who would like to see a larger, more activist government; there are smart and thoughtful economists who would prefer a smaller government; and there is a continuum of thinkers in between.

In some cases, the experts disagree over factual questions, just as eminent surgeons may disagree over the appropriate remedy for opening a clogged artery. For example, there is an ongoing dispute over the effects of raising the minimum wage. Theory suggests that there must be a trade-off: A higher minimum wage obviously helps those workers whose wages are raised; at the same time, it hurts some low-wage workers who lose their jobs (or never get hired in the first place) because firms cut back on the number of workers they employ at the new higher wage. Economists disagree (and present competing research) over how many jobs are lost when the minimum wage goes up. This is a crucial piece of information if one is to make an informed decision on whether or not raising the minimum wage is a good policy for helping low-wage workers. Over time, it is a question that can be answered with good data and solid research. (As one policy analyst once pointed out to me, it may be easy to lie with statistics, but it's a lot easier to lie without them.)

More often, economics can merely frame issues that require judgments based on morals, philosophy, and politics—somewhat as a doctor lays out the options to a patient. The physician can outline the medical issues related to treating an advanced cancer with chemotherapy. The treatment decision ultimately resides with the patient, who will interject his or her own views on quality of life versus longevity, willingness to experience discomfort, family situation, etc.—all perfectly legitimate considerations that have nothing to do with medicine or science. Yet making that decision still requires excellent medical advice.

In that vein of thought, we can present a framework for thinking about the role of the government in the economy.

Government has the potential to enhance the productive capacity of the economy and make us much better off as a result. Government creates and sustains the legal framework that makes markets possible; it raises our utility by providing public goods that we are unable to purchase for ourselves; it fixes the rough edges of capitalism by correcting externalities, particularly in the environmental realm. Thus, the notion that smaller government is always better government is simply wrong.

That said, reasonable people can agree with everything above and still disagree over whether the U.S. government should be bigger or smaller. It is one thing to believe, in theory, that government has the capacity to spend resources in ways that will make us better off; it is another to believe that the fallible politicians who make up Congress are going to choose to spend money that way. Is a German-Russian museum in Lawrence Welk's birthplace of Strasburg, North Dakota, really a public good? Congress allocated $500,000 for the museum in 1990 (and then withdrew it in 1991 when there was a public outcry). How about a $100 million appropriation to search for extraterrestrial life? Searching for ET meets the definition of a public good, since it would be impractical for each of us to mount his or her own individual search for life in outer space. Still, I suspect that many Americans would prefer to see their money spent elsewhere.

If I were to poll one hundred economists, nearly every one of them would tell me that significantly improving primary and secondary education in this country would lead to large economic gains. But the same group would be divided over whether or not we should spend more money on public education. Why? Because they would disagree sharply over whether pouring more money into the existing system would improve student outcomes.

Some government activity shrinks the size of the pie but still may be socially desirable. Transferring money from the rich to the poor is technically "inefficient" in the sense that sending a check for $1 to a poor family may cost the economy $1.25 when the deadweight costs of taxation are taken into account. The relatively high taxation necessary to support a strong social safety net falls most heavily on those with productive assets, including human capital, making countries like France a good place to be a child born into a poor family and a bad place to be an Internet entrepreneur (which in turn makes it a bad place to be a high-tech worker). Overall, policies that guarantee some pie for everybody will slow the growth of the pie itself. Per capita income in the United States is higher than per capita income in France; the United States also has a higher proportion of children living in poverty.

Having said all that, reasonable people can disagree over the appropriate level of social spending. First, they may have different preferences about how much wealth they are willing to trade off for more equality. The United States is a richer but more unequal place than most of Europe. Second, the notion of a simple trade-off between wealth and equality oversimplifies the dilemma of helping the most disadvantaged. Economists who care deeply about the poorest Americans may disagree over whether the poor would be helped more by expensive government programs, such as universal health care, or by lower taxes that would encourage economic growth and put more low-income Americans to work at higher wages.

Last, some government involvement in the economy is purely destructive. Heavy-handed government can be like a millstone around the neck of a market economy. Good intentions can lead to government programs and regulations whose benefits are grossly outweighed by their costs. Bad intentions can lead to all kinds of laws that serve special interests or corrupt politicians. This is especially true in the developing world, where much good could be done just by getting government out of areas of the economy where it does not belong. As Jerry Jordan, former president and CEO of the Federal Reserve Bank of Cleveland, has noted, "What separates the economic 'haves' from the 'have-nots' is whether the role of an economy's institutions— particularly its public institutions—is to facilitate production or to confiscate it."[17]

In short, government is like a surgeon's scalpel: It is an intrusive tool that can be used for good or for ill. Wielded carefully and judiciously, it will facilitate the body's remarkable ability to heal itself. In the wrong hands, or wielded overzealously with even the best of intentions, it can cause great harm.

CHAPTER 5

Economics of Information:

McDonald's didn't create a better hamburger

When Bill Clinton ran for president in 1992, he floated the idea of Hope Scholarships. The Clinton plan (based on an earlier experiment at Yale) was seemingly elegant: Students could borrow money for college and then repay the loans after graduation with a percentage of their annual income rather than the usual fixed payments of principal plus interest. Graduates who went on to become investment bankers would owe more in student loans than graduates who counseled disadvantaged teens in poor neighborhoods, which was exactly the point. The plan was designed to address the concern that students graduating with large debts are forced to do well rather than do good. After all, it is hard to become a teacher or a social worker after graduating with $75,000 in student loans.

In theory, the program would finance itself. Administrators could determine the average postgraduation salary for eligible students and then calculate the percentage of income they would have to pay in order for the program to recoup its costs—say 1.5 percent of annual income for fifteen years. Students who became brain surgeons would pay back more than average; students who fought tropical diseases in

Togo would pay less. On average, the high and low earners would cancel each other out and the program would break even.

There was just one problem: The Hope Scholarships had no hope of working, at least not without a large, ongoing government subsidy. The problem was a crucial asymmetry of information: Students know more about their future career plans than loan administrators do. College students never know their future plans with certainty, but most have a good idea whether their postgraduation income will be more or less than average—which is enough to determine if a Hope Scholarship would be more or less expensive than a conventional loan. Aspiring Wall Street barons would avoid the program because it's a bad deal for them. Who wants to pay back 1.5 percent of $5 million every year for fifteen years when a conventional loan would be much cheaper? Meanwhile, the world's future kindergarten teachers and Peace Corps volunteers would opt in.

The result is called adverse selection; future graduates sort themselves in or out of the program based on private information about their career plans. In the end, the program attracts predominantly low earners. The repayment calculations, based on the average postgraduation salary, no longer apply and the program cannot recover its costs. One may assume that Mr. Clinton ignored what his advisers almost certainly told him about the Yale experiment: It was quietly canceled after five years, both because repayments fell short of projections and because the administrative costs were prohibitive.

What we don't know *can* hurt us. Economists study how we acquire information, what we do with it, and how we make decisions when all we get to see is a book's cover. Indeed, the Swedish Academy of Sciences recognized this point in 2001 by awarding the Nobel Prize in Economics to George Akerlof, Michael Spence, and Joseph Stiglitz for their seminal work on the economics of information. Their work explores the problems that arise when rational people are forced to make decisions based on incomplete information, or when one party to a transaction knows more than another. Their insights are relevant to some of our most pressing social issues, from genetic screening to discrimination in the workplace.

Consider a small law firm interviewing two job candidates, one male and one female. Both candidates are recent Harvard Law School graduates and are eminently qualified for the position. If the "best" candidate for the job is the one who will earn the most money for the firm, which seems a reasonable assumption, then I will argue that the rational choice is to hire the man. The interviewer has no specific information on the family plans of the candidates at hand (and is forbidden by law from asking about them), but can make a reasonable inference based on what everyone knows about America at the beginning of the twenty-first century: Women still bear the bulk of child-rearing responsibilities. Demographics suggest that both candidates are likely to start families in the near future. Yet only the female candidate will take paid maternity leave. More important, she may not return to work after having the child, which leaves the firm with the cost of finding, hiring, and training another lawyer.

Is any of this certain? No. The male candidate may have dreams of staying home with his five children; the female candidate may have decided years ago that she has no interest in having children. But these are not the most likely scenarios. The female candidate is punished because the firm has no information on her specific circumstances but good data on broad social trends. Is this fair? No. (And it's not legal either.) *Yet the firm's logic makes sense.* In other words, it is rational to discriminate in this case, which turns the whole idea of discrimination on its head. Discrimination is usually irrational. As Nobel laureate Gary Becker pointed out in *The Economics of Discrimination*, employers with a "taste for discrimination" sacrifice profits because they pass over minorities in favor of less qualified whites.[1] A patient who refuses to see an eminent black doctor because of his skin color is a fool. A law firm that minimizes employee turnover by playing the statistical averages may offend our sensibilities and violate federal law—but it is not foolish.

When we approach this situation as an information problem, there are several crucial insights. First, firms are not the only villains. When professional women choose to have a child, take paid maternity leave, and then quit their companies, they impose a cost, arguably unfair, on their firms. *More important, they impose a cost on other women.* Firms that feel they have been "burned" by employees who take maternity leave and then quit are more likely to discriminate against young women in the hiring process (particularly those who are already pregnant) and less likely to offer generous maternity benefits. The good news is that there is a quick and easy solution: a generous but refundable maternity package. Keep it if you come back to work, return it if you don't. That simple policy change gives us nearly everything we want. Firms no longer have to be concerned about paying benefits to women who will not return to work. Indeed, it becomes possible to offer more generous benefits without providing an incentive for workers to take the money and run. Women, in turn, do not face the same level of discrimination in the hiring process.

Statistical discrimination, or so-called "rational discrimination," takes place when an individual makes an inference that is defensible based on broad statistical patterns but (1) is likely to be wrong in the specific case at hand; and (2) has a discriminatory effect on some group. Suppose an employer has no racial prejudice but does have an aversion to hiring workers with a criminal background. That's certainly a reasonable preference, for all kinds of reasons. If this employer has to make a hiring decision without access to applicants' criminal backgrounds (either because he doesn't have the time or resources to gather such information, or perhaps because he is forbidden by law from asking), then it's entirely plausible that he will discriminate against black male applicants, who are far more likely to have served time in prison (28 percent) than white male applicants (4 percent).

Of course, all this employer cares about is whether or not the person standing in front of him has a criminal record. If he can acquire that information with certainty, then the broader social patterns don't matter. In theory, we would expect access to criminal background checks to reduce discrimination against black men without criminal records. In fact, that is what the data show us. A group of economists compared hiring decisions at firms that conduct criminal background checks with hiring decisions at firms that don't. They concluded, "We find that employers who check criminal backgrounds are more likely to hire African-American workers, especially men. This effect is stronger among those employers who report an aversion to hiring those with criminal records than among those who do not."[2]

With race, more information is usually better. The corresponding implication is that less information can be worse. The United States has a huge ex-offender population. (America has a high incarceration rate, and most people who go to prison eventually get out; the median sentence is less than two years.) Policies that seek to help ex-offenders by suppressing information on their criminal backgrounds may be bad for a much wider population. The authors of the study cited above warned that their results "suggest that curtailing access to criminal history records may actually harm more people than it helps and aggravate racial differences in labor market outcomes."

This chapter is not about discrimination. It is about information, which lies at the heart of many discrimination-related problems. Information matters, particularly when we don't have all that we need. Markets tend to favor the party that knows more. (Have you ever bought a used car?) But if the imbalance, or asymmetry of information, becomes too large, then markets can break down entirely. This was the fundamental insight of 2001 Nobel laureate George Akerlof, an economist at the University of California, Berkeley. His paper entitled "The Market for Lemons" used the used-car market to make its central point. Any individual selling a used car knows more about its quality than someone looking to buy it. This creates an adverse selection problem, just as it did with the Hope Scholarships. Car owners who are happy with their vehicles are less likely to sell them. Thus, used-car buyers anticipate hidden problems and demand a discount. But once there is a discount built into the market, owners of high-quality cars become even less likely to sell them—which guarantees the market will be full of lemons. In theory, the market for high-quality used cars will not work, much to the detriment of anyone who may want to buy or sell such a car. (In practice, such markets often do work for reasons explained by the gentlemen with whom Mr. Akerlof shared his Nobel prize; more on that in a moment.)

"The Market for Lemons" is characteristic of the kinds of ideas recognized by the Nobel committee. It is, in the words of the Royal Swedish Academy of Sciences, "a simple but profound and universal idea, with numerous implications and widespread applications." Health care, for example, is plagued with information problems. Consumers of health care—the patients—almost always have less information about their care than their doctors do. Indeed, even after we see a doctor, we may not know whether we were treated properly. This asymmetry of information is at the heart of our health care woes.

Under any "fee for service" system, doctors charge a fee for each procedure they perform. Patients do not pay for these extra tests and procedures; their insurance companies (or the federal government, in the case of older Americans who are eligible for Medicare) do. At the same time, medical technology continues to present all kinds of new medical options, many of which are fabulously expensive. This combination is at the heart of rapidly rising medical costs: Doctors have an incentive to perform expensive medical procedures and patients have no reason to disagree. If you walk into your doctor's office with a headache and the doctor suggests a CAT scan, you would almost certainly agree "just to be sure." Neither you nor your doctor is acting unethically. When cost is not a factor, it makes perfect sense to rule out brain cancer even when the only symptom is a headache the morning after the holiday office party. Your doctor might also reasonably fear that if she doesn't order a CAT scan, you might sue for big bucks later if something turns out to be wrong with your head.

Medical innovation is terrific in some cases and wasteful in others. Consider the current range of treatments for prostate cancer, a cancer that afflicts many older men. One treatment option is "watchful waiting," which involves doing nothing unless and until tests show that the cancer is getting worse. This is a reasonable course of action because prostate cancer is so slow-growing that most men die of something else before the prostate cancer becomes a serious problem. Another treatment option is proton radiation therapy, which involves shooting atomic particles at the cancer using a proton accelerator that is roughly the size of a football field. Doing nothing essentially costs nothing (more or less); shooting protons from an accelerator costs somewhere in the range of $100,000.

The cost difference is not surprising; the shocking thing is that proton therapy has not been proven any more effective than watchful waiting. An analysis by the RAND Corporation concluded, "No therapy has been shown superior to another."[3]

Health maintenance organizations were designed to control costs by changing the incentives. Under many HMO plans, general practitioners are paid a fixed fee per patient per year, regardless of what services they provide. Doctors may be restricted in the kinds of tests and services they can prescribe and may even be paid a bonus if they refrain from sending their patients to see specialists. That changes things. Now when you walk into the doctor's office (still at a disadvantage in terms of information about your own health) and say, "I'm dizzy, my head hurts, and I'm bleeding out my ear," the doctor consults the HMO treatment guidelines and tells you to take two aspirin. As exaggerated as that example may be, the basic point is valid: The person who knows most about your medical condition may have an economic incentive to deny you care. Complaints about too much spending are replaced by complaints about too little spending. Every HMO customer has a horror story about wrangling with bureaucrats over acceptable expenses. In the most extreme (and anecdotal) stories, patients are denied lifesaving treatments by HMO bean counters.

Some doctors are willing to do battle with the insurance companies on behalf of their patients. Others simply break the rules by disguising treatments that are not covered by insurance as treatments that are. (Patients aren't the only ones suffering from an asymmetry of information.) Politicians have jumped into the fray, too, demanding things like disclosure of the incentives paid to doctors by insurance companies and even a patient's bill of rights.

The information problem at the heart of health care has not gone away: (1) The patient, who does not pay the bill, demands as much care as possible; (2) the doctor maximizes income and minimizes lawsuits by delivering as much care as possible; (3) the insurance company maximizes profits by paying for as little care as possible; (4) technology has introduced an array of massively expensive options, some of which are miracles and others of which are a waste of money; and (5) it is very costly for either the patient or the insurance company to prove the "right" course of treatment. In short, information makes health care different from the rest of the economy. When you walk into an electronics store to buy a big-screen TV, you can observe which picture looks clearest. You then compare price tags, knowing that the bill will arrive at your house eventually. In the end, you weigh the benefits of assorted televisions (whose quality you can observe) against the costs (that you will have to pay) and you pick one. *Brain surgery really is different.*

The fundamental challenge of health care reform is paying for the "right" treatment—the "product" that makes the most sense relative to what it costs. This is an exercise that consumers perform on their own everywhere else in the economy. Bean counters should not automatically say no to super-expensive treatments; some may be wonderfully effective and worth every penny. They *should* say no to expensive treatments that are not demonstrably better than less expensive options. They should also say no to doing some tests "just to be sure," both because these diagnostics are expensive, but also because when administered to healthy people they tend to generate "false positives," which can breed expensive, unnecessary, and potentially dangerous follow-up care.

There is an old aphorism in advertising: "I know I'm wasting half my money; I just wish I knew which half." Health care is similar, and if the goal of health care reform is to restrain rapidly rising costs, then any policy change will have to focus on quality and outcomes rather than just paying for inputs. *New York Times* financial columnist David Leonhardt describes the treatment for prostate cancer (where fabulously expensive technology does not appear to be delivering better health) as his own "personal litmus test" for health care reform. He writes, "The prostate cancer test will determine whether President Obama and Congress put together a bill that begins to fix the fundamental problem with our medical system: the combination of soaring costs and mediocre results. If they don't, the medical system will remain deeply troubled, no matter what other improvements they make."

But we're not done with health care yet. The doctor may know more about your health than you do, but you know more about your long-term health than your insurance company does. You may not be able to diagnose rare diseases, but you know whether or not you lead a healthy lifestyle, if certain diseases run in your family, if you are engaging in risky sexual behavior, if you are likely to become pregnant, etc. This information advantage has the potential to wreak havoc on the insurance market.

Insurance is about getting the numbers right. Some individuals require virtually no health care. Others may have chronic diseases that require hundreds of thousands of dollars of treatment. The insurance company makes a profit by determining the average cost of treatment for all of its policyholders and then charging slightly more. When Aetna writes a group policy for 20,000 fifty-year-old men, and the average cost of health care for a fifty-year-old man is $1,250 a year, then presumably the company can set the annual premium at $1,300 and make $50—*on average*—for each policy underwritten. Aetna will make money on some policies and lose money on others, but overall the company will come out ahead—if the numbers are right.

Is this example starting to look like the Hope Scholarships or the used-car market? It should. The $1,300 policy is a bad deal for the healthiest fifty-year-old men and a very good deal for the overweight smokers with a family history of heart disease. So, the healthiest men are most likely to opt out of the program; the sickest guys are most likely to opt in. As that happens, the population of men on which the original premium was based begins to change; on average, the remaining men are less healthy. The insurance company studies its new pool of middle-aged men and reckons that the annual premium must be raised to $1,800 in order to make a profit. Do you see where this is going? At the new price, more men—the most healthy of the unhealthy—decide that the policy is a bad deal, so they opt out. The sickest guys cling to their policies as tightly as their disease-addled bodies will allow. Once again the pool changes and now even $1,800 does not cover the cost of insuring the men who sign up for the program. In theory, this adverse selection could go on until the market for health insurance fails entirely.

That does not actually happen. Insurance companies usually insure large groups whose individuals are not allowed to select in or out. If Aetna writes policies for all General Motors employees, for example, then there will be no adverse selection. The policy comes with the job, and all workers, healthy and unhealthy, are covered. They have no choice. Aetna can calculate the average cost of care for this large pool of men and women and then charge a premium sufficient to make a profit.

Writing policies for individuals, however, is a much scarier undertaking. Companies rightfully fear that the people who have the most demand for health coverage (or life insurance) are those who need it most. *This will be true no matter how much an insurance company charges for its policies.* At any given price—even $5,000 a month—the individuals who expect their medical costs to be higher than the cost of the policy will be the most likely to sign up. Of course, the insurance companies have some tricks of their own, such as refusing coverage to individuals who are sick or likely to become sick in the future. This is often viewed as some kind of cruel and unfair practice perpetrated on the public by the insurance industry. On a superficial level, it does seem perverse that sick people have the most trouble getting health insurance. But imagine if insurance companies did not have that legal privilege. A (highly contrived) conversation with your doctor might go something like this:

DOCTOR: I'm afraid I have bad news. Four of your coronary arteries are fully or partially blocked. I would recommend open-heart surgery as soon as possible.

PATIENT: Is it likely to be successful?

DOCTOR: Yes, we have excellent outcomes.

PATIENT: Is the operation expensive?

DOCTOR: Of course it's expensive. We're talking about open-heart surgery.

PATIENT: Then I should probably buy some health insurance first.

DOCTOR: Yes, that would be a very good idea.

Insurance companies ask applicants questions about family history, health habits, smoking, dangerous hobbies, and all kinds of other personal things. When I applied for term life insurance, a representative from the company came to my house and drew blood to make sure that I was not HIV-positive. He asked whether my parents were alive, if I scuba dive, if I race cars. (Yes, yes, no.) I peed in a cup; I got on a scale; I answered questions about tobacco and illicit drug use—all of which seemed reasonable given that the company was making a commitment to pay my wife a large sum of money should I die in the near future.

Insurance companies have another subtle tool. They can design policies, or "screening" mechanisms, that elicit information from their potential customers. This insight, which is applicable to all kinds of other markets, earned Joseph Stiglitz, an economist at Columbia University and a former chief economist of the World Bank, a share of the 2001 Nobel Prize. How do firms screen customers in the insurance business? They use a deductible. Customers who consider themselves likely to stay healthy will sign up for policies that have a high deductible. In exchange, they are offered cheaper premiums. Customers who privately know that they are likely to have costly bills will avoid the deductible and pay a higher premium as a result. (The same thing is true when you are shopping for car insurance and you have a sneaking suspicion that your sixteen-year-old son is an even worse driver than most sixteen-year-olds.) In short, the deductible is a tool for teasing out private information; it forces customers to sort themselves.

Any insurance question ultimately begs one explosive question: How much information is too much? I guarantee that this will become one of the most nettlesome policy problems in coming years. Here is a simple exercise. Pluck one hair from your head. (If you are totally bald, take a swab of saliva from your cheek.) That sample contains your entire genetic code. In the right hands (or the wrong hands), it can be used to determine if you are predisposed to heart disease, certain kinds of cancer, depression, and—if the science continues at its current blistering pace—all kinds of other diseases. With one strand of your hair, a researcher (or insurance company) may soon be able to determine if you are at risk for Alzheimer's disease—twenty-five years before the onset of the disease. This creates a dilemma. If genetic information is shared widely with insurance companies, then it will become difficult, if not impossible, for those most prone to illness to get any kind of coverage. In other words, the people who need health insurance most will be the least likely to get it—not just the night before surgery, but ever. Individuals with a family history of Huntington's disease, a hereditary degenerative brain disorder that causes premature death, are already finding it hard or impossible to get life insurance. On the other hand, new laws are forbidding insurance companies from gathering such information, leaving them vulnerable to serious adverse selection. Individuals who know that they are at high risk of getting sick in the future will be the ones who load up on generous insurance policies.

An editorial in *The Economist* noted this looming quandary: "Governments thus face a choice between banning the use of test results and destroying the industry, or allowing their use and creating an underclass of people who are either uninsurable or cannot afford to insure themselves." *The Economist*, which is hardly a bastion of left-wing thought, suggested that the private health insurance market may eventually find this problem intractable, leaving government with a much larger role to play. The editorial concluded: "Indeed, genetic testing may become the most potent argument for state-financed universal health care."[4]

Any health care reform that seeks to make health insurance both more accessible and more affordable, particularly for those who are sick or likely to get sick, will have devastating adverse selection problems. Think about it: If I promise that you can buy affordable insurance, regardless of whether or not you are already sick, then the optimal time to buy that insurance is in the ambulance on the way to the hospital. The only fix for this inherent problem is to combine guaranteed access to affordable insurance with a requirement that everyone buy insurance—healthy and sick, young and old—a so-called "personal mandate." The insurance companies will still lose money on the policies that they are forced to sell to bad risks, but those losses can be offset by the profits earned from healthy people who are forced to buy insurance. (Any country with a national health care system effectively has a personal mandate; all citizens are forced to pay taxes, and in return they all get government-funded health care.)

This is the approach that Massachusetts took as part of a state plan to provide universal access to health insurance. State residents who can afford health insurance but don't buy it are fined on their state tax return. Hillary Clinton supported a personal mandate in the 2008

Democratic presidential primaries; Barack Obama did not, though that arguably had more to do with distinguishing himself from his toughest Democratic opponent than it did with his analysis of adverse selection. Obviously, forcing healthy people to buy something that they would otherwise not buy is a heavy-handed use of government; it's also the only way to pool risk (which is the purpose of insurance) when the distribution of risk is not random.

Here are the relevant economics: (1) We know who is sick; (2) increasingly we know who will become sick; (3) sick people can be extremely expensive; and (4) private insurance doesn't work well under these circumstances. That's all straightforward. The tough part is philosophical/ideological: To what extent do we want to share health care expenses anyway (if at all), and how should we do it? Those were the fundamental questions when Bill Clinton sought to overhaul health care in 1993, and again when the Obama administration took it up in 2009.

This chapter started with the most egregious information-related problems—cases in which missing information cripples markets and causes individuals to behave in ways that have serious social implications. Economists are also intrigued by more mundane examples of how markets react to missing information. We spend our lives shopping for products and services whose quality we cannot easily determine. (You had to pay for this book before you were able to read it.) In the vast majority of cases, consumers and firms create their own mechanisms to solve information problems. Indeed, therein lies the genius of McDonald's that inspired the title of this chapter. The "golden arches" have as much to do with information as they do with hamburgers. Every McDonald's hamburger tastes the same, whether it is sold in Moscow, Mexico City, or Cincinnati. That is not a mere curiosity; it is at the heart of the company's success. Suppose you are driving along Interstate 80 outside of Omaha, having never been in the state of Nebraska, when you see a McDonald's. Immediately you know all kinds of things about the restaurant. You know that it will be clean, safe, and inexpensive. You know that it will have a working bathroom. You know that it will be open seven days a week. You may even know how many pickles are on the double cheeseburger. *You know all of these things before you get out of your car in a state you've never been in.*

Compare that to the billboard advertising Chuck's Big Burger. Chuck's may offer one of the best burgers west of the Mississippi. Or it might be a likely spot for the nation's next large *E. coli* outbreak. How would you know? If you lived in Omaha, then you might be familiar with Chuck's reputation. But you don't; you are driving through Nebraska at nine o'clock at night. (What time does Chuck's close, anyway?) If you are like millions of other people, even those who find fast food relatively unappealing, you will seek out the golden arches because you know what lies beneath them. McDonald's sells hamburgers, fries, and, most important, predictability.

This idea underlies the concept of "branding," whereby companies spend enormous sums of money to build an identity for their products. Branding solves a problem for consumers: How do you select products whose quality or safety you can determine only after you use them (and sometimes not even then)? Hamburgers are just one example. The same rule applies in everything from vacations to fashion. Will you have fun on your cruise? Yes, because it is Royal Caribbean—or Celebrity or Viking or Cunard. I have a poor sense of fashion, so I am reassured that when I buy a Tommy Hilfiger shirt I will look reasonably presentable when I leave the house. Michelin tire advertisements feature babies playing inside of Michelin tires with the tag line "Because so much is riding on your tires." The implicit message is clear enough. Meanwhile, Firestone has most likely destroyed much of the value of its brand as the result of the link between faulty tires and deadly rollovers in Ford Explorers.

Branding has come under assault as a tool by which avaricious multinational corporations persuade us to pay extortionate premiums for goods that we don't need. Economics tells a different story:

Branding helps to provide an element of trust that is necessary for a complex economy to function. Modern business requires that we conduct major transactions with people whom we've never met before. I regularly mail off checks to Fidelity even though I do not know a single person at the company. Harried government regulators can only protect me from the most egregious kinds of fraud. They do not protect me from shoddy business practices, many of which are perfectly legal. Businesses routinely advertise their longevity. That sign outside the butcher proclaiming "Since 1927" is a politic way of saying, "We wouldn't still be here if we ripped off our customers."

Brands do the same thing. Like reputations, they are built over time. Indeed, sometimes the brand becomes more valuable than the product itself. In 1997, Sara Lee, a company that sells everything from underwear to breakfast sausages, declared that it would begin selling off its manufacturing facilities. No more turkey farms or textile mills. Instead, the company would focus on attaching its prestigious brand names—Champion, Hanes, Coach, Jimmy Dean—to products manufactured by outside firms. One business magazine noted, "Sara Lee believes that its soul is in its brands, and that the best use of its energies is to breathe commercial life into the inert matter supplied by others."[5] The irony is lovely: Sara Lee's strategy for growth and profits is to produce nothing.

Branding can be a very profitable strategy. In competitive markets, prices are driven relentlessly toward the cost of production. If it costs 10 cents to make a can of soda and I sell it for $1, someone is going to come along and sell it for 50 cents. Soon enough, someone else will be peddling it for a quarter, then 15 cents. Eventually, some ruthlessly efficient corporation will be peddling soda for 11 cents a can. From the consumer's standpoint, this is the beauty of capitalism. From the producer's standpoint, it is "commodity hell." Consider the sorry lot of the American farmer. A soybean is a soybean; as a result, an Iowa farmer cannot charge even one penny above the market price for his crop. Once transportation costs are taken into account, every soybean in the world sells for the same price, which, in most years, is not a whole lot more than it cost to produce.

How does a firm save its profits from the death spiral of competition? By convincing the world (rightfully or not) that its mixture of corn syrup and water is different from everyone else's mixture of corn syrup and water. Coca-Cola is not soda; it's Coke. Producers of branded goods create a monopoly for themselves—and price their products accordingly—by persuading consumers that their products are like no other. Nike clothes are not pieces of fabric sewn together by workers in Vietnam; they are Tiger Woods's clothes. Even farmers have taken this message to heart. At the supermarket, one finds (and pays a premium for) Sunkist oranges, Angus beef, Tyson chickens.

Sometimes we gather information by paying outsiders to certify quality. Roger Ebert's job is to see lots of bad movies so that I don't have to. When he sees the occasional gem, he gives it a "thumbs up." In the meantime, I am spared from seeing the likes of *Tomcats*, a film that Mr. Ebert awarded zero stars. I pay for this information in the form of my subscription to the *Chicago Sun-Times* (or by looking at ads that the *Sun-Times* is paid to display on its free website). *Consumer Reports* provides the same kind of information on consumer goods; Underwriters Laboratories certifies the safety of electrical appliances; Morningstar evaluates the performance of mutual funds. And then there is Oprah's book club, which has the capacity to send obscure books rocketing up the best-seller lists.

Meanwhile, firms will do whatever they can to "signal" their own quality to the market. This was the insight of 2001 Nobel laureate Michael Spence, an economist at Stanford University. Suppose that you are choosing an investment adviser after a good stroke of fortune in the Powerball lottery. The first firm you visit has striking wood paneling, a marble lobby, original Impressionist paintings, and executives wearing handmade Italian suits. Do you think: (1) My fees will pay for all this very nice stuff—what a ripoff!; or (2) wow, this firm must be extremely successful and I hope they will take me on as a client. Most people would choose 2. (If you're not convinced, think about it the other way: How would you feel if your investment adviser worked in a dank office with twenty-year-old government-surplus WANG word processors?)

The trappings of success—the paneling, the marble, the art collection—have no inherent relation to the professional conduct of the firm. Rather, we interpret them as "signals" that reassure us that the firm is top-notch. They are to markets what a peacock's bright feathers are to a prospective mate: a good sign in a world of imperfect information.

What signals success when you walk into an office in parts of Asia? Ridiculously cold temperatures. The blast of frigid air tells you immediately that this firm can afford lots of air-conditioning. Even when the temperature is more than ninety degrees outside, office temperatures are sometimes so cold that some workers use space heaters. The *Wall Street Journal* reports, "Frosty air conditioning is a way for businesses and building owners to show that they're ahead of the curve on comfort. In ostentatious Asian cities, bosses like to send out the message: We are so luxurious, we're arctic."[6]

Here is a related question that economists like to ponder: Harvard graduates do very well in life, but is that because they learned things at Harvard that made them successful, or is it because Harvard finds and admits talented students who would have done extraordinarily well in life anyway? In other words, does Harvard add great value to its students, or does it simply provide an elaborate "signaling" mechanism that allows bright students to advertise their talents to the world by being admitted to Harvard? Alan Krueger, a Princeton economist, and Stacy Dale, an economist at the Mellon Foundation, have done an interesting study to get at this question.[7] They note that graduates of highly selective colleges earn higher salaries later in life than graduates of less selective colleges. For example, the average student who entered Yale, Swarthmore, or the University of Pennsylvania in 1976 earned $92,000 in 1995; the average student who entered a moderately selective college, such as Penn State, Denison, or Tulane, earned $22,000 less. That is not a particularly surprising finding, nor does it get at the question of whether the students at schools like Yale and Princeton would earn more than their peers at less competitive schools even if they played beer pong and watched television for four years.

So Mr. Krueger and Ms. Dale took their analysis one step further. They examined the outcomes of students who were admitted to both a highly selective school and a moderately selective school. Some of those students headed to places like the Ivy League; others chose their less selective option. Mr. Krueger and Ms. Dale's chief finding is best summarized by the title of the paper: "Children Smart Enough to Get into Elite Schools May Not Need to Bother." The average earnings of students admitted to both a highly selective school and a moderately selective school were roughly the same regardless of which type of college they attended. (The one exception was students from lower-income families for whom attending a more selective school increased earnings significantly.) Overall, the quality of student appears to matter more later in life than the quality of the university he or she attended.

Is it irrational to spend $150,000 or more to attend an Ivy League university? Not necessarily. At a minimum, a Princeton or Yale diploma is the résumé equivalent of Roger Ebert's "thumbs up." It pronounces you highly qualified so that others in life—employers, spouses, in-laws—will have fewer doubts. And there is always the possibility that you may learn something while huddling for four years with the world's great minds. Still, Mr. Krueger offers this advice to students applying to college: "Don't believe that the only school worth attending is one that would not admit you. . . . Recognize that your own motivation, ambition and talents will determine your success more than the college name on your diploma."

The notion that bright, motivated individuals (with similarly motivated parents) will do well, however or wherever they are schooled, is often lost on America's school reformers. In Illinois, each fall is greeted with the release of the state's school report cards. Every school in the state is evaluated based on how well its students have performed on a battery of standardized exams. The media quickly seize on these school report cards to identify the state's "best" schools, most of which are usually in affluent suburbs. But does this process really tell us anything about which schools are the most effective? Not necessarily. "In many suburban communities, students would do well on standardized tests even if they went to school and sat in a closet every day for four years," says University of Rochester economist Eric Hanushek, an expert on the somewhat tenuous relationship between school inputs and student outcomes. There is a fundamental piece of missing information: How much value is really being added at these "high-performing schools"? Do they have exceptional teachers and administrators, or are they repositories for privileged students who would do well on standardized tests regardless of where they went to school? It's the Harvard question all over again.

This chapter started with a serious social issue, and so it will end. Racial profiling is an information problem. There are two simple questions at the heart of the issue. First, does race or ethnicity—alone or in conjunction with some other circumstance—convey meaningful information related to potential criminal activity? If so, what do we do about it? The answer to the first question gets most of the attention. After the attacks of September 11, one could certainly make the case that thirty-five-year-old Arab men posed a greater risk to the country than sixty-five-year-old Polish women. Police officers have long argued that race can be a tip-off; well-dressed white kids in poor black neighborhoods are often looking to buy drugs. Criminal organizations have racial or ethnic affiliations. At the same time President Clinton was declaring racial profiling "morally indefensible," the website of his drug czar, Barry McCaffrey, was doing just that. In Denver, the site noted, the heroin dealers are predominantly Mexican nationals.

In Trenton, crack dealers are predominantly African-American males and the powdered cocaine dealers are predominantly Latino.[8]

Indeed, we all profile in our own way. We are taught from a young age that one should never judge a book by its cover. *But we must; it is often all we get to see.* Imagine you are walking in a parking garage at night when you hear footsteps behind you. Ideally, you would ask this person for a résumé; you and he would sit down for coffee and discuss his goals, his job, his family, his political philosophy, and, most important, the reason he is walking behind you in a dark parking garage. You would do a criminal background check. Then, with all this information in hand, you would decide whether or not to hit the panic button on your key ring. The reality, of course, is different. You get one quick glance over your shoulder. What information matters? Sex? Race? Age? Briefcase? Clothing?

I'll never forget my own experience as a victim of racial profiling. I boarded a westbound bus from downtown Chicago just as it started to get dark. Chicago is a very segregated city; most of the neighborhoods west of downtown are predominantly African-American. I was wearing a suit, and after a few blocks I was the only white guy on the bus. Around that time, an older black woman asked kindly, "Oh, are the Bulls playing tonight?" The Chicago Bulls play at the Chicago Stadium, which is also directly west of the city center. This woman had inferred, innocently enough, that the only reason a white guy in a suit would be on this bus around 7:00 p.m. would be to go to a Bulls game. Obviously it was unfair and potentially hurtful for her to draw any conclusion about my destination based only on my skin color and style of dress. The really weird thing is that I was on my way to the Bulls game.

Race, age, ethnicity, and/or country of origin can convey information in some circumstances, particularly when other better information is lacking. From a social policy standpoint, however, the fact that these attributes may convey meaningful information is a red herring. The question that matters is: Are we willing to systematically harass individuals who fit a broad racial or ethnic profile that may, on average, have some statistical support but will still be wrong far more often than it is right? Most people would answer no in most circumstances. We've built a society that values civil liberties even at the expense of social order. Opponents of racial profiling always seem to get dragged into the quagmire of whether or not it is good police work or an effective counterterrorism tool. That's not the only relevant point—and it may be completely irrelevant in some cases. If economics teaches us anything, it's that we ought to weigh costs and benefits. The costs of harassing ten or twenty or one hundred law-abiding people to catch one more drug dealer are not worth it. Terrorism is trickier because the potential costs of letting just one person slip through the cracks are so devastatingly high. So what exactly should we do about it? That is one of the tough trade-offs in the post–September 11 world.

In the world of Econ 101, all parties have "perfect information." The graphs are neat and tidy; consumers and producers know everything they could possibly want to know. The world outside of Econ 101 is more interesting, albeit messier. A state patrolman who has pulled over a 1990 Grand Am with a broken taillight on a deserted stretch of Florida highway does not have perfect information. Nor does a young family looking for a safe and dependable nanny, or an insurance company seeking to protect itself from the extraordinary costs of HIV/AIDS. Information matters. Economists study what we do with it, and, sometimes more important, what we do without it.

CHAPTER 6

Productivity and Human Capital:

Why is Bill Gates so much richer than you are?

L
ike many people, Bill Gates found his house a little cramped once he had children. The software mogul moved into his $100 million dollar mansion in 1997; not long after, it needed some tweaking. The 37,000-square-foot home has a twenty-seat theater, a reception hall, parking for twenty-eight cars, an indoor trampoline pit, and all kinds of computer gadgetry, such as phones that ring only when the person being called is nearby. But the house was not quite big enough.[1] According to documents filed with the zoning board in suburban Medina, Washington, Mr. Gates and his wife added another bedroom and some additional play and study areas for their children.

There are a lot of things one might infer from Mr. Gates's home addition, but one of them is fairly obvious: It is good to be Bill Gates. The world is a fascinating playground when you have $50 billion or so. One might also ponder some larger questions: Why do some people have indoor trampolines and private jets while others sleep in bus station bathrooms? How is it that roughly 13 percent of Americans are poor, which is an improvement from a recent peak of 15 percent in 1993 but not significantly better than it was during any year in the 1970s? Meanwhile, one in five American children—and a staggering

35 percent of black children—live in poverty. Of course, America is the rich guy on the block. At the dawn of the third millennium, vast swathes of the world's population—some three billion people—are desperately poor.

Economists study poverty and income inequality. They seek to understand who is poor, why they are poor, and what can be done about it. Any discussion of why Bill Gates is so much richer than the men and women sleeping in steam tunnels must begin with a concept economists refer to as human capital. Human capital is the sum total of skills embodied within an individual: education, intelligence, charisma, creativity, work experience, entrepreneurial vigor, even the ability to throw a baseball fast. It is what you would be left with if someone stripped away all of your assets—your job, your money, your home, your possessions—and left you on a street corner with only the clothes on your back. How would Bill Gates fare in such a situation? Very well. Even if his wealth were confiscated, other companies would snap him up as a consultant, a board member, a CEO, a motivational speaker. (When Steve Jobs was fired from Apple, the company that he founded, he turned around and founded Pixar; only later did Apple invite him back.) How would Tiger Woods do? Just fine. If someone lent him golf clubs, he could be winning a tournament by the weekend.

How would Bubba, who dropped out of school in tenth grade and has a methamphetamine addiction, fare? Not so well. The difference is human capital; Bubba doesn't have much. (Ironically, some very rich individuals, such as the sultan of Brunei, might not do particularly well in this exercise either; the sultan is rich because his kingdom sits atop an enormous oil reserve.) The labor market is no different from the market for anything else; some kinds of talent are in greater demand than others. The more nearly unique a set of skills, the better compensated their owner will be. Alex Rodriguez will earn $275 million over ten years playing baseball for the New York Yankees because he can hit a round ball traveling ninety-plus miles an hour harder and more often than other people can. "A-Rod" will help the Yankees win games, which will fill stadiums, sell merchandise, and earn television revenues. Virtually no one else on the planet can do that as well as he can.

As with other aspects of the market economy, the price of a certain skill bears no inherent relation to its social value, only its scarcity. I once interviewed Robert Solow, winner of the 1987 Nobel Prize in Economics and a noted baseball enthusiast. I asked if it bothered him that he received less money for winning the Nobel Prize than Roger Clemens, who was pitching for the Red Sox at the time, earned in a single season. "No," Solow said. "There are a lot of good economists, but there is only one Roger Clemens." That is how economists think.

Who is wealthy in America, or at least comfortable? Software programmers, hand surgeons, nuclear engineers, writers, accountants, bankers, teachers. Sometimes these individuals have natural talent; more often they have acquired their skills through specialized training and education. In other words, they have made significant investments in human capital. Like any other kind of investment—from building a manufacturing plant to buying a bond—money invested today in human capital will yield a return in the future. A very good return. A college education is reckoned to yield about a 10 percent return on investment, meaning that if you put down money today for college tuition, you can expect to earn that money back plus about 10 percent a year in higher earnings. Few people on Wall Street make better investments than that on a regular basis.

Human capital is an economic passport—literally, in some cases. When I was an undergraduate in the late 1980s, I met a young Palestinian man named Gamal Abouali. Gamal's family, who lived in Kuwait, were insistent that their son finish his degree in three years instead of four. This required taking extra classes each quarter and attending school every summer, all of which seemed rather extreme to me at the time. What about internships and foreign study, or even a winter in Colorado as a ski bum? I had lunch with Gamal's father once, and he explained that the Palestinian existence was itinerant and precarious. Mr. Abouali was an accountant, a profession that he could practice nearly anywhere in the world—because, he explained, that is where he might end up. The family had lived in Canada before moving to Kuwait; they could easily be somewhere else in five years, he said.

Gamal was studying engineering, a similarly universal skill. The sooner he had his degree, his father insisted, the more secure he would be. Not only would the degree allow him to earn a living, but it might also enable him to find a home. In some developed countries, the right to immigrate is based on skills and education—human capital.

Mr. Abouali's thoughts were strikingly prescient. After Saddam Hussein's retreat from Kuwait in 1990, most of the Palestinian population, including Gamal's family, was expelled because the Kuwaiti government felt that the Palestinians had been sympathetic to the Iraqi aggressors. Mr. Abouali's daughter gave him a copy of the first edition of this book. When he read the above section, he exclaimed, "See, I was right!"

The opposite is true at the other end of the labor pool. The skills necessary to ask "Would you like fries with that?" are not scarce. There are probably 150 million people in America capable of selling value meals at McDonald's. Fast-food restaurants need only pay a wage high enough to put warm bodies behind all of their cash registers. That may be $7.25 an hour when the economy is slow or $11 an hour when the labor market is especially tight; it will never be $500 an hour, which is the kind of fee that a top trial lawyer can command. Excellent trial lawyers are scarce; burger flippers are not. The most insightful way to think about poverty, in this country or anywhere else in the world, is as a dearth of human capital. True, people are poor in America because they cannot find good jobs. But that is the symptom, not the illness. The underlying problem is a lack of skills, or human capital. The poverty rate for high school dropouts in America is 12 times the poverty rate for college graduates. Why is India one of the poorest countries in the world? Primarily because 35 percent of the population is illiterate (down from almost 50 percent in the early 1990s).[2] Or individuals may suffer from conditions that render their human capital less useful. A high proportion of America's homeless population suffers from substance abuse, disability, or mental illness.

A healthy economy matters, too. It was easier to find a job in 2001 than it was in 1975 or 1932. A rising tide does indeed lift all boats; economic growth is a very good thing for poor people. Period. But even at high tide, low-skilled workers are clinging to driftwood while their better-skilled peers are having cocktails on their yachts. A robust economy does not transform valet parking attendants into college professors. Investments in human capital do that. Macroeconomic factors control the tides; human capital determines the quality of the boat. Conversely, a bad economy is usually most devastating for workers at the shallow end of the labor pool.

Consider this thought experiment. Imagine that on some Monday morning we dropped off 100,000 high school dropouts on the corner of State Street and Madison Street in Chicago. It would be a social calamity. Government services would be stretched to capacity or beyond; crime would go up. Businesses would be deterred from locating in downtown Chicago. Politicians would plead for help from the state or the federal government: *Either give us enough money to support these people or help us get rid of them.* When business leaders in Sacramento, California, decided to crack down on the homeless, one strategy was to offer them one-way bus tickets out of town.[3] (Atlanta reportedly did the same before the 1996 Olympics.)

Now imagine the same corner and let's drop off 100,000 graduates from America's top universities. The buses arrive at the corner of State and Madison and begin unloading lawyers, doctors, artists, geneticists, software engineers, and a lot of smart, motivated people with general skills. Many of these individuals would find jobs immediately. (Remember, human capital embodies not only classroom training but also perseverance, honesty, creativity—virtues that lend themselves to finding work.) Some of these highly skilled graduates would start their own businesses; entrepreneurial flair is certainly an important component of human capital. Some of them would leave for other places; highly skilled workers are more mobile than their low-skilled peers. In some cases, firms would relocate to Chicago or open up offices and plants in Chicago to take advantage of this temporary glut of talent. Economic pundits would later describe this freak unloading of buses as a boon for Chicago's economic development, much as waves of immigration helped America to develop.

If this example sounds contrived, consider the case of the Naval Air Warfare Center (NAWC) in Indianapolis, a facility that produced advanced electronics for the navy until the late 1990s. NAWC, which employed roughly 2,600 workers, was slated to be closed as part of the military's downsizing. We're all familiar with these plant-closing stories. Hundreds or thousands of workers lose their jobs; businesses in the surrounding community begin to wither because so much purchasing power has been lost. Someone comes on camera and says, "When the plant closed back in [some year], this town just began to die." But NAWC was a very different story.[4] One of its most valuable assets was its workforce, some 40 percent of whom were scientists or engineers. Astute local leaders, led by Mayor Stephen Goldsmith, believed that the plant could be sold to a private buyer. Seven companies filed bids; Hughes Electronics was the winner.

On a Friday in January 1997, the NAWC employees went home as government employees; the following Monday, 98 percent of them came to work as Hughes employees. (And NAWC became HAWC.) The Hughes executives I interviewed said that the value of the acquisition lay in the people, not just the bricks and mortar. Hughes was buying a massive amount of human capital that it could not easily find anywhere else. This story contrasts sharply with the plant closings that Bruce Springsteen sings about, where workers with limited education find that their narrow sets of skills have no value once the mill/mine/factory/plant is gone. The difference is human capital. Indeed, economists can even provide empirical support for those Springsteen songs. Labor economist Robert Topel has estimated that experienced workers lose 25 percent of their earnings capacity in the long run when they are forced to change jobs by a plant closing.

Now is an appropriate time to dispatch one of the most pernicious notions in public policy: the lump of labor fallacy. This is the mistaken belief that there is a fixed amount of work to be done in the economy, and therefore every new job must come at the expense of a job lost somewhere else. If I am unemployed, the mistaken argument goes, then I will find work only if someone else works less, or not at all. This is how the French government used to believe the world worked, and it is wrong. Jobs are created anytime an individual provides a new good or service, or finds a better (or cheaper) way of providing an old one.

The numbers prove the point. The U.S. economy produced tens of millions of new jobs over the past three decades, including virtually the entire Internet sector. (Yes, the recession that began in 2007 destroyed lots of jobs, too.) Millions of women entered the labor force in the second half of the twentieth century, yet our unemployment rate was still extremely low by historical standards until the beginning of the recent downturn. Similarly, huge waves of immigrants have come to work in America throughout our history without any long-run increase in unemployment. Are there short-term displacements? Absolutely; some workers lose jobs or see their wages depressed when they are forced to compete with new entrants to the labor force. But more jobs are created than lost. Remember, new workers must spend their earnings elsewhere in the economy, creating new demand for other products. The economic pie gets bigger, not merely resliced.

Here is the intuition: Imagine a farming community in which numerous families own and farm their own land. Each family produces just enough to feed itself; there is no surplus harvest or unfarmed land. Everyone in this town has enough to eat; on the other hand, no one lives particularly well. Every family spends large amounts of time doing domestic chores. They make their own clothes, teach their own children, make and repair their own farm implements, etc. Suppose a guy wanders into town looking for work. In scenario one, this guy has no skills. There is no extra land to farm, so the community tells him to get back on the train. Maybe they even buy him a one-way ticket out of town. This town has "no jobs."

Now consider scenario two: The guy who ambles into town has a Ph.D. in agronomy. He has designed a new kind of plow that improves corn yields. He trades his plow to farmers in exchange for a small share of their harvests. Everybody is better off. The agronomist can support himself; the farmers have more to eat, even after paying for their new plows (or else they wouldn't buy the plows). And this community has just created one new job: plow salesman. Soon thereafter, a carpenter arrives at the train station. He offers to do all the odd jobs that limit the amount of time farmers can spend tending to their crops. Yields go up again because farmers are able to spend more time doing what they do best: farming. And another new job is created.

At this point, farmers are growing more than they can possibly eat themselves, so they "spend" their surplus to recruit a teacher to town. That's another new job. She teaches the children in the town, making the next generation of farmers better educated and more productive than their parents. Over time, our contrived farming town, which had "no jobs" at the beginning of this exercise, has romance novelists, fire-fighters, professional baseball players, and even engineers who design iPhones and Margarita Space Paks. This is the one-page economic history of the United States. Rising levels of human capital enabled an agrarian nation to evolve into places as rich and complex as Manhattan and Silicon Valley.

Not all is rosy along the way, of course. Suppose one of our newly educated farmers designs a plow that produces even better yields, putting the first plow salesman out of business—creative destruction. True, this technological breakthrough eliminates one job in the short run. In the long run, though, the town is still better off. Remember, all the farmers are now richer (as measured by higher corn yields), enabling them to hire the unemployed agronomist to do something else, such as develop new hybrid seeds (which will make the town richer yet).

Technology displaces workers in the short run but does not lead to mass unemployment in the long run. Rather, we become richer, which creates demand for new jobs elsewhere in the economy. Of course, educated workers fare much better than uneducated workers in this process. They are more versatile in a fast-changing economy, making them more likely to be left standing after a bout of creative destruction.

Human capital is about much more than earning more money. It makes us better parents, more informed voters, more appreciative of art and culture, more able to enjoy the fruits of life. It can make us healthier because we eat better and exercise more. (Meanwhile, good health is an important component of human capital.) Educated parents are more likely to put their children in car seats and teach them about colors and letters before they begin school. In the developing world, the impact of human capital can be even more profound. Economists have found that a year of additional schooling for a woman in a low-income country is associated with a 5 to 10 percent reduction in her child's likelihood of dying in the first five years of life.[5]

Similarly, our total stock of human capital—everything we know as a people—defines how well off we are as a society. We benefit from the fact that we know how to prevent polio or make stainless steel—even if virtually no one reading this book would be able to do either of those things if left stranded on a deserted island. Economist Gary Becker, who was awarded the Nobel Prize for his work in the field of human capital, reckons that the stock of education, training, skills, and even the health of people constitutes about 75 percent of the wealth of a modern economy. Not diamonds, buildings, oil, or fancy purses—but things that we carry around in our heads. "We should really call our economy a 'human capitalist economy,' for that is what it mainly is," Mr. Becker said in a speech. "While all forms of capital—physical capital, such as machinery and plants, financial capital, and human capital—are important, human capital is the most important. Indeed, in a modern economy, human capital is by far the most important form of capital in creating wealth and growth."[6]

There is a striking correlation between a country's level of human capital and its economic well-being. At the same time, there is a striking *lack* of correlation between natural resources and standard of living. Countries like Japan and Switzerland are among the richest in the world despite having relatively poor endowments of natural resources. Countries like Nigeria are just the opposite; enormous oil wealth has done relatively little for the nation's standard of living. In some cases, the mineral wealth of Africa has financed bloody civil wars that would have otherwise died out. In the Middle East, Saudi Arabia has most of the oil while Israel, with no natural resources to speak of, has a higher per capita income.

High levels of human capital create a virtuous cycle; well-educated parents invest heavily in the human capital of their children. Low levels of human capital have just the opposite effect. Disadvantaged parents beget disadvantaged children, as any public school teacher will tell you. Mr. Becker points out, "Even small differences among children in the preparation provided by their families are frequently multiplied over time into large differences when they are teenagers. This is why the labor market cannot do much for school dropouts who can hardly read and never developed good work habits, and why it is so difficult to devise policies to help these groups."[7]

Why does human capital matter so much? To begin with, human capital is inextricably linked to one of the most important ideas in economics: productivity. Productivity is the efficiency with which we convert inputs into outputs. In other words, how good are we at making things? Does it take 2,000 hours for a Detroit autoworker to make a car or 210 hours? Can an Iowa corn farmer grow thirty bushels of corn on an acre of land or 210 bushels? The more productive we are, the richer we are. The reason is simple: The day will always be twenty-four hours long; the more we produce in those twenty-four hours the more we consume, either directly or by trading it away for other stuff. Productivity is determined in part by natural resources—it is easier to grow wheat in Kansas than it is in Vermont—but in a modern economy, productivity is more affected by technology, specialization, and skills, all of which are a function of human capital.

America is rich because Americans are productive. We are better off today than at any other point in the history of civilization because we are better at producing goods and services than we have ever been, including things like health care and entertainment. The bottom line is that we work less and produce more. In 1870, the typical household required 1,800 hours of labor just to acquire its annual food supply; today, it takes about 260 hours of work. Over the course of the twentieth century, the average work year has fallen from 3,100 hours to about 1,730 hours. All the while, real gross domestic product (GDP) per capita—an inflation-adjusted measure of how much each of us produces, on average—has increased from $4,800 to more than $40,000. Even the poor are living extremely well by historical standards. *The poverty line is now at a level of real income that was attained only by those in the top 10 percent of the income distribution a century ago.* As John Maynard Keynes once noted, "In the long run, productivity is everything."

Productivity is the concept that takes the suck out of Ross Perot's "giant sucking sound." When Ross Perot ran for president in 1992 as an independent, one of his defining positions was opposition to the North American Free Trade Agreement (NAFTA). Perot reasoned that if we opened our borders to free trade with Mexico, then millions of jobs would flee south of the border. Why wouldn't a firm relocate to Mexico when the average Mexican factory worker earns a fraction of the wages paid to American workers? The answer is productivity. Can American workers compete against foreign workers who earn half as much or less? *Yes, most of us can.* We produce more than Mexican workers—much more in many cases—because we are better-educated, because we are healthier, because we have better access to capital and technology, and because we have more efficient government institutions and better public infrastructure. Can a Vietnamese peasant with two years of education do your job? Probably not.

Of course, there are industries in which American workers are not productive enough to justify their relatively high wages, such as manufacturing textiles and shoes. These are industries that require relatively unskilled labor, which is more expensive in this country than in the developing world. Can a Vietnamese peasant sew basketball shoes together? Yes—and for a lot less than the American minimum wage. American firms will look to "outsource" jobs to other countries only if the wages in those countries are cheap relative to what those workers can produce. A worker who costs a tenth as much and produces a tenth as much is no great bargain. A worker who costs a tenth as much and produces half as much probably is.

While Ross Perot was warning that most of the U.S. economy would migrate to Guadalajara, mainstream economists predicted that NAFTA would have a modest but positive effect on American employment. Some jobs would be lost to Mexican competition; more jobs would be created as exports to Mexico increased. We are now more than a decade into NAFTA, and that is exactly what happened. Economists reckon that the effect on overall employment was positive, albeit very small relative to the size of the U.S. economy.

Will our children be better off than we are? Yes, if they are more productive than we are, which has been the pattern throughout American history. Productivity *growth* is what improves our standard of living. If productivity grows at 2 percent a year, then we will become 2 percent richer every year. Why? Because we can take the same inputs and make 2 percent more stuff. (Or we could make the same amount of stuff with 2 percent fewer inputs.) One of the most interesting debates in economics is whether or not the American economy has undergone a sharp increase in the rate of productivity growth. Some economists, including Alan Greenspan during his tenure as Fed chairman, have argued that investments in information technology have led to permanently higher rates of productivity growth. Others, such as Robert Gordon at Northwestern University, believe that productivity growth has not changed significantly when one interprets the data properly.

The answer to that debate matters enormously. From 1947 to 1975, productivity grew at an annual rate of 2.7 percent a year. From 1975 until the mid-1990s, for reasons that are still not fully understood, productivity growth slowed to 1.4 percent a year. Then it got better again; from 2000 to 2008, productivity growth returned to a much healthier 2.5 percent annually. That may seem like a trivial difference; in fact, it has a profound effect on our standard of living. One handy trick in finance and economics is the rule of 72; divide 72 by a rate of growth (or a rate of interest) and the answer will tell you roughly how long it will take for a growing quantity to double (e.g., the principal in a bank account paying 4 percent interest will double in roughly 18 years). When productivity grows at 2.7 percent a year, our standard of living doubles every twenty-seven years. At 1.4 percent, it doubles every fifty-one years.

Productivity growth makes us richer, regardless of what is going on in the rest of the world. If productivity grows at 4 percent in Japan and 2 percent in the United States, *then both countries are getting richer*. To understand why, go back to our simple farm economy. If one farmer is raising 2 percent more corn and hogs every year and his neighbor is raising 4 percent more, then they are eating more every year (or trading more away). If this disparity goes on for a long time, one of them will become significantly richer than the other, which may become a source of envy or political friction, but they are both growing steadily better off. The important point is that productivity growth, like so much else in economics, is not a zero-sum game.

What would be the effect on America if 500 million people in India became more productive and gradually moved from poverty to the middle class? We would become richer, too. Poor villagers currently subsisting on $1 a day cannot afford to buy our software, our cars, our music, our books, our agricultural exports. If they were wealthier, they could. Meanwhile, some of those 500 million people, whose potential is currently wasted for lack of education, would produce goods and services that are superior to what we have now, making us better off.

One of those newly educated peasants might be the person who discovers an AIDS vaccine or a process for reversing global warming. To paraphrase the United Negro College Fund, 500 million minds are a terrible thing to waste.

Productivity growth depends on investment—in physical capital, in human capital, in research and development, and even in things like more effective government institutions. These investments require that we give up consumption in the present in order to be able to consume more in the future. If you skip buying a BMW and invest in a college education instead, your future income will be higher. Similarly, a software company may forgo paying its shareholders a dividend and plow its profits back into the development of a new, better product. The government may collect taxes (depriving us of some current consumption) to fund research in genetics that improves our health in the future. In each case, we spend resources now so that we will become more productive later. When we turn to the macroeconomy—our study of the economy as a whole—one important concern will be whether or not we are investing enough as a nation to continue growing our standard of living.

Our legal, regulatory, and tax structures also affect productivity growth. High taxes, bad government, poorly defined property rights, or excessive regulation can diminish or eliminate the incentive to make productive investments. Collective farms, for example, are a very bad way to organize agriculture. Social factors, such as discrimination, can profoundly affect productivity. A society that does not educate its women or that denies opportunities to members of a particular race or caste or tribe is leaving a vast resource fallow. Productivity growth also depends a great deal on innovation and technological progress, neither of which is understood perfectly. Why did the Internet explode onto the scene in the mid-1990s rather than the late 1970s? How is it that we have cracked the human genome yet we still do not have a cheap source of clean energy? In short, fostering productivity growth is like raising children: We know what kinds of things are important even if there is no blueprint for raising an Olympic athlete or a Harvard scholar.

The study of human capital has profound implications for public policy. Most important, it can tell us why we haven't all starved to death. The earth's population has grown to six billion; how have we been able to feed so many mouths? In the eighteenth century, Thomas Malthus famously predicted a dim future for humankind because he believed that as society grew richer, it would continuously squander those gains through population growth—having more children. These additional mouths would gobble up the surplus. In his view, humankind was destined to live on the brink of subsistence, recklessly procreating during the good times and then starving during the bad. As Paul Krugman has pointed out, for fifty-five of the last fifty-seven centuries, Malthus was right. The world population grew, but the human condition did not change significantly.

Only with the advent of the Industrial Revolution did people begin to grow steadily richer. Even then, Malthus was not far off the mark. As Gary Becker points out, "Parents did spend more on children when their incomes rose—as Malthus predicted—but they spent a lot more on each child and had fewer children, as human capital theory predicts."[8] The economic transformations of the Industrial Revolution, namely the large productivity gains, made parents' time more expensive. As the advantages of having more children declined, people began investing their rising incomes in the *quality* of their children, not merely the *quantity*.

One of the fallacies of poverty is that developing countries are poor because they have rapid population growth. In fact, the causal relationship is best understood going the other direction: Poor people have many children because the cost of bearing and raising children is low. Birth control, no matter how dependable, works only to the extent that families prefer fewer children. As a result, one of the most potent weapons for fighting population growth is creating better economic opportunities for women, which starts by educating girls.

Taiwan doubled the number of girls graduating from high school between 1966 and 1975. Meanwhile, the fertility rate dropped by half. In the developed world, where women have enjoyed an extraordinary range of new economic opportunities for more than a half century, fertility rates have fallen near or below replacement level, which is 2.1 births per woman.

We began this chapter with a discussion of Bill Gates's home, which is, I am fairly certain, bigger than yours. At the dawn of the third millennium, America is a profoundly unequal place. Is the nation growing more unequal? That answer, by almost any measure, is yes. According to analysis by the Congressional Budget Office, American households in the bottom fifth of the income distribution were earning only 2 percent more in 2004 (adjusted for inflation) than they were in 1979. That's a quarter century with no real income growth at all. Americans in the middle of the income distribution did better over the same stretch; their average household income grew 15 percent in real terms. Those in the top quintile—the top 20 percent—saw household income growth of 63 percent (adjusted for inflation).[9]

As America's longest economic boom in history unfolded, the rich got richer while the poor ran in place, or even got poorer. Wages for male high school dropouts have fallen by roughly a quarter compared to what their dads earned if they were also high school dropouts. The recession that began in 2007 has narrowed the gap between America's rich and poor slightly (by destroying wealth at the top, not by making the typical worker better off). Most economists would agree that the long-term trend is a growing gap between America's rich and poor. The most stunning action has been at the top of the top. In 1979, the wealthiest 1 percent of Americans earned 9 percent of the nation's total income; now they get 16 percent of America's annual collective paycheck.

Why? Human capital offers the most insight into this social phenomenon. The last several decades have been a real-life version of *Revenge of the Nerds.* Skilled workers in America have always earned higher wages than unskilled workers; that difference has started to grow at a remarkable rate. In short, human capital has become more important, and therefore better rewarded, than ever before. One simple measure of the importance of human capital is the gap between the wages paid to high school graduates and the wages paid to college graduates. College graduates earned an average of 40 percent more than high school graduates at the beginning of the 1980s; now they earn 80 percent more. Individuals with graduate degrees do even better than that. The twenty-first century is an especially good time to be a rocket scientist.

Our economy is evolving in ways that favor skilled workers. For example, the shift toward computers in nearly every industry favors workers who either have computer skills or are smart enough to learn them on the job. Technology makes smart workers more productive while making low-skilled workers redundant. ATMs replaced bank tellers; self-serve pumps replaced gas station attendants; automated assembly lines replaced workers doing mindless, repetitive tasks. Indeed, the assembly line at General Motors encapsulates the major trend in the American economy. Computers and sophisticated robots now assemble the major components of a car—which creates high-paying jobs for people who write software and design robots while reducing the demand for workers with no specialized skills other than a willingness to do an honest day's work.

Meanwhile, international trade puts low-skilled workers in greater competition with other low-skilled workers around the globe. In the long run, international trade is a powerful force for good; in the short run, it has victims. Trade, like technology, makes high-skilled workers better off because it provides new markets for our high-tech exports. Boeing sells aircraft to India, Microsoft sells software to Europe, McKinsey & Company sells consulting services to Latin America. Again, this is more good news for people who know how to design a fuel-efficient jet engine or explain total quality management in Spanish. On the other hand, it puts our low-tech workers in competition with low-priced laborers in Vietnam. Nike can pay workers $1 a day to make shoes in a Vietnamese sweatshop. You can't make Boeing airplanes that way. Globalization creates more opportunities for skilled workers (*Naked Economics* is published in eleven languages!) and more competition for unskilled workers.

There is still disagreement about the degree to which different causes are responsible for this shifting gap in wages. Unions have grown less powerful, giving blue-collar workers less clout at the bargaining table. Meanwhile, high-wage workers are logging more hours on the job than their low-wage counterparts, which exacerbates the total earnings gap.[10] More and more industries are linking pay to performance, which increases wage gaps between those who are more and less productive. In any case, the rise in income inequality is real. Should we care? Economists have traditionally argued that we should not, for two basic reasons. First, income inequality sends important signals in the economy. The growing wage gap between high school and college graduates, for example, will motivate many students to get college degrees. Similarly, the spectacular wealth earned by entrepreneurs provides an incentive to take the risks necessary for leaps in innovation, many of which have huge payoffs for society. Economics is about incentives, and the prospect of getting rich is a big incentive.

Second, many economists argue that we should not care about the gap between rich and poor as long as everybody is living better. In other words, we should care about how much pie the poor are getting, not how much pie they are getting relative to Bill Gates. In his 1999 presidential address to the American Economics Association, Robert Fogel, a Nobel Prize–winning economic historian, pointed out that our poorest citizens have amenities unknown even to royalty a hundred years ago. (More than 90 percent of public housing residents have a color television, for example.) Envy may be one of the seven deadly sins, but it is not something to which economists have traditionally paid much attention. My utility should depend on how much I like my car, not on whether or not my neighbor is driving a Jaguar.

Of course, common sense suggests otherwise. H. L. Mencken once noted that a wealthy man is a man who earns $100 a year more than his wife's sister's husband. Some economists have belatedly begun to believe that he was on to something.[11] David Neumark and Andrew Postlewaite looked at a large sample of American sisters in an effort to understand why some women choose to work outside of the home and others do not. When the researchers controlled for all the usual explanations—unemployment in the local labor market, a woman's education and work experience, etc.—they found powerful evidence to support H. L. Mencken's wry observation: A woman in their sample was significantly more likely to seek paid employment if her sister's husband earned more than her own.

Cornell economist Robert Frank, author of *Luxury Fever*, has made a persuasive case that relative wealth—the size of my pie compared to my neighbor's—is an important determinant of our utility. He offered survey respondents a choice between two worlds: (A) You earn $110,000 and everyone else earns $200,000; or (B) you earn $100,000 and everyone else earns $85,000. As he explains, "The income figures represent real purchasing power. Your income in World A would command a house 10 percent larger than the one you could afford in World B, 10 percent more restaurant dinners and so on. By choosing World B, you'd give up a small amount of absolute income in return for a large increase in relative income." You would be richer in World A; you would be less wealthy in World B but richer than everyone else. Which scenario would make you happier? Mr. Frank found that a majority of Americans would choose B. In other words, relative income does matter. Envy may be part of the explanation. It is also true, Mr. Frank points out, that in complex social environments we seek ways to evaluate our performance. Relative wealth is one of them.

There is a second, more pragmatic concern about rising income inequality. Might the gap between rich and poor—ethics aside— become large enough that it begins to inhibit economic growth? Is there a point at which income inequality stops motivating us to work harder and becomes counterproductive? This might happen for all kinds of reasons. The poor might become disenfranchised to the point that they reject important political and economic institutions, such as property rights or the rule of law. A lopsided distribution of income may cause the rich to squander resources on increasingly frivolous luxuries (e.g., doggy birthday cakes) when other kinds of investments, such as human capital for the poor, would yield a higher return. Or class warfare may lead to measures that punish the rich without making the poor any better off.[12] Some studies have indeed found a negative relationship between income inequality and economic growth; others have found just the opposite. Over time, data will inform this relationship. But the larger philosophical debate will rage on: If the pie is growing, how much should we care about the size of the pieces?

The subject of human capital begs some final questions. Will the poor always be with us, as Jesus once admonished? Does our free market system make poverty inevitable? Must there be losers if there are huge economic winners? No, no, and no. Economic development is not a zero-sum game; the world does not need poor countries in order to have rich countries, nor must some people be poor in order for others to be rich. Families who live in public housing on the South Side of Chicago are not poor because Bill Gates lives in a big house. *They are poor despite the fact that Bill Gates lives in a big house.* For a complex array of reasons, America's poor have not shared in the productivity gains spawned by Microsoft Windows. Bill Gates did not take their pie away; he did not stand in the way of their success or benefit from their misfortunes. Rather, his vision and talent created an enormous amount of wealth that not everybody got to share. There is a crucial distinction between a world in which Bill Gates gets rich by stealing other people's crops and a world in which he gets rich by growing his own enormous food supply that he shares with some people and not others. The latter is a better representation of how a modern economy works.

In theory, a world in which every individual was educated, healthy, and productive would be a world in which every person lived comfortably. Perhaps we will never cure the world of the assorted physical and mental illnesses that prevent some individuals from reaching their full potential. But that is biology, not economics. Economics tells us that there is no theoretical limit to how well we can live or how widely our wealth can be spread.

Can that really be true? If we all had Ph.D.s, who would pass out the towels at the Four Seasons? Probably no one. As a population becomes more productive, we begin to substitute technology for labor. We use voice mail instead of secretaries, washing machines instead of maids, ATMs instead of bank tellers, databases instead of file clerks, vending machines instead of shopkeepers, backhoes instead of ditch diggers. The motivation for this development harks back to a concept from Chapter 1: opportunity cost. Highly skilled individuals can do all kinds of productive things with their time. Thus, it is fabulously expensive to hire an engineer to bag groceries. (How much would you have to be paid to pass out towels at the Four Seasons?) There are far fewer domestic servants in the United States than in India, even though the United States is a richer country. India is awash with low-skilled workers who have few other employment options; America is not, making domestic labor relatively expensive (as anyone with a nanny can attest). Who can afford a butler who would otherwise earn $50 an hour writing computer code?

When we cannot automate menial tasks, we may relegate them to students and young people as a means for them to acquire human capital. I caddied for more than a decade (most famously for George W. Bush, long before he ascended to the presidency); my wife waited tables. These jobs provide work experience, which is an important component of human capital. But suppose there was some unpleasant task that could not be automated away, nor could it be done safely by young people at the beginning of their careers. Imagine, for example, a highly educated community that produces all kinds of valuable goods and services but generates a disgusting sludge as a by-product. Further imagine that collecting the sludge is horrible, mind-numbing work. Yet if the sludge is not collected, then the whole economy will grind to a halt. If everyone has a Harvard degree, who hauls away the sludge?

The sludge hauler does. And he or she, incidentally, would be one of the best-paid workers in town. If the economy depends on hauling this stuff away, and no machine can do the task, then the community would have to induce someone to do the work. The way to induce people to do anything is to pay them a lot. The wage for hauling sludge would get bid up to the point that some individual—a doctor, or an engineer, or a writer—would be willing to leave a more pleasant job to haul sludge. Thus, a world rich in human capital may still have unpleasant tasks—proctologist springs to mind—but no one has to be poor. Conversely, many people may accept less money to do particularly enjoyable work—teaching college students comes to mind (especially with the summer off).

Human capital creates opportunities. It makes us richer and healthier; it makes us more complete human beings; it enables us to live better while working less. Most important from a public policy perspective, human capital separates the haves from the have-nots. Marvin Zonis, a professor at the University of Chicago Graduate School of Business and a consultant to businesses and governments around the world, made this point wonderfully in a speech to the Chicago business community. "Complexity will be the hallmark of our age," he noted. "The demand everywhere will be for ever higher levels of human capital. The countries that get that right, the companies that understand how to mobilize and apply that human capital, and the schools that produce it . . . will be the big winners of our age. For the rest, more backwardness and more misery for their own citizens and more problems for the rest of us."[13]

CHAPTER 7

Financial Markets:

What economics can tell us about getting rich quick (and losing weight, too!)

When I was an undergraduate many years ago, a new diet swept through one of the sororities on campus. This was no ordinary diet; it was the grapefruit and ice cream diet. The premise, as the name would suggest, was that one could lose weight by eating large amounts of grapefruit and ice cream. The diet did not work, of course, but the incident has always stuck with me. I was fascinated that a very smart group of women had tossed aside common sense to embrace a diet that could not possibly work. No medical or dietary information suggested that eating grapefruit and ice cream would cause weight loss. Still, it was an appealing thought. Who wouldn't want to lose weight by eating ice cream?

I was reminded of the grapefruit and ice cream diet recently when one of my neighbors began to share his investment strategy. He had taken a big hit over the past year because his portfolio was laden with Internet and tech stocks, he explained, but he was plunging back into the market with a new and improved strategy. He was studying the charts of past market movements for shapes that would signal where the market was going next. I cannot remember the specific shapes he was looking for. I was distracted at the time, both because I was watering flowers and because my mind was screaming, "Grapefruit and ice cream!" My smart neighbor, who is both a doctor and a university faculty member, was venturing far from the halls of science with his investment strategy, and that is the broader lesson. When it comes to personal finance (and losing weight), intelligent people will toss good sense aside faster than you can say "miracle diet." The rules for investing successfully are strikingly simple, but they require discipline and short-term sacrifice. The payoff is a slow, steady accumulation of wealth (with plenty of setbacks along the way) rather than a quick windfall. So, faced with the prospect of giving up consumption in the present for plodding success in the future, we eagerly embrace faster, easier methods—and are then shocked when they don't work.

This chapter is not a primer on personal finance. There are some excellent books on investment strategies. Burton Malkiel, who was kind enough to write the foreword for this book, has written one of the best: *A Random Walk Down Wall Street*. Rather, this chapter is about what a basic understanding of markets—the ideas covered in the first two chapters—can tell us about personal investing. Any investment strategy must obey the basic laws of economics, just as any diet is constrained by the realities of chemistry, biology, and physics. To borrow the title of Wally Lamb's best-selling novel: I know this much is true.

At first glance, the financial markets are remarkably complex. Stocks and bonds are complicated enough, but then there are options, futures, options on futures, interest rate swaps, government "strips," and the now infamous credit default swaps. At the Chicago Mercantile Exchange, it is now possible to buy or sell a futures contract based on the average temperature in Los Angeles. At the Chicago Board of Trade, one can buy and sell the right to emit SO_2. Yes, it's actually possible to make (or lose) money by trading smog. The details of these contracts can be mind-numbing, yet at bottom, most of what is going on is fairly straightforward. Financial instruments, like every other good or service in a market economy, must create some value. Both the buyer and seller must perceive themselves as better off by entering into the deal. All the while, entrepreneurs seek to introduce financial products that are cheaper, faster, easier, or otherwise better than what already exists. Mutual funds were a financial innovation; so were the index funds that Burt Malkiel helped to make popular. At the height of the financial crisis in 2008, it became clear that even Wall Street executives did not fully understand some of the products that their firms were buying and selling. Still, all financial instruments—no matter how complex the bells and whistles—are based on four simple needs:

Raising capital. One of the fascinating things in life, particularly in America, is that we can spend large sums of money that don't belong to us. Financial markets enable us to borrow money. Sometimes this means that Visa and MasterCard indulge our eagerness to consume today what we cannot afford until next year (if then); more often—and more significant to the economy—borrowing makes possible all kinds of investment. We borrow to pay college tuition. We borrow to buy homes. We borrow to build plants and equipment or to launch new businesses. We borrow to do things that make us better off even after we've paid the cost of borrowing.

Sometimes we raise capital without borrowing; we may sell shares of our business to the public. Thus, we trade an ownership stake (and therefore a claim on future profits) in exchange for cash. Or companies and governments may borrow directly from the public by issuing bonds. These transactions may be as simple as a new car loan or as complex as a multibillion-dollar bailout by the International Monetary Fund. *The bottom line never changes: Individuals, firms, and governments need capital to do things today that they could not otherwise afford; the financial markets provide it to them—at a price.*

Modern economies cannot survive without credit. Indeed, the international development community has begun to realize that making credit available to entrepreneurs in the developing world, even loans as small as $50 or $100, can be a powerful tool for fighting poverty. Opportunity International is one such "microcredit" lender. In 2000, the organization made nearly 325,000 low-collateral or non-collateral loans in twenty-four developing countries. The average loan size was a seemingly paltry $195. Esther Gelabuzi, a widow in Uganda with six children, represents a typical story. She is a professional midwife, and she used a tiny loan by Western standards to set up a clinic (still without electricity). She has since delivered some fourteen hundred babies, charging patients from $6 to $14 each. Opportunity International claims to have created some 430,000 jobs. As impressive, the repayment rate on the micro-loans is 96 percent.

Storing, protecting, and making profitable use of excess capital. The sultan of Brunei earned billions of dollars in oil revenues in the 1970s. Suppose he had stuffed that cash under his mattress and left it there. He would have had several problems. First, it is very difficult to sleep with billions of dollars stuffed under the mattress. Second, with billions of dollars stuffed under the mattress, the dirty linens would not be the only thing that disappeared every morning. Nimble fingers, not to mention sophisticated criminals, would find their way to the stash. Third, and most important, the most ruthless and efficient thief would be inflation. If the sultan of Brunei stuffed $1 billion under his mattress in 1970, it would be worth only $180 million today.

Thus, the sultan's first concern would be protecting his wealth, both from theft and from inflation, each of which diminishes his purchasing power in its own way. His second concern would be putting his excess capital to some productive use. The world is full of prospective borrowers, all of whom are willing to pay for the privilege. When economists slap fancy equations on the chalkboard, the symbol for the interest rate is r, not i. Why? Because the interest rate is considered to be the rental rate—r—on capital. And that is the most intuitive way to think about what is going on. Individuals, companies, and institutions with surplus capital are renting it to others who can make more productive use of it. The Harvard University endowment is roughly $25 billion.

This is the Ivy League equivalent of rainy-day money; stuffing it under the mattresses of students and faculty would be both impractical and a waste of a tremendous resource. Instead, Harvard employs nearly two hundred professionals to manage this hoard in a way that generates a healthy return for the university while providing capital to the rest of the world.[1] Harvard buys stocks and bonds, invests in venture capital funds, and otherwise puts $25 billion in the hands of people and institutions around the globe who can do productive things with it. From 1995 to 2005, the endowment earned an average 16 percent annual return, which is a lot more productive for the university than leaving the cash lying around campus. (Harvard also managed to lose 30 percent of its endowment during the financial crisis, so we'll come back to the Harvard endowment when we talk about "risk and reward.")[2]

Financial markets do more than take capital from the rich and lend it to everyone else. They enable each of us to smooth consumption over our lifetimes, which is a fancy way of saying that we don't have to spend income at the same time we earn it. Shakespeare may have admonished us to be neither borrowers nor lenders; the fact is that most of us will be both at some point. If we lived in an agrarian society, we would have to eat our crops reasonably soon after the harvest or find some way to store them. Financial markets are a more sophisticated way of managing the harvest. We can spend income now that we have not yet earned—as by borrowing for college or a home—or we can earn income now and spend it later, as by saving for retirement. The important point is that earning income has been divorced from spending it, allowing us much more flexibility in life.

Insuring against risk. Life is a risky proposition. We risk death just getting into the bathtub, not to mention commuting to work or bungee jumping with friends. Let us consider some of the ways you might face financial ruin: natural disaster, illness or disability, fraud or theft. One of our primary impulses as human beings is to minimize these risks. Financial markets help us to do that. The most obvious examples are health, life, and auto insurance. As we noted in Chapter 4, insurance companies charge more for your policy than they expect to pay out to you, on average. But "average" is a really important term here. You are not worried about average outcomes; you are worried about the worst things that could possibly happen to you. A bad draw—the tree that falls in an electrical storm and crushes your home—could be devastating. Thus, most of us are willing to pay a predictable amount—even one that is more than we expect to get back—in order to protect ourselves against the unpredictable.

Almost anything can be insured. Are you worried about pirates? You should be, if you ship goods through the South China Sea or the Malacca Strait. As *The Economist* explains, "Pirates still prey on ships and sailors. And far from being jolly sorts with wooden legs and eye patches, today's pirates are nasty fellows with rocket-propelled grenades and speedboats." There were 266 acts of piracy (or attempts) reported to the International Maritime Organization in 2005. This is why firms sending cargo through dangerous areas buy marine insurance (which also protects against other risks at sea). When the French oil tanker *Limberg* was rammed by a suicide bomber in a speedboat packed with explosives off the coast of Yemen in 2002, the insurance company ended up writing a check for $70 million—just like when someone backs into your car in the Safeway parking lot, only a much bigger claim.[3]

The clothing and shoe company Fila should have bought insurance before the 2009 U.S. Open tennis tournament, but didn't. Like other such companies, Fila endorses athletes and pays them large bonuses when they do great things. Fila endorses Belgian tennis player Kim Clijsters, winner of the U.S. Open, but opted not to buy "win insurance" for the roughly $300,000 in bonus money they had promised her for a victory. (This was an expensive decision, but perhaps also an insulting one for Ms. Clijsters.) The insurance would have been cheap; Clijsters was unseeded, had played only two tournaments since leaving the game to have a baby, and was considered a 40–1 long shot by bookies before the tournament.[4]

The financial markets provide an array of other products that look complicated but basically function like an insurance policy. A futures contract, for example, locks in a sale price for a commodity—anything from electrical power to soybean meal—at some defined date in the future. On the floor of the Board of Trade, one trader can agree to sell another trader a thousand bushels of corn for $3.27 a bushel in March of 2010. What's the point? The point is that producers and consumers of these commodities have much to fear from future price swings. Corn farmers can benefit from locking in a sale price while their corn is still in the ground—or even before they plant it. Might the farmers get a better price by waiting to sell the crop until harvest? Absolutely. Or they might get a much lower price, leaving them without enough money to pay the bills. They, like the rest of us, are willing to pay a price for certainty.

Meanwhile, big purchasers of commodities can benefit from being on the other side of the trade. Airlines use futures contracts to lock in a predictable price for jet fuel. Fast-food restaurants can enter into futures contracts for ground beef, pork bellies (most of which are made into bacon), and even cheddar cheese. I don't know any Starbucks executives personally, but I have a pretty good idea what keeps them awake at night: the world price of coffee beans. Americans will pay $3.50 for a grande skim decaf latte, but probably not $6.50, which is why I would be willing to bet the royalties from this book that Starbucks uses the financial markets to protect itself from sudden swings in the price of coffee.

Other products deal with other risks. Consider one of my personal favorites: catastrophe bonds.[5] Wall Street dreamed up these gems to help insurance companies hedge their natural disaster risk. Remember, the insurance company writes a check when a tree falls on your house; if a lot of trees fall on a lot of houses, then the company, or even the entire industry, has a problem. Insurance companies can minimize that risk by issuing catastrophe bonds. These bonds pay a significantly higher rate of interest than other corporate bonds because there is a twist: If hurricanes or earthquakes do serious damage to a certain area during a specified period of time, then the investors forfeit some or all of their principal. The United Services Automobile Association did one of the first deals in the late 1990s tied to the hurricane season on the East Coast. If a single hurricane caused $1.5 billion in claims or more, then the catastrophe bond investors lost all of their principal. The insurance company, on the other hand, was able to offset its claims losses by avoiding repayment on its debt. If a hurricane did between $1 billion and $1.5 billion in damage, then investors lost a fraction of their principal. If hurricanes did relatively little damage that year, then the bondholders got their principal back plus nearly 12 percent in interest—a very nice return for a bond.

The same basic idea is now being used to protect against terrorism. The World Football Federation, which governs international soccer, insured the 2006 World Cup against disruption due to terrorism (and other risks) by issuing $260 million in "cancellation bonds." If the tournament went off without a hitch (as it did), the investors get their capital back along with a handsome profit. If there had been a disruption serious enough to cancel the World Cup, the investors lose some or all of their money, which is used instead to compensate the World Football Federation for the lost revenue. The beauty of these products lies in the way they spread risk. The party selling the bonds avoids ruin by sharing the costs of a natural disaster or a terrorist attack with a broad group of investors, each of whom has a diversified portfolio and will therefore take a relatively small hit even if something truly awful happens.

Indeed, one role of the financial markets is to allow us to spread our eggs around generously. I must recount one of those inane experiences that can happen only in high school. Some expert in adolescent behavior at my high school decided that students would be less likely to become teen parents if they realized how much responsibility it required. The best way to replicate parenthood, the experts reckoned, would be to have each student carry an egg around school. The egg represented a baby and was to be treated as such—handled delicately, never left out of sight, and so on. But this was high school. Eggs were dropped, crushed, left in gym lockers, hurled against the wall by bullies, exposed to secondhand smoke in the bathrooms, etc. The experience taught me nothing about parenthood; it did convince me forever that carrying eggs is a risky proposition.

The financial markets make it cheap and easy to put our eggs into many different baskets. With a $1,000 investment in a mutual fund, you can invest in five hundred or more companies. If you were forced to buy individual stocks from a broker, you could never afford so much diversity with a mere $1,000. For $10,000, you can diversify across a wide range of assets: big stocks, small stocks, international stocks, long-term bonds, short-term bonds, junk bonds, real estate. Some of those assets will perform well at the same time others are doing poorly, protecting you from Wall Street's equivalent of bullies hurling eggs against the wall. One attraction of catastrophe bonds for investors is that their payout is determined by the frequency of natural disasters, which is not correlated with the performance of stocks, bonds, real estate, or other traditional investments.

Even the much-maligned credit default swaps have a legitimate investment purpose. A credit default swap is really just an insurance policy on whether or not some third party will pay back its debts. Suppose your husband pressures you to loan $25,000 to your ne'er-do-well brother-in-law so that he can finally complete his court-mandated anger management program and turn his life around. You have grave concerns about whether you will ever see any of this money again. What you need is a credit default swap. You can pay some other party (presumably with a more favorable view of your brother-in-law's creditworthiness) to enter into a contract with you that promises to pay you $25,000 in the event that your brother-in-law does not pay back the cash. The contract functions as insurance against default. Like any other kind of insurance, you pay for this protection. If your brother-in-law gets his act together and pays back the loan, you will have purchased the credit default swap for nothing (which is how the other party to the transaction, or the counterparty, makes its money). How could something so simple and seemingly useful contribute to the near collapse of the global financial system? Read on.

Speculation. Of course, once any financial product is created, it fulfills another basic human need: the urge to speculate, or bet on short-term price movements. One can use the futures market to mitigate risk—or one can use the futures market to bet on the price of soybeans next year. One can use the bond market to raise capital—or one can use it to bet on whether or not Ben Bernanke will cut interest rates next month. One can use the stock market to invest in companies and share their future profits—or one can buy a stock at 10:00 a.m. in hopes of making a few bucks by noon. Financial products are to speculation what sporting events are to gambling. They facilitate it, even if that is not their primary purpose.

This is what went wrong with credit default swaps. The curious thing about these contracts is that anyone can get into the action, regardless of whether or not they are a party to the debt that is being guaranteed. Let's stick with the example of your loser brother-in-law. It makes sense for you to use a credit default swap to protect yourself against loss. However, that same market also allows the rest of us to bet on whether or not your brother-in-law will pay back the loan. That's not hedging a bet; that's speculation. So for any single debt, there may be hundreds or thousands of contracts tied to whether or not it gets repaid. Think about what that means if your brother-in-law starts skipping his anger management classes and defaults. At that point, a $25,000 loss gets magnified thousands of times over.

If the parties guaranteeing that debt haven't done their homework (so they don't truly understand what a loser your brother-in-law is), or if they don't care (because they earn big bonuses for making dubious bets with the firm's capital), then an otherwise small set of economic setbacks can explode into something bigger. That's what happened when the American economy hit a real-estate-related speed bump in 2007. AIG was the firm at the heart of the credit default debacle because it guaranteed a lot of debt that went bad. In his excellent 2009 assessment of the financial crisis, former chief economist for the International Monetary Fund Simon Johnson writes:

> Regulators, legislators, and academics almost all assumed that the managers of these banks knew what they were doing. In retrospect, they didn't. AIG's Financial Products division, for instance, made $2.5 million in pretax profits in 2005, largely by selling underpriced insurance on complex, poorly understood securities. Often described as "picking up nickels in front of a steamroller," this strategy is profitable in ordinary years, and catastrophic in bad ones. As of last fall, AIG had outstanding insurance on more than $400 billion in securities. To date, the U.S. government, in an effort to rescue the company, has committed to about $180 billion in investments and loans to cover losses that AIG's sophisticated risk modeling had said were virtually impossible.[6]

Raising capital. Protecting capital. Hedging risk. Speculating. That's it. All the frantic activity on Wall Street or LaSalle Street (home of the futures exchanges in Chicago) fits into one or more of those buckets. The world of high finance is often described as a rich man's version of Las Vegas—risk, glamour, interesting personalities, and lots of money changing hands. Yet the analogy is terribly inappropriate. Everything that happens in Las Vegas is a zero-sum game. If the house wins a hand of blackjack, you lose. And the odds are stacked heavily in favor of the house. If you play blackjack long enough—at least without counting cards—it is a mathematical certainty that you will go broke. Las Vegas provides entertainment, but it does not serve any broader social purpose. Wall Street does. Most of what happens is a positive-sum game. Things get built; companies are launched; individuals and companies manage risk that might otherwise be devastating.

Not every transaction is a winner, of course. Just as individuals make investments they later regret, the capital markets are perfectly capable of squandering huge amounts of capital; choose your favorite failed dot-com and think of that as an example. Billions of dollars of capital flowed into businesses that didn't work. The real estate bubble and the Wall Street meltdown did the same on an even bigger scale. Adam Smith's invisible hand has hurled a lot of capital into the ocean, never to be seen again. Meanwhile, some potentially profitable enterprises are starved for capital because they have insufficient collateral. Economists worry, for example, that too little credit is available for poor families who would like to invest in human capital. A college degree is an excellent investment, but it is not something that can be repossessed in the event of default.

Still, the financial markets do for capital what other markets do for everything else: allocate it in a highly productive, albeit imperfect, way. Capital flows to where it can earn the highest return, which is not a bad place to have it flowing (as opposed to, say, into businesses run by top communist officials or friends of the king). As with the rest of the economy, government can be enemy or friend. Government can mess up the capital markets in the same ways it can mess up anything else—with overly burdensome taxes and regulations, by diverting capital into pet projects, by refusing to allow creative destruction to work its harshly efficient ways. Or government can make the financial markets work better: by minimizing fraud, forcing transparency on the system, creating and enforcing a regulatory framework, providing public goods that lower the cost of doing business, and so on. Once again, the wisdom lies in telling the difference.

Obviously the current crisis has presented some teachable moments. The financial regulatory system needs to be patched up, if not completely overhauled. The challenge will be to protect what a modern financial system does best—allocating capital to productive investments and protecting us from risks we can't afford—while curtailing the excesses—stupid bets that enrich the folks making them before eventually leaving a mess for the rest of us to clean up.

All that is well and good. *But how does one get rich in the markets?* One of my former colleagues at *The Economist* suggested that this book should be called *Are You Rich Enough?* His logic was that most people would answer no and rip the book off the shelves. Sadly, I'm not a big believer in surefire strategies to trade your way to riches. Just as miracle weight-loss programs violate nearly everything we know about health and nutrition, get-rich-quick schemes violate the most basic principles of economics.

Let me begin with an example. Suppose you are shopping for a home in the Lincoln Park neighborhood of Chicago. After many weeks of searching, you find that a three-story single-family brownstone will cost you somewhere in the range of $500,000. Some homes are listed for $450,000 but they need work; others are listed for $600,000 because they have extra amenities. Just when you begin to despair that you will have to spend $500,000 for a home, you find a brownstone listed for $250,000 that meets all of your specifications. When you investigate, you learn that this home is every bit as nice as the ones you've been looking at—same location, same size, same structural integrity. Still wary, you ask your real estate agent for her assessment. She assures you that this house is indeed a remarkable bargain and should be selling for $500,000. In her professional opinion, there is no doubt that you could buy this house for $250,000 and sell it only months later for $500,000 or more. Then you see the final piece of evidence. An article on page 3 of *Crain's Chicago Business* has a screaming headline: "Bargain of the Month: Lincoln Park Brownstone Listed for $250,000."

So you snap up the house for $250,000. Sure enough, six months later you sell it for $500,000—doubling your money.*

---

* Your actual return would be much higher, since much of the purchase would be financed. If you put $50,000 down, for example, you would have earned $250,000

How many things are wrong with this story? Quite a few. A reasonable person might begin by asking some of the following questions:

1. If this house was really worth $500,000, who was the moron selling it for $250,000? Was this person not willing or able to do the three minutes of work necessary to determine that comparable houses in the neighborhood were selling for twice as much? If not, wasn't there a family member or a real estate agent—whose commission is based on the sale price—willing to point out this enormous discrepancy?

2. Maybe not. In that case, why hasn't my real estate agent bought this house for herself? If this house is a "sure thing" to double in price, why is she working for my 3 percent commission when $250,000 is staring her in the face?

3. Perhaps my real estate agent is a moron, too. In that case, where are all of the other buyers looking for bargains, especially after this house is featured in *Crain's Chicago Business?* If this brownstone is a tremendous bargain—and has been widely advertised as such—then presumably all kinds of people are going to want to buy it. A bidding war would result, with potential buyers offering larger and larger sums until the price reached its fair market value, which is around $500,000.

In other words, there is virtually no chance that you will find a Lincoln Park brownstone (without some surprise lurking in the basement) for $250,000. Why? Because of the most basic idea in economics. You are trying to maximize your utility—and so is everyone else. In a world in which everyone is looking to make profitable investments, no one is going to leave $250,000 sitting on the table. *Yet people assume the stock market works like this all the time.* We believe that after

---

on a $50,000 investment (minus the interest you paid to carry the mortgage during the period you owned the house).

reading about a "hot stock" in *BusinessWeek*, or reading a Wall Street analyst's buy recommendation (offered to all the firm's clients), we can load up on stocks that will trounce the market average. But those supposed "hot stocks" are merely the Lincoln Park brownstone in different clothing. Here's why:

Let's start with a stunningly simple but often overlooked point: Every time you buy a stock (or any other asset), someone has to sell it to you. The guy who sells you this "hot stock" has decided that he would rather have cash. He has looked at the current "bargain price" and he wants out—right when you are getting in. Sure, he may need the money for something else, but he is still going to demand a fair market price, just as we would expect someone who has to move out of Lincoln Park to ask $500,000 for a brownstone, not $250,000. The stock market, as the name would suggest, is a market. The price of a stock at any given time is the price at which the number of buyers equals the number of sellers. Half of the investors trading your "hot stock" are trying to get rid of it.

Or maybe you know something that the sellers don't. Perhaps all the people unloading XYZ Corp. missed the *Wall Street Journal* article about XYZ's new blockbuster drug for male-pattern baldness. Okay, that might happen. But where are the world's other sophisticated buyers? This stock is a sure thing at $45, yet for some reason Warren Buffett, the traders at Goldman Sachs, and the top Fidelity portfolio managers are not snapping it up. (If they were, the stock would be bid up to a much higher price, just like the Lincoln Park brownstone.) Do you know something that no one else on Wall Street knows (bearing in mind that trading on any information not available to the public is against the law)?

Or maybe someone on Wall Street is pitching you this stock idea. America's brokerage houses employ a cadre of analysts who spend their days kicking the tires of corporate America. Is all that information wrong? No—though there are plenty of cases of incompetence and conflict of interest. Analysts provide all kinds of legitimate information, just like your real estate agent. When you are shopping for a home, your agent can tell you about neighborhoods, schools, taxes, crime—the kinds of things that matter. Wall Street analysts do the same things for companies; they report on management, future products, the industry, the competition. But that does nothing to guarantee that you are going to earn an above-average return on the stock.

The problem is that everyone else has access to the same information. This is the essence of the efficient markets theory. The main premise of the theory is that asset prices already reflect all available information. Thus it is difficult, if not impossible, to choose stocks that will outperform the market with any degree of consistency. Why can't you buy a brownstone in Lincoln Park for $250,000? Because buyers and sellers recognize that such a home is worth much more. A share of XYZ Corp. is no different. Stock prices settle at a fair price given everything that we know or can reasonably predict; prices will rise or fall in the future only in response to unanticipated events—things that we cannot know in the present.

Picking stocks is a lot like trying to pick the shortest checkout line at the grocery store. Do some lines move faster than others? Absolutely, just as some stocks outperform others. Are there things that you can look for that signal how fast one line will move relative to another? Yes. You don't want to be behind the guy with two full shopping carts or the old woman clutching a fistful of coupons. So why is it that we seldom end up in the shortest line at the grocery store (and most professional stock pickers don't beat the market average)? Because everyone else is looking at the same things we are and acting accordingly. They can see the guy with two shopping carts, the cashier in training at register three, the coupon queen lined up at register six. Everybody at the checkout tries to pick the fastest line. Sometimes you will be right; sometimes you will be wrong. Over time they will average out, so that if you go to the grocery store often enough, you'll probably spend about the same amount of time waiting in line as everyone else.

Indeed, we can take the analogy one step further. Suppose that somewhere near the produce aisle you saw an old woman stuffing wads of coupons in her pockets. When you arrive at the checkout and see her in line, you wisely steer your cart somewhere else. As she gets out her coin purse and begins slowly handing coupons to the cashier, you smugly congratulate yourself. Moments later, however, you realize the guy ahead of you forgot to weigh his avocados. "Price check on avocados at register three!" your cashier barks repeatedly as you watch the coupon lady push her groceries out of the store. Who could have predicted that? No one, just as no one would have predicted that MicroStrategy, a high-flying software company, would restate its income on March 19, 2000, essentially wiping millions of dollars of earnings off its books. The stock fell $140 in one day, a 62 percent plunge. Did the investors and portfolio managers who bought MicroStrategy shares think this was going to happen? Of course not. *It's the things you can't predict that matter.* Indeed, the next time you are tempted to invest a large sum of money in a single stock, even that of a large and well-established firm, repeat these magic words: Enron, Enron, Enron. Or Lehman, Lehman, Lehman.

Proponents of the efficient markets theory have advice for investors: Just pick a line and stand in it. If assets are priced efficiently, then a monkey throwing darts at the stock pages should choose a porfolio that will perform as well, on average, as the portfolios picked by the Wall Street stars. (Burton Malkiel has pointed out that since diversification is important, the monkey should actually throw a wet towel at the stock pages.) Indeed, investors now have access to their own monkey with a towel: index funds. Index funds are mutual funds that do not purport to pick winners. Instead, they buy and hold a predetermined basket of stocks, such as the S&P 500, the index that comprises America's largest five hundred companies. Since the S&P 500 is a broad market average, we would expect half of America's actively managed mutual funds to perform better, and half to perform worse. But that is before expenses. Fund managers charge fees for all the tire-kicking they do; they also incur costs as they trade aggressively. Index funds, like towel-throwing monkeys, are far cheaper to manage.

But that's all theory. What do the data show? It turns out that the monkey with a towel can be an investor's best friend. According to Morningstar, a firm that tracks mutual funds, slightly fewer than half of the U.S. actively managed diversified funds beat the S&P 500 over the past year. A more impressive 66 percent of actively-managed funds beat the S&P 500 over the past five years. But look what happens as the time frame gets longer: Only 45 percent of actively managed funds beat the S&P over a twenty-year stretch, which is the most relevant time frame for people saving for retirement or college. *In other words, 55 percent of the mutual funds that claim to have some special stock-picking ability did worse over two decades than a simple index fund, our modern equivalent of a monkey throwing a towel at the stock pages.*

If you had invested $10,000 in the average actively managed equity fund in 1973, when Malkiel's heretical book *A Random Walk Down Wall Street* first came out, it would be worth $355,091 today (many editions later). If you had invested the same amount of money in an S&P 500 index fund, it would now be worth $364,066.

Data notwithstanding, the efficient markets theory is obviously not the most popular idea on Wall Street. There is an old joke about two economists walking down the street. One of them sees a $100 bill lying in the street and points it out to his friend. "Is that a $100 bill lying in the gutter?" he asks.

"No," his friend replies. "If it were a $100 bill, someone would have picked it up already."

So they walk on by.

Neither the housing market nor the stock market has behaved lately in ways consistent with such a sensible and orderly view of human behavior. Some of the brightest minds in finance have been chipping away at the efficient markets theory. Behavioral economists have documented the ways in which individuals make flawed decisions: We are prone to herd-like behavior, we have too much confidence in our own abilities, we place too much weight on past trends when predicting the future, and so on. Given that a market is just a collection of individuals' decisions, it stands to reason that if individuals get things wrong in systematic ways (like overreacting to good and bad news), then markets can get things wrong, too (like bubbles and busts).

There is even a new field, neuroeconomics, that combines economics, cognitive neuroscience, and psychology to explore the role that biology plays in our decision making. One of the most bizarre and intriguing findings is that people with brain damage may be particularly good investors. Why? Because damage to certain parts of the brain can impair the emotional responses that cause the rest of us to do foolish things. A team of researchers from Carnegie Mellon, Stanford, and the University of Iowa conducted an experiment that compared the investment decisions made by fifteen patients with damage to the areas of the brain that control emotions (but with intact logic and cognitive functions) to the investment decisions made by a control group. The brain-damaged investors finished the game with 13 percent more money than the control group, largely, the authors believe, because they do not experience fear and anxiety. The impaired investors took more risks when there were high potential payoffs and got less emotional when they made losses.[7]

This book is not prescribing brain injury as an investment strategy. However, behavioral economists do believe that by anticipating the flawed decisions that regular investors are likely to make, we can beat the market (or at least avoid being ravaged by it). Yale economist Robert Shiller first challenged the theory of efficient markets in the early 1980s. He became much more famous for his book *Irrational Exuberance*, which argued in 2000 that the stock market was overvalued. He was right. Five years later he argued that there was a bubble in the housing market. He was right again.

If irrational investors are leaving $100 bills strewn about, shouldn't we be able to pick them up somehow? Yes, argues Richard Thaler, a University of Chicago economist (and the guy who took away the bowl of cashews from his guests back in Chapter 1). Thaler has even been willing to put his money where his theory is. He and some collaborators created a mutual fund that would take advantage of our human imperfections: the behavioral growth fund. I will even admit that after I interviewed Mr. Thaler for Chicago public radio, I decided to toss aside my strong belief in efficient markets and invest a small sum in his fund. How has it done? Very well. The behavioral growth fund has produced an average return of 4.5 percent a year since its inception, compared to an average annual return of 2.3 percent for the S&P 500.

The efficient markets theory isn't going anywhere soon. In fact, it's still a crucial concept for any investor to understand, for two reasons. First, markets may do irrational things, but that doesn't make it easy to make money off those crazy movements, at least not for long. As investors take advantage of a market anomaly, say by buying up stocks that have been irrationally underpriced, they will fix the very inefficiency that they exploited (by bidding up the price of the underpriced stocks until they aren't underpriced anymore). Think about the original analogy of trying to find the fastest checkout line at the grocery store. Suppose you do find one line that moves predictably faster than the others—maybe it has a really fast cashier and a nimble bagger. This outcome is observable to other shoppers; they are going to pile into your special line until it's not particularly fast anymore. The chances of you picking the shortest line week after week are essentially nil. Mutual funds work the same way. If a portfolio manager starts beating the market, others will see his oversized returns and copy the strategy, making it less effective in the process. So even if you believe that there will be an occasional $100 bill lying on the ground, you should also recognize that it won't be lying there for long.

Second, the most effective critics of the efficient markets theory think the average investor probably can't beat the market and shouldn't try. Andrew Lo of MIT and A. Craig MacKinlay of the Wharton School are the authors of a book entitled *A Non-Random Walk Down Wall Street* in which they assert that financial experts with extraordinary resources, such as supercomputers, can beat the market by finding and exploiting pricing anomalies. A *BusinessWeek* review of the book noted, "Surprisingly, perhaps, Lo and MacKinlay actually agree with Malkiel's advice to the average investor. If you don't have any special expertise or the time and money to find expert help, they say, go ahead and purchase index funds."[8]

Warren Buffett, arguably the best stock picker of all time, says the same thing.[9] Even Richard Thaler, the guy beating the market with his behavioral growth fund, told the *Wall Street Journal* that he puts most of his retirement savings in index funds.[10] Indexing is to investing what regular exercise and a low-fat diet are to losing weight: a very good starting point. The burden of proof should fall on anyone who claims to have a better way.

As I've already noted, this chapter is not an investment guide. I'll leave it to others to explain the pros and cons of college savings plans, municipal bonds, variable annuities, and all the other modern investment options. That said, basic economics can give us a sniff test. It provides us with a basic set of rules to which any decent investment advice must conform:

Save. Invest. Repeat. Let's return to the most basic idea in this chapter: Capital is scarce. This is the only reason that any kind of investing yields returns. If you have spare capital, then someone will pay you to use it. But you've got to have the spare capital first, and the only way to generate spare capital is to spend less than you earn—i.e., save. The more you save, and the sooner you begin saving it, the more rent you can command from the financial markets. Any good book on personal finance will dazzle you with the virtues of compound interest. Suffice it here to note that Albert Einstein is said to have called it the greatest invention of all time.

The flip side, of course, is that if you are spending more cash than you earn, then you will have to "rent" the difference somewhere. And you will have to pay for that privilege. Paying the rent on capital is no different from paying the rent on anything else: It is an expense that crowds out other things you may want to consume later. The cost of living better in the present is living less well in the future. Conversely, the payoff for living frugally in the present is living better in the future. So for now, set aside questions about whether your 401(k) should be in stocks or bonds. The first step is far more simple: Save early, save often, and pay off the credit cards.

Take risk, earn reward. Okay, now we'll talk about whether your 401(k) should be in stocks or bonds. Suppose you have capital to rent, and you are deciding between two options: lending it to the federal government (a treasury bond), or lending it to your neighbor Lance, who has been tinkering in his basement for three years and claims to have invented an internal combustion engine that runs on sunflower seeds. Both the federal government and your neighbor Lance are willing to pay you 6 percent interest on the loan. What to do? Unless Lance has photos of you in a compromising position, you should buy the government bond. The sunflower combustion engine is a risky proposition; the government bond is not. Lance may eventually attract the capital necessary to build his invention, but not by offering a 6 percent return. *Riskier investments must offer a higher expected return in order to attract capital.* That is not some arcane law of finance; it is simply markets at work. No rational person will invest money somewhere when he or she can earn the same expected return with less risk somewhere else.

The implication for investors is clear: You will be compensated for taking more risk. Thus, the more risky your portfolio, the higher your return—*on average.* Yes, it's that pesky concept of "average" again. If your portfolio is risky, it also means that some very bad things will occasionally happen. Nothing encapsulates this point better than an old headline in the *Wall Street Journal:* "Bonds Let You Sleep at Night but at a Price."[11] The story examined stock and bond returns from 1945 to 1997. Over that period, a portfolio of 100 percent stocks earned an average annual return of 12.9 percent; a portfolio of 100 percent bonds earned a relatively meager 5.8 percent average annual return over the same period. So you might ask yourself, who are the chumps holding bonds? Not so fast. The same story then examined how the different portfolios performed in their worst years. The stock portfolio lost 26.5 percent of its value in its worst year; the bond portfolio never lost more than 5 percent of its value in a single bad year. Similarly, the stock portfolio had negative annual returns eight times between 1945 and 1997; the bond portfolio lost money only once. The bottom line: Risk is rewarded—if you have a tolerance for it.

That brings us back to the Harvard endowment, which lost about a third of its value during the 2008 financial crisis. And Yale lost a quarter of its endowment in one year alone. Meanwhile, over the same stretch of dismal economic circumstances, my mother-in-law earned about a 3 percent return by keeping nearly all of her assets in certificates of deposit and a checking account. Is my mother-in-law an investment genius? Should Harvard have directed more of its assets to a giant checking account? No and no. My mother-in-law always keeps her assets in safe but low-yielding investments because she has a small appetite for risk. She is protected when times are bad; of course, that also means that if the stock market posts an 18 percent gain one year, she earns . . . 3 percent. Meanwhile, Harvard and Yale and other schools with large endowments earned enormous returns during the boom years by taking large risks and making relatively illiquid investments. (Liquidity is the reflection of how quickly and predictably something can be turned into cash. Illiquid investments, like rare art or Venezuelan corporate bonds, must pay a premium to compensate for this drawback; of course, when you need to get rid of them quickly to raise cash, it's a problem.) These institutions pay an occasional price for their aggressive portfolios, but those bumps should be more than offset in the long run with returns that are a heck of a lot better than a certificate of deposit. Most important, the endowments are different than the typical investor planning for college or retirement; their investment horizon is theoretically infinite, meaning that they can afford some really bad years, or even decades, if it maximizes returns over the next one hundred or two hundred years (although both Harvard and Yale have had to make serious budget cuts lately to make up for lost endowment revenue). Yale President Richard Levin told the *Wall Street Journal*, "We made huge excess returns on the way up. When it's all over and things stabilize I think we'll find the overall long-run performance [of the endowment] is better than if we didn't."[12] I suspect he's right, but that doesn't necessarily make it a wise strategy for my mother-in-law.

Diversify. When I teach finance, I like to have my students flip coins. It is the best way to make certain points. Here is one of them: A well-diversified portfolio will significantly lower the risk of serious losses without lowering your expected return. Let's turn to the coins. Suppose the return on the $100,000 you have tucked away in a 401(k) depends on the flip of a coin: Heads, it quadruples in value; tails, you lose everything. The average outcome of this exercise is very good. (Your expected return is 100 percent.)* The problem, of course, is that the downside is unacceptably bad. You have a 50 percent chance of losing your whole nest egg. Try explaining that to a spouse.

So let's bring in some more coins. Suppose you spread the $100,000 in your 401(k) into ten different investments, each with the same payoff scheme: Heads, the investment quadruples in value; tails, it becomes worthless. Your expected return has not changed at all: On average, you will flip five heads and five tails. Five of your investments would quadruple in value, and five would become worthless. That works out to the same handsome 100 percent return. But look at what has happened to your downside risk. The only way you can lose your entire 401(k) is by flipping ten tails, which is highly unlikely. (The probability is less than one in a thousand.) Now imagine the same exercise if you buy several index funds that include thousands of stocks from around the world.† That many coins will never come up all tails.

---

* The expected return is 0.5($400,000) + 0.5($0) = $200,000, which is a 100 percent return on your $100,000 investment.

† This exercise is somewhat oversimplified. The flips of a coin are independent,

Of course, you better make darn sure that all those investments have outcomes that are truly independent of one another. It's one thing to flip coins, where the outcome of one flip is uncorrelated with the outcome of the next flip. It's quite another to buy shares of Microsoft and Intel and then assume that you've safely split your portfolio into two baskets. Yes, they are different companies with different products and different management, but if Microsoft has a really bad year, there is a pretty good chance that Intel will suffer, too. One of the mistakes that compounded the financial crisis was the belief that bundling lots of mortgages together into a single mortgage-backed security created an investment that was safer and more predictable than any single mortgage—like flipping one hundred coins instead of just one. If you are a bank with one mortgage loan outstanding, it could go into default, taking all of your capital with it. But if you buy a financial product constructed from thousands of mortgages, most of them will be fine, which offsets the risk of the occasional default.

During normal times, that's probably true. A mortgage goes into default when someone gets sick or loses a job. That's not likely to be highly correlated across households; if one house on the block goes into foreclosure, there is no reason to believe that others will, too. When a real estate bubble pops, everything is different. Housing prices were plummeting all over the country, and the accompanying recession meant that lots and lots of people were losing jobs. The seemingly clever securities backed by real estate loans morphed into the "toxic assets" that we've been trying to clean up ever since.

Invest for the long run. Have you ever been in a casino when someone wins big? The casino operators are just as happy as everybody else.

---

while the performance of individual stocks are not. Some events, such as an interest rate hike, will affect the whole market. Thus, buying two stocks will not offer as much diversification as would splitting your portfolio between two flips of a coin. Nonetheless, the broader point is valid.

Why? Because they are going to make an extraordinary amount of money in the long run; this is just one minor hiccup along the way. The beauty of running a casino is that the numbers are stacked in your favor. If you are willing to wait long enough—and pose happily for photos as you give a giant check to the occasional big winner—then you will get rich.

Investing has the same benefits as running a casino: The odds are stacked in your favor if you are patient and willing to endure the occasional setback. Any reasonable investment portfolio must have a positive expected return. Remember, you've rented capital to assorted entities and you expect to get something back in return. Indeed, the riskier the ventures, the more you expect to get back, on average. So the longer you hold your (diversified) investments, the longer you have for probability to work its magic. Where will the Dow close tomorrow? I have no clue. Where will it be next year? I don't know. Where will it be in five years? Probably higher than it is today, but that's no sure thing. Where will it be in twenty-five years? Significantly higher than it is today; I'm reasonably certain of it. The idiocy of day trading—buying a stock in hopes of selling it several hours later at a profit—is that it incurs all the costs of trading stocks (commissions and taxes, not to mention your time) without any of the benefits that come from holding equities for the long run.

So there you have it—the sniff test for personal investing. The next time an investment adviser comes to you promising a 20 or 40 percent return, you know that one of three things must be true: (1) This must be a very risky investment in order to justify such a high expected return—think Harvard endowment; (2) your investment adviser has stumbled upon an opportunity still undiscovered by all the world's sophisticated investors, and he has been kind enough to share it with you—please call me; or (3) your investment adviser is incompetent and/or dishonest—think Bernie Madoff. All too often the answer is (3).

The fascinating thing about economics is that the fundamental ideas don't change. Monarchs in the Middle Ages needed to raise capital (usually to fight wars), just as biotech startups do today. I have no idea what the planet will look like in one hundred years. Perhaps we will be settling Mars or converting salt water into a clean, renewable source of energy. I do know that either of those undertakings would use the financial markets to raise capital and to mitigate risk. And I'm positive that Americans will not have become thin and healthy by eating only grapefruit and ice cream.

CHAPTER 8

The Power of Organized Interests:

What economics can tell us about politics

Many years ago I took a vacation with a group of friends. As the sole academic among the bunch, I was the object of mild curiosity. When I explained that I was studying public policy, one of my peers asked skeptically, "If people know so much about public policy, then why is everything so messed up?" On the one hand, the question was idiotic; it's a bit like asking, "If we know so much about medicine, why do people keep dying all the time?" One can always come up with clever rejoinders a decade later. (At the time, I mumbled something like "Well, it's complicated.") I might have pointed out that in the realm of public policy, as in medicine, we have achieved some pretty good wins. Americans are healthier, richer, better-educated, and less vulnerable to economic booms and busts than at any time in our history—the recent economic downturn notwithstanding.

Still, the question has stuck with me for years, in large part because it hints at an important point: Even when economists reach consensus on policies that would make us better off, those policies often run into a brick wall of political opposition. International trade is a perfect example. I am not aware of a single mainstream economist who believes that international trade is anything less than crucial to the well-being of rich and poor countries alike. There is just one small problem: It's an issue that literally causes riots in the streets. Even before the violent antiglobalization protests in places like Seattle and Genoa, agreements to expand trade, such as the North American Free Trade Agreement, caused ferocious political battles.

Meanwhile, pork-barrel legislation sails through Congress, lavishing money on small projects that cannot possibly be described as promoting the national interest. For nearly forty years, the federal budget included a cash payment to American mohair farmers. (Mohair comes from the Angora goat and is a wool substitute.) The mohair subsidy was created in 1955 at the behest of the armed forces to ensure a sufficient supply of yarn for military uniforms in the event of a war. I won't quibble with that. *But the military switched to synthetic fibers for its uniforms around 1960.* The government continued to give large cash payments to mohair farmers for another thirty-five years. The mohair subsidy was eventually eliminated when it became the poster child for pork-barrel politics and was doomed by its sheer absurdity.

And then, when the rest of us turned our attention elsewhere, *it came back.* The 2008 farm bill includes subsidies for wool and mohair producers for the crop years 2008 to 2012. How does this happen?

It is not because the mohair farmers are enormously powerful, well funded, or politically sophisticated. They are not any of those things. In fact, the small number of mohair farmers is an advantage. What the mohair farmers have going for them is that they can get large payments from the government without taxpayers ever really noticing. Suppose there are a thousand mohair farmers, each of whom gets a check from the federal government for $100,000 every spring, just for being a mohair farmer. The farmers who get that subsidy care a lot about it—probably more than they care about any other government policy. Meanwhile, the rest of us, who pay mere pennies extra in taxes to preserve an unnecessary supply of mohair, don't care much about it at all. Any politician with a preference for job security can calculate that a vote for the mohair subsidy will earn the strong support of the mohair farmers while costing nothing among other voters. It's a political no-brainer.

The problem is that mohair farmers aren't the only group lining up to get a subsidy, or a tax break, or trade protection, or some other government policy that puts money in their pockets. Indeed, the most savvy politicians can trade favors with one another—if you support the mohair farmers in my district, then I'll support the Bingo Hall of Fame in your district. During my days as a speechwriter for the governor of Maine, we used to refer to the state budget as a Christmas tree. Every legislator could hang an ornament or two. I currently live in the Illinois Fifth Congressional District, the seat held for decades by Dan Rostenkowski (and later by Rahm Emanuel). We Chicagoans can drive around the city and literally point to the things that Rosty built. When the Museum of Science and Industry needed tens of millions of dollars to build an underground parking garage, Dan Rostenkowski found federal funds.[1] Should taxpayers in Seattle or rural Vermont have paid for a parking garage at a Chicago museum? Of course not. But when I took my children to the museum last weekend in a downpour, I was delighted to be able to park indoors. That helps to explain why Dan Rostenkowski, not long out of federal prison, can still command a standing ovation at political gatherings in Chicago.

The stimulus bill passed by the Obama administration during the depths of the financial crisis was a giant legislative Christmas tree. I will argue in the next chapter that the stimulus was a reasonable thing to do under the circumstances. No sane person, however, would have designed that particular bill, which included funding for things ranging from "green" golf carts to a polar ice breaker. Yes, the process that has generated decades of cash payments for mohair farmers is alive and well. Let's talk about ethanol, a corn-based gasoline additive with putative environmental benefits. Gasoline blended with ethanol is taxed 5.4 cents less per gallon than pure gasoline, ostensibly because it burns more cleanly than pure gasoline and because it lowers our dependence on foreign oil. Of course, neither scientists nor environmentalists are convinced that ethanol is such a great thing. A 1997 study by the General Accounting Office (which later changed its name to the Government Accountability Office), the nonpartisan research arm of Congress, found that ethanol had little effect on either the environment or our dependence on foreign oil. The ethanol subsidy had, however, cost the Treasury $7.1 billion in forgone tax revenues. Worse, ethanol may actually make some kinds of air pollution worse. It evaporates faster than pure gasoline, contributing to ozone problems in hot temperatures. A 2006 study published in the Proceedings of the National Academy of Sciences concluded that ethanol does reduce greenhouse gas emissions by 12 percent relative to gasoline, but it calculated that devoting the entire U.S. corn crop to make ethanol would replace only a small fraction of American gasoline consumption. Corn farming also contributes to environmental degradation due to runoff from fertilizer and pesticides.[2]

But to dwell on the science is to miss the point. As the *New York Times* noted in the throes of the 2000 presidential race, "Regardless of whether ethanol is a great fuel for cars, it certainly works wonders in Iowa campaigns."[3] The ethanol tax subsidy increases the demand for corn, which puts money in farmers' pockets. Just before the Iowa caucuses, corn farmer Marvin Flier told the *Times*, "Sometimes I think [the candidates] just come out and pander to us," he said. Then he added, "Of course, that may not be the worst thing." The National Corn Growers Association figures that the ethanol program increases the demand for corn, which adds 30 cents to the price of every bushel sold.

Bill Bradley opposed the ethanol subsidy during his three terms as a senator from New Jersey (not a big corn-growing state). Indeed, some of his most important accomplishments as a senator involved purging the tax code of subsidies and loopholes that collectively do more harm than good. But when Bill Bradley arrived in Iowa as a Democratic presidential candidate back in 1992, he "spoke to some farmers" and suddenly found it in his heart to support tax breaks for ethanol. In short, he realized that ethanol is crucial to Iowa voters, and Iowa is crucial to the presidential race. Since then, every mainstream presidential candidate has supported the ethanol subsidy, except one: John McCain. To his credit, Senator McCain generally opposed ethanol subsidies during his presidential runs in both 2000 and 2008. While Senator McCain's "straight talk" is admirable, let us remind ourselves of one important detail: John McCain is not currently president of the United States. That would be Barack Obama—an ethanol subsidy supporter.

Ethanol is not a case of a powerful special interest pounding the rest of us into submission. Farmers are a scant 2 or 3 percent of the population; even fewer of them actually grow corn. If squeezing favors out of the political process were simply a matter of brute strength, then those of us who can't tell a heifer from a steer should be kicking the farmers around. Indeed, America's right-handed voters could band together and demand tax breaks at the expense of the lefties. And we could really have our way with those mohair farmers. But that's not what happens.

Economists have come up with a theory of political behavior that fits better with what we actually observe. *When it comes to interest group politics, it pays to be small.* Gary Becker, the same University of Chicago Nobel Prize winner who figured so prominently in our thinking about human capital, wrote a seminal paper in the early 1980s that nicely encapsulated what had become known as the economics of regulation. Building on work that went all the way back to Milton Friedman's doctoral dissertation, Becker theorized that, all else equal, small, well-organized groups are most successful in the political process. Why? Because the costs of whatever favors they wrangle out of the system are spread over a large, unorganized segment of the population.

Think about ethanol again. The benefits of that $7 billion tax subsidy are bestowed on a small group of farmers, making it quite lucrative for each one of them. Meanwhile, the costs are spread over the remaining 98 percent of us, putting ethanol somewhere below good oral hygiene on our list of everyday concerns. The opposite would be true with my plan to have left-handed voters pay subsidies to right-handed voters. There are roughly nine right-handed Americans for every lefty, so if every right-handed voter were to get some government benefit worth $100, then every left-handed voter would have to pay $900 to finance it. The lefties would be hopping mad about their $900 tax bills, probably to the point that it became their preeminent political concern, while the righties would be only modestly excited about their $100 subsidy. An adept politician would probably improve her career prospects by voting with the lefties.

Here is a curious finding that makes more sense in light of what we've just discussed. In countries where farmers make up a small fraction of the population, such as America and Europe, the government provides large subsidies for agriculture. But in countries where the farming population is relatively large, such as China and India, the subsidies go the other way. Farmers are forced to sell their crops at below-market prices so that urban dwellers can get basic food items cheaply. In the one case, farmers get political favors; in the other, they must pay for them. What makes these examples logically consistent is that in both cases the large group subsidizes the smaller group.

In politics, the tail can wag the dog. This can have profound effects on the economy.

Death by a thousand subsidies. The cost of Dan Rostenkowski's underground parking garage at the Museum of Science and Industry is insignificant in the face of our $14 trillion economy. So is the ethanol subsidy. So is the trade protection for sugar producers, and the tax break for pharmaceutical companies with operations in Puerto Rico, and the price supports for dairy farmers. But in total, these things—and the tens of thousands of others like them—*are* significant. Little inefficiencies begin to disrupt the most basic function of a market economy: taking inputs and producing goods and services as efficiently as possible. If the government has to support the price of milk, the real problem is that there are too many dairy farmers. The best definition I've ever heard of a tax shelter is some kind of investment or behavior that would not make sense in the absence of tax considerations. And that is exactly the problem here: Governments should not be in the business of providing incentives for people to do things that would not otherwise make sense.

Chapter 3 outlined all the reasons why good government is not just important, but essential. Yet it is also true that when Congress turns its attention to a problem, a lot of ornaments end up on the Christmas tree. The late George Stigler, a University of Chicago economist who won the Nobel Prize in 1982, proposed and defended a counterintuitive notion: Firms and industries often benefit from regulation. In fact, they can use the political process to generate regulation that either helps them or hobbles their competitors.

Does that sound unlikely? Consider the case of teacher certification. Every state requires public school teachers to do or achieve certain things before becoming licensed. Most people consider that to be quite reasonable. In Illinois, the requirements for certification have risen steadily over time. Again, that seems reasonable given our strong emphasis on public school reform. But when one begins to scrutinize the politics of certification, things become murkier. The teachers' unions, one of the most potent political forces in America, always support reforms that require more rigorous training and testing for teachers. Read the fine print, though. Almost without exception, these laws exempt current teachers from whatever new requirement is being imposed. In other words, individuals who would like to become teachers have to take additional classes or pass new exams; existing teachers do not. That doesn't make much sense if certification laws are written for the benefit of students. If doing certain things is necessary in order to teach, then presumably anyone standing at the front of a classroom should have to do them.

Other aspects of certification law don't make much sense either. Private school teachers, many of whom have decades of experience, cannot teach in public schools without jumping through assorted hoops (including student teaching) that are almost certainly unnecessary. Nor can university professors. When Albert Einstein arrived in Princeton, New Jersey, he was not legally qualified to teach high school physics.

The most striking (and frustrating) thing about all of this is that researchers have found that certification requirements have virtually no correlation with performance in the classroom whatsoever. The best evidence on this point (which is consistent with all other evidence that I've seen) comes from Los Angeles. When California passed a law in the late 1990s to reduce class size across the state, Los Angeles had to hire a huge number of new teachers, many of whom were uncertified. Los Angeles also collected classroom-level data on the performance of students assigned to any given teacher. A study done for the Hamilton Project, a public policy think tank, looked at the performance of 150,000 students over three years and came to two conclusions: (1) Good teachers matter. Students assigned to the best quarter of teachers ended up 10 percentile points ahead of students given the worst quarter of teachers (controlling for the students' initial level of achievement); and (2) certification doesn't matter. The study "found no statistically significant achievement differences between students assigned to certified teachers and students assigned to uncertified teachers." The authors of the study recommend that states eliminate entry barriers that keep talented people from becoming public schoolteachers.[4] Most states are doing the opposite.

Mr. Stigler would have argued that all of this is easy to explain. Just think about how the process benefits teachers, not students. Making it harder to become a teacher reduces the supply of new entrants into the profession, which is a good thing for those who are already there. Any barrier to entry looks attractive from the inside.

I have a personal interest in all kinds of occupational licensure (cases in which states require that individuals become licensed before practicing certain professions). My doctoral dissertation set out to explain a seemingly anomalous pattern in Illinois: The state requires barbers and manicurists to be licensed, but not electricians. A shoddy electrical job could burn down an entire neighborhood; a bad manicure or haircut seems relatively more benign. Yet the barbers and manicurists are the ones regulated by the state. The short explanation for the pattern is two words: interest groups. The best predictor of whether or not a profession is licensed in Illinois is the size and budget of its professional association. (Every profession is small relative to the state's total population, so all of these groups have the mohair advantage. The size and budget of the professional association reflects the extent to which members of the profession have organized to exploit it.) Remarkably, political organization is a better predictor of licensure than the danger members of the profession pose to the public (as measured by their liability premium). George Stigler was right: *Groups seek to get themselves licensed.*

Small, organized groups fly under the radar and prevail upon legislators to do things that do not necessarily make the rest of us better off. Economists, particularly those among the more free-market "Chicago school," are sometimes perceived to be hostile toward government. It would be more accurate to describe them as skeptical. The broader the scope of government, the more room there is for special interests to carve out deals for themselves that have nothing to do with the legitimate functions of government described in Chapter 3.

Tyranny of the status quo. If small groups can get what they want out of the legislative process, they can also stop what they don't want, or at least try. Joseph Schumpeter, who coined the term "creative destruction," described capitalism as a process of incessantly destroying the old structure and creating a new one. That may be good for the world; it is bad for the firms and industries that make up the "old structure." The individuals standing in capitalism's path of progress—or destruction, from their standpoint—will use every tool they have to avoid it, including politics. And why shouldn't they? The legislative process helps those who help themselves. Groups under siege from competition may seek trade protection, a government bailout, favorable tax considerations, limitations on a competing technology, or some other special treatment. With layoffs or bankruptcy looming, the plea to politicians for help can be quite compelling.

So what's the problem? The problem is that we don't get the benefits of the new economic structure if politicians decide to protect the old one. Roger Ferguson, Jr., former vice chairman of the board of governors of the Federal Reserve, explains, "Policymakers who fail to appreciate the relationship between the relentless churning of the competitive environment and wealth creation will end up focusing their efforts on methods and skills that are in decline. In so doing, they establish policies that are aimed at protecting weak, outdated technologies, and in the end, they slow the economy's march forward."[5]

Both politics and compassion suggest that we ought to offer a hand to those mowed over by competition. If some kind of wrenching change generates progress, then the pie must get bigger. And if the pie gets bigger, then at least some of it ought to be offered to the losers—be it in the form of transition aid, job retraining, or whatever else will help those who have been knocked over to get back on their feet. One of the features that made the North American Free Trade Agreement more palatable was a provision that offered compensation to workers whose job losses could be tied to expanded trade with Mexico. Similarly, many states are using money from the massive legal settlement with the tobacco industry to compensate tobacco farmers whose livelihoods are threatened by declining tobacco use.

There is a crucial distinction, however, between using the political process to build a safety net for those harmed by creative destruction and using the political process to stop that creative destruction in the first place. Think about the telegraph and the Pony Express. It would have been one thing to help displaced Pony Express workers by retraining them as telegraph operators; it would have been quite another to help them by banning the telegraph. Sometimes the political process does the equivalent of the latter for reasons related to the mohair problem. The economic benefits of competition are huge but spread over a large group; the costs tend to be smaller but highly concentrated. As a result, the beneficiaries of creative destruction hardly notice; the losers chain themselves to their congressman's office door seeking protection, as any of us might if our livelihood or community were at risk.

Such is the case in the realm of international trade. Trade is good for consumers. We pay less for shoes, cars, electronics, food, and everything else that can be made better or more cheaply somewhere else in the world (or is made more cheaply in this country because of foreign competition). Our lives are made better in thousands of little ways that have a significant cumulative effect. Looking back on the Clinton presidency, former Treasury secretary Robert Rubin reflected, "The economic benefits of the tariff reductions we negotiated over the last eight years represent the largest tax cut in the history of the world."[6]

Cheaper shoes here, a better television there—still probably not enough to get the average person to fly somewhere and march *in favor* of the World Trade Organization (WTO). Meanwhile, those most directly affected by globalization have a more powerful motivation. In one memorable case, the AFL-CIO and other unions did send some thirty thousand members to Seattle in 1999 to protest against broadening the WTO. The flimsy pretext was that the union is concerned about wages and working conditions in the developing world. Nonsense. The AFL-CIO is worried about American jobs. More trade means cheaper goods for millions of American consumers *and* lost jobs and shuttered plants. That is something that will motivate workers to march in the streets, as it has been throughout history. The original Luddites were bands of English textile workers who destroyed textile-making machinery to protest the low wages and unemployment caused by mechanization. What if they had gotten their way?

Consider that at the beginning of the fifteenth century, China was far more technologically advanced than the West. China had a superior knowledge of science, farming, engineering, even veterinary medicine. The Chinese were casting iron in 200 B.C., some fifteen hundred years before the Europeans. Yet the Industrial Revolution took place in Europe while Chinese civilization languished. Why? One historical interpretation posits that the Chinese elites valued stability more than progress. As a result, leaders blocked the kinds of wrenching societal changes that made the Industrial Revolution possible. In the fifteenth century, for example, China's rulers banned long-sea-voyage trade ventures, choking off trade as well as the economic development, discovery, and social change that come with them.

We have designed some institutions to help the greater good prevail over narrow (if eminently understandable) interests. For example, the president will often seek "fast-track authority" from Congress when the administration is negotiating international trade agreements. Congress must still ratify whatever agreement is reached, but only with an up or down vote. The normal process by which legislators can add amendments is waived. The logic is that legislators are not allowed to eviscerate the agreement by exempting assorted industries; a trade agreement that offers protection to a few special interests in every district is no trade agreement at all. The fast-track process forces politicians who talk the talk of free trade to walk the walk, too.

The unfairly maligned World Trade Organization is really just an international version of the fast-track process. Negotiating to bring down trade barriers among many countries—each laden with domestic interest groups—is a monumental task. The WTO makes the process more politically manageable by defining the things that countries must do in order to join: open markets, eliminate subsidies, phase out tariffs, etc. That is the price of membership. Countries that are admitted gain access to the markets of all the existing members—a huge carrot that gives politicians an incentive to say no to the mohair farmers of the world.

Cut the politicians a break. In the fall of 2000, a promising political career was launched. I was elected president of the Seminary Townhouse Association. (Perhaps "elected" is too strong a word; the outgoing president asked if I would do it, and I was too naive to say no.) At about that time, the Chicago Transit Authority (CTA) announced plans to expand an elevated train station very close to our homes. The proposed expansion would bring the station into compliance with the Americans with Disabilities Act and allow the CTA to accommodate more riders. It would also move the elevated train tracks (and all the accompanying noise) thirty feet closer to our homes. In short, this plan was good for Chicago public transportation and bad for our townhouse association. Under my excellent leadership, we wrote letters, we held meetings, we consulted architects, we presented alternative plans (some of which would have required condemning and demolishing homes elsewhere in the neighborhood). Fullerton Avenue eventually got a new elevated train station, but not before we did everything in our power to disrupt the project.

Yes, ladies and gentlemen, we are the special interests. All of us. You may not raise Angora goats (the source of mohair); you may not grow corn (the source of ethanol). But you are part of some group— probably many of them—that has unique interests: a profession, an ethnic group, a demographic group, a neighborhood, an industry, a part of the country. As the old saying puts it, "Where you stand depends on where you sit." It is facile to declare that politicians should just do the right thing. The hoary old cliché about tough decisions is true. Doing the right thing—making a decision that generates more benefits for the nation than costs—will not cause people to stand up and cheer. It is far more likely that the many people you have made better off will hardly notice while the small group you have harmed will pelt your car with tomatoes.

In 2008, my unpromising political career got more interesting (but not necessarily any more promising). President Obama appointed Congressman Rahm Emanuel to be his chief of staff, which left an opening in the Illinois Fifth Congressional District. That's my congressional district, and I, along with more than twenty other candidates, decided to run in the special election to fill the seat. (Our race should not be confused with the vacant Illinois Senate seat that former Governor Rod Blagojevich tried to sell.) I figured that if I was going to write books like this one that criticized public policies, then I ought to be willing to step into the ring, rather than just cast rocks from the outside. (For the record, I opposed the ethanol subsidy—a relatively meaningless position given that the Fifth Congressional District is entirely urban and has not a single farmer.)

The punch line of this chapter can be encapsulated in a single experience from that campaign. At the first candidates' forum, the moderator, a political columnist for a Chicago newspaper, asked each candidate to comment on his or her view of federal earmarks. Earmarks are the mechanism by which members of Congress insert pork into bills; an earmark directs federal money to a specific project in a member's district and is therefore insulated from any formal review as to whether the project makes sense or not. For example, an earmark in a transportation bill, such as the notorious "bridge to nowhere" in Alaska, allocates money for the bridge even if the Department of Transportation never would have funded it. The subject of earmarks had come up because the first spending bill signed by President Obama had nearly nine thousand earmarks. (No, that is not an exaggeration.)

One by one, each candidate excoriated both the concept of earmarks and the politicians who support them. One candidate even proposed arresting members of Congress who cut such deals. But the earmark question was a trap, and a clever one at that. The moderator asked a follow-up question, something like, "So each of you would oppose an earmark to support Children's Memorial Hospital?" As you may have inferred, this particular children's hospital is in the Fifth Congressional District, about 300 yards from where we were sitting. The answers to the follow-up question were less emphatic than the original assault on earmarks and included comments like, "Of course, a hospital is different" and "That particular earmark involves children" and "I will do everything I can as a congressman to support Children's Memorial Hospital" and so on. No one suggested that politicians who support an earmark for the hospital should go to prison.

Everyone despises earmarks, except for their own. A member of Congress who secures special funding to expand Children's Memorial Hospital is a success. A ribbon-cutting ceremony will celebrate the project, with cupcakes and juice and speeches lauding this politician's hard work in Congress. How did the funding come to pass? Not because this one politician gave a speech on the floor of the House that was so emotional and inspiring that the other 534 members decided to lavish funds on a children's hospital in Illinois. He did it by supporting a bill with nine thousand earmarks, one of which was his. Such is the political reality in a democratic system: We love our congressman who finds funding for the hospital; what we hate are politicians who support earmarks.

Would campaign finance reform change anything? At the margins, if that. Money is certainly one tool for grabbing a politician's attention, but there are others. If the dairy farmers (who benefit from federal price supports) can't give money, they will hire lobbyists, ring doorbells, hold meetings, write letters, threaten hunger strikes, and vote as a bloc. Campaign finance reform does not change the fact that the dairy farmers care deeply about their subsidy while the people who pay for it don't care much at all. The democratic process will always favor small, well-organized groups at the expense of large, diffuse groups. It's not just how many people care one way or the other; it's how *much* they care. Two percent who care deeply about something are a more potent political force than the 98 percent who feel the opposite but aren't motivated enough to do anything about it.

Bob Kerrey, former Democratic senator from Nebraska, has said that he doesn't think campaign finance reform would lead to much change at all. "The most important corruption that happens in politics doesn't go away even if you had full public financing of campaigns," he told *The New Yorker*. "And that is: I don't want to tell you something that's going to make you not like me. If I had a choice between getting a round of applause by delivering a twenty-six-second applause line and getting a round of boos by telling you the truth, I'd rather get the round of applause."[7]

So, if I were asked again why our growing knowledge of public policy does not always translate into a perfect world, this chapter would be my more complete answer.

CHAPTER 9

Keeping Score:

Is my economy bigger than your economy?

A
s I have mentioned, in the late 1980s I was a young speechwriter working for the governor of Maine. One of my primary responsibilities was finding jokes. "Funny jokes," he would admonish me. "Belly laughs, not chuckles." Two decades later, one of those jokes stands out, not so much because it is funny now, but rather for what it tells us about what we were thinking then. Recall that George Bush, Sr., was president and Dan Quayle was vice president. New England was in the midst of an economic slump and Maine was particularly hard hit. Meanwhile, Japan appeared to be the world's economic powerhouse. The joke goes like this:

While vacationing at Kennebunkport, George H. W. Bush is hit on the head with one of his beloved horseshoes. He slips into a coma. Nine months later, he awakens and President Quayle is standing at his bedside. "Are we at peace?" Mr. Bush asks.

"Yes. The country is at peace," says President Quayle.

"What is the unemployment rate?" Mr. Bush asks.

"About 4 percent," says President Quayle.

"Inflation?" queries Mr. Bush.

"Under control," says President Quayle.

"Amazing," says Mr. Bush. "How much does a loaf of bread cost?"

President Quayle scratches his head nervously and says, "About 240 yen."

Believe it or not, that was good for a belly laugh. Some of the humor derived from the prospect of Dan Quayle as president, but mostly it was an outlet for anxiety over the popular notion that Japan was on the brink of world economic domination. Obviously times change. We now know that Japan went on to suffer from more than a decade of economic stagnation while the United States moved into what would become the longest economic expansion in the nation's history. The Nikkei Index, which reflects prices on the Japanese stock market, peaked at 38,916 just around the time the governor of Maine was telling that joke. Today the Nikkei is just over 10,000.

Of course, Americans aren't gloating about that these days. After fifteen years of a generally strong economy in the United States, we stumbled into the worst economic downturn since the Great Depression. Why is it that all economies, rich and poor, proceed in fits and starts, stumbling from growth to recession and back to growth again? During the robust growth of the 1990s, the labor market was so tight that fast-food restaurants were paying signing bonuses, college graduates were getting stock options worth millions, and anyone with a pulse was earning double-digit returns in the stock market. Consumers were buoyed by rising home and stock prices. Capital flowed in from the rest of the world, most notably China, making it easy for Americans to borrow cheaply.

And then everything went wildly off track, like one of those NASCAR wrecks. Consumers were suddenly overburdened with debt and stuck with homes they couldn't sell. The stock market plunged. The unemployment rate climbed toward 10 percent. America's biggest banks were on the brink of insolvency. The Chinese started musing publicly about whether they should continue to buy American treasury bonds. We liked it better the first way. What happened?

To understand the cycle of recession and recovery—the "business cycle," as economists call it—we need to first learn about the tools for measuring a modern economy. If the president really did wake up from a coma after suffering a horseshoe accident, it's a fair bet that he would ask for one number first: gross domestic product, or GDP, which represents the total value of all goods and services produced in an economy. When the headlines proclaim that the economy grew 2.3 percent in a particular year, they are referring to GDP growth. It means simply that we as a country produced 2.3 percent more goods and services than we did the year before. Similarly, if we say that public education promotes economic growth, we are saying that it raises the rate of GDP growth. Or if we were asked whether an African country is better off in 2010 than it was in 2000, our answer would begin (though certainly not end) with a description of what happened to GDP over the course of the decade.

Can we really gauge our collective well-being by the quantity of goods and services that we produce? Yes and no. We'll start with "yes," though we will come to "no" before the chapter is done. GDP is a decent measure of our well-being for the simple reason that what we can consume is constrained by what we can produce—either because we consume those goods directly or because we trade them away for goods produced somewhere else. A country with a GDP per capita of $1,000 cannot consume $20,000 per capita. Where exactly are the other $19,000 worth of goods and services going to come from? What we consume can deviate from what we produce for short stretches, just as family spending can deviate from family income for a while. In the long run, however, what a country produces and what it consumes are going to be nearly identical.

I must make two important qualifications. First, what we care about is *real* GDP, which means that the figure has been adjusted to account for inflation. In contrast, *nominal* figures have not been adjusted for inflation. If nominal GDP climbs 10 percent in 2012 but inflation is also 10 percent, then we haven't actually produced more of anything. We've just sold the same amount of stuff at higher prices, which has not made us any better off. Your salary will have most likely gone up 10 percent as well, but so will have the price of everything you buy. It's the economic equivalent of swapping a $10 bill for ten $1 bills—it looks good in your wallet, but you're not any richer. We will explore inflation in greater depth in the next chapter. For now, suffice it to say that our standard of living depends on the quantity of goods and services we take home with us, not on the price that shows up at the register.

Second, we care about GDP *per capita*, which is a nation's GDP divided by its population. Again, this adjustment is necessary to prevent wildly misleading conclusions. India has a GDP of $3.3 trillion while Israel has a GDP of $201 billion. Which is the richer country? Israel by far. India has more than a billion people while Israel has only seven million; GDP per capita in Israel is $28,300 compared to only $2,900 in India. Similarly, if a country's economy grows 3 percent in a given year but the population grows 5 percent, then GDP per capita will fall. The country is producing more goods and services, but not enough more to keep up with a population that is growing faster.

If we look at real GDP in America, it tells us several things. First, the American economy is massive by global standards. American GDP is roughly $14 trillion, which is only slightly smaller than all the countries of the European Union combined. The next-largest single economy is China, which has a GDP of around $8 trillion. On a per capita basis, we are rich, both by global standards and by our own historical standards. In 2008, America's GDP per capita was roughly $47,000, slightly less than Norway, Singapore, and a few small countries with a lot of oil, but still nearly the highest in the world. Our real GDP per capita is more than twice what it was in 1970 and five times what it was in 1940.

In other words, the average American is five times as rich as he or she would have been in 1940. How could that be? The answer is back in Chapter 5: We're more productive. The day is not any longer, but what we can get done in twenty-four hours has changed dramatically. The Federal Reserve Bank of Dallas came up with a novel way to express our economic progress over the course of the twentieth century: Compare how long we had to work in 2000 to buy basic items with how long we had to work to buy the same items in 1900. As the officials at the Dallas Fed explain, "Making money takes time, so when we shop, we're really spending time. The real cost of living isn't measured in dollars and cents but in the hours and minutes we must work to live."[1]

So here goes: A pair of stockings cost 25 cents in 1900. Of course, the average wage at the time was 14.8 cents an hour, so the real cost of stockings at the beginning of the twentieth century was one hour and forty-one minutes of work for the average American. If you walk into a department store today, stockings (pantyhose) are seemingly more expensive than they were in 1900—but they're not. By 2000, the price had gone up, but our wages had gone up even faster. Stockings in 2000 cost around $4, while America's average wage was over $13 an hour. As a result, a pair of stockings cost the average worker only eighteen minutes of time, a stunning improvement from an hour and forty-one minutes a century earlier.

The same is true for most goods over most long stretches of time. If your grandmother were to complain that a chicken costs more today than it did when she was growing up, she would be correct only in the most technical sense. The price of a three-pound chicken has indeed climbed from $1.23 in 1919 to $3.86 in 2009. But grandma really has nothing to complain about. The "work time" necessary to earn a chicken has dropped remarkably. In 1919, the average worker spent two hours and thirty-seven minutes to earn enough money to buy a chicken (and, I'm guessing, at least another forty-five minutes for the mashed potatoes). In short, you would work most of your morning just to earn lunch. How long does it take to "earn" a chicken these days? Just under thirteen minutes. Cut out one personal phone call and you've got Sunday dinner taken care of. Skip surfing the web for a little while and you could probably feed the neighbors, too.

Do you remember the days when it was novel, perhaps even mildly impressive, to see someone speaking on a cellular phone in a restaurant? (Okay, it was a short stretch of time, but a cell phone did have a certain cachet in the mid-1980s.) No wonder; back then a cell phone "cost" about 456 hours of work for the average American. Almost three decades later, cell phones are just plain annoying, in large part because everyone has one. The reason everyone has one is that they now "cost" about nine hours of work for the average worker—98 percent less than they cost twenty years ago.

We take this material progress for granted; we shouldn't. A rapidly rising standard of living has not been the norm throughout history. Robert Lucas, Jr., winner of the Nobel Prize in 1995 for his numerous contributions to macroeconomics, has argued that even in the richest countries, the phenomenon of sustained growth in living standards is only a few centuries old. Other economists have concluded that the growth rate of GDP per capita in Europe between 500 and 1500 was essentially zero.[2] They don't call it the Dark Ages for nothing.

We should also make clear what it means for a country to be poor by global standards at the beginning of the twenty-first century. As I've noted, India has a per capita GDP of $2,900. But let's translate that into something more than just a number. Modern India has more than 100,000 cases of Hansen's disease, better known to the world as leprosy. Leprosy is a contagious disease that attacks the body's tissues and nerves, leaving horrible scars and limb deformities. The striking thing about Hansen's disease is that it is easily cured, and, if caught early, recovery is complete. How much does it cost to treat leprosy? One $3 dose of antibiotic will cure a mild case; a $20 regimen of three antibiotics will cure a more severe case. The World Health Organization even provides the drugs free, but India's health care infrastructure is not good enough to identify the afflicted and get them the medicine they need.[3]

So, more than 100,000 people in India are horribly disfigured by a disease that costs $3 to cure. That is what it means to have a per capita GDP of $2,900.

Having said all that, GDP is, like any other statistic, just one measure. Figure skating and golf notwithstanding, it is hard to collapse complex entities into a single number. The list of knocks against GDP as a measure of social progress is a long one. GDP does not count any economic activity that is not paid for, such as work done in the home. If you cook dinner, take care of the kids, and tidy up around the house, none of that counts toward the nation's official output. However, if you order out food, drop your kids off at a child care center, and hire a cleaning lady, all of that does. Nor does GDP account for environmental degradation; if a company clear-cuts a virgin forest to make paper, the value of the paper shows up in the GDP figures without any corresponding debit for the forest that is now gone.

China has taken this last point to heart. Chinese GDP growth over the past decade has been the envy of the world, but it has come at the cost of significant environmental degradation. Of the twenty-five most polluted cities in the world, sixteen are in China (you've never heard of most of them). China's State Environmental Protection Administration has begun to calculate "Green GDP" figures, which seek to evaluate the true quality of economic growth by subtracting the costs of environmental damage. Using this metric, China's 10 percent GDP growth in 2004 was really closer to 7 percent when the $64 billion in pollution costs are taken into account. Green GDP has an obvious logic. The *Wall Street Journal* explains, "While GDP looks at the market value of goods and services produced in a country each year, it ignores the fact that a nation might be fueling its expansion by polluting or burning through natural resources in an unsustainable way. In fact, the usual methods of calculating GDP make destroying the environment look good for the economy. If an industry pollutes in the process of manufacturing products, and the government pays to clean up the mess, both activities add to GDP."[4]

There are no value judgments whatsoever attached to traditional GDP calculations. A dollar spent building a prison or cleaning up after a natural disaster boosts GDP, even though we would be better off if we did not need prisons and if there were no disasters to clean up after. Leisure counts for nothing. If you spend a glorious day walking in the park with your grandmother, you are not contributing to GDP and may actually be subtracting from it if you've taken the day off to do it. (True, if you take grandma bowling or to the movies, the money you spend will show up in the GDP figures.) GDP does not take into account the distribution of income; GDP per capita is a simple average that can mask enormous disparities between rich and poor. If a small minority of a country's population grow fabulously rich while most citizens are getting steadily poorer, per capita GDP growth could still look impressive.

The United Nations has created the Human Development Index (HDI) as a broader indicator of national economic health. The HDI uses GDP as one of its components but also adds measures of life expectancy, literacy, and educational attainment. The United States ranked thirteenth in the 2009 report; Norway was number one, followed by Australia and Iceland. HDI is a good tool for assessing progress in developing countries; it tells us less about overall well-being in rich countries where life expectancy, literacy, and educational attainment are already relatively high.

The most effective knock against GDP may simply be that it is an imperfect measure of how well off we really consider ourselves to be. Economics has an overly tautological view of happiness: The things we do must make us happy; otherwise we would not do them. Similarly, growing richer must make us better off because we can do and have more of the things that we enjoy. Yet survey results tell us something different. Richer may not be happier. Remember that robust growth of the 1990s? It didn't seem to do much good for our psyches. In fact, the period of rising real incomes from 1970 to 1999 coincided with a decrease in those who described themselves as "very happy" from 36 percent to 29 percent.[5] Economists are belatedly beginning to probe this phenomenon, albeit in their own perversely quantitative way. For example, David Blanchflower and Andrew Oswald, economists at Dartmouth College and the University of Warwick, respectively, found that a lasting marriage is worth $100,000 a year, since married people report being as happy, on average, as divorced (and not remarried) individuals who have incomes that are $100,000 higher. So, before you go to bed tonight, be sure to tell your spouse that you would not give him or her up for anything less than $100,000 a year.

Some economists are studying happiness directly, by asking participants to keep daily journals in which they record what they are doing at various times and how it makes them feel. Not surprisingly, "intimate relations" is at the top of the list in terms of positive experiences; the morning commute is at the bottom, lower than cooking, housework, the evening commute, and everything else.[6] The findings are not trivial, as they can illuminate ways in which individuals think they are making themselves happy but aren't really. (Yes, you should see the influence of the behavioral economists here.) For example, that long commute may not be worth what it buys (usually a bigger house and a higher salary). Not only is the commute unpleasant, but it often carries a high opportunity cost: less time spent socializing, exercising, or relaxing—all of which rate as highly pleasurable activities. Meanwhile, we quickly become inured to the benefits of the goods that we previously coveted (kind of like getting used to a hot bath), whereas the happiness generated by experiences (family vacations and their lingering memories) is more durable. *The Economist* summarizes the prescriptions of the research so far: "In general, the economic arbiters of taste recommend 'experiences' over commodities, pastimes over knick-knacks, doing over having."[7]

If GDP is a flawed measure of economic progress, why can't we come up with something better?

We can, argues Marc Miringhoff, a professor of social sciences at Fordham University, who believes that the nation should have a "social report card."[8] He proposed a social health index that would combine sixteen social indicators, such as child poverty, infant mortality, crime, access to health care, and affordable housing. Conservative author and commentator William Bennett agrees with half of that analysis. We do need a measure of progress that is broader than GDP, he argues. But ditch all that liberal claptrap. Mr. Bennett's "index of leading cultural indicators" includes the kinds of things that he considers important: out-of-wedlock births, divorce rates, drug use, participation in church groups, and the level of trust in government.

French President Nicolas Sarkozy instructed the French national statistics agency in 2009 to develop an indicator of the nation's economic health that incorporates broader measures of quality of life than GDP alone. Two prominent economists and former Nobel Prize winners, Joseph Stiglitz and Amartya Sen, chaired a panel convened by Sarkozy to examine a seeming paradox: Rising GDP seems to come with a perception that life is getting more stressful and difficult, not less. Sarkozy wants a measure that incorporates the joys of art and leisure and the sorrows of environmental destruction and stress.[9] Measuring these elements of the human condition is a noble gesture—but a single number? The *Wall Street Journal* commented, "Chapeaus off to Messrs. Stiglitz and Sen if they can put a number on such spiritual matters—but don't hold your breath."

So you begin to see the problem. Any measure of economic progress depends on how you define progress. GDP just adds up the numbers. There is something to be said for that. All else equal, it is better for a nation to produce more goods and services than fewer. When GDP turns negative, the damage is real: jobs lost, businesses closed, productive capacity turned idle. But why should we ever have to deal with that anyway? Why should a modern economy switch from forward to reverse? If we can produce and consume $14 trillion worth of stuff, and put most Americans to work doing it, why should we toss a bunch of people out of work and produce 5 percent less the following year?

The best answer is that recessions are like wars: If we could prevent them, we would. Each one is just different enough from the last to make it hard to ward off. (Though presumably policymakers have prevented both wars and recessions on numerous occasions; it's only when they fail that we notice.) In general, recessions stem from some shock to the economy. That is, something bad happens. It may be the collapse of a stock market or property bubble (the United States in 1929 and 2007, Japan in 1989); a steep rise in the price of oil (the United States in 1973); or even a deliberate attempt by the Federal Reserve to slow down an overheated economy (the United States in 1980 and 1990). In developing countries, the shock may come from a sudden fall in the price of a commodity on which the economy is heavily dependent. Obviously there may be a combination of causes. The American slowdown that began in 2001 had its roots in the "tech wreck"—the overinvestment in technology that ultimately ended with the bursting of the Internet bubble. That trouble was compounded by the terrorist attacks of September 11 and their aftermath.

No matter the cause, the most fascinating thing about recessions is how they spread. Let's start with a simple one, and then work our way to the "Great Recession" of 2007. You probably didn't notice, but around 2001 the price of coffee beans plunged from $150 to $50 per hundred pounds.[10] Although that drop may have made your Starbucks latte habit modestly more affordable, Central America, a major coffee-producing region, was reeling. The *New York Times* reported:

> The collapse of the [coffee] market has set off a chain reaction that is felt throughout the region. Towns have been left to scrape by as tax receipts drop, forcing them to scale back services and lay off workers. Farms have scaled back or closed, leaving thousands of the area's most vulnerable people with no money to buy food or clothes or to pay their rent. Small growers, in debt to banks and coffee processors who lent

them money to care for the crops and workers, have been idled, and some of them are facing the loss of their land.

Whether you live in Central America or Santa Monica, someone else's economic distress can become your problem very quickly. The recession of 2007 (which erupted into a financial crisis in 2008) has been the scariest in a long time. The economic "shock" in this case originated with sharp drops in both the stock and housing markets, both of which left American households poorer. Christina Romer, chair of President Obama's Council of Economic Advisers, estimates that U.S. household wealth fell 17 percent between December 2007 and December 2008—five times the size of the decline in 1929 (when fewer families owned stocks or houses).[11] When consumers sustain a shock to their income, they spend less, which spreads the economic damage. This is an intriguing paradox: Our natural (and rational) reaction to precarious economic times is to become more cautious with our spending, which makes our collective situation worse. The loss of confidence caused by a shock to the economy may turn out to be worse than the shock itself. My thrift—a decision to curtail my advertising budget or to buy a car next year instead of this year—may cost you your job, which will in turn hurt my business! Indeed, if we all believe the economy is likely to get worse, then it will get worse. And if we all believe it will get better, then it will get better. Our behavior—to spend or not to spend—is conditioned on our expectations, and those expectations can quickly become self-fulfilling. Franklin Delano Roosevelt's admonition that we have "nothing to fear but fear itself" was both excellent leadership and good economics. Similarly, Rudy Giuliani's exhortation that New Yorkers should go out and do their holiday shopping in the weeks after the World Trade Center attack was not as wacky as it sounded. Spending can generate confidence that generates spending that causes a recovery.

Unfortunately the Great Recession that began in 2007 had other aspects to it that spread the economic damage in virulent and scary ways. Many American households were "excessively leveraged," meaning that they had borrowed far more than they could manage. The housing boom had encouraged ever bigger houses with ever bigger mortgages. Meanwhile, the down payments—the amount of their own money buyers had to spend to get a loan—were getting smaller relative to what was being borrowed. Subprime mortgages (a financial innovation, one must admit) made it easier for people to borrow who were otherwise not creditworthy and for other people to borrow in particularly aggressive ways (e.g., with no down payment at all). This all works fine when housing prices are going up; someone who falls behind on their mortgage payments can always sell the house to repay the loan. When the housing bubble burst, however, the numbers became a disaster. Overleveraged American families found that they could not afford their mortgage payments, nor could they sell their homes. Millions of houses and condos were thrown into foreclosure by whatever bank or financial institution owned the mortgage. When these properties were dumped on the market, it drove prices down further and exacerbated all the real estate–induced problems.

But we haven't even arrived at the scary part yet. America's mortgage problem spread to the financial sector through two related channels. First, banks were plagued with lots of bad real estate loans, which made them less able and willing to make new loans. Anyone looking to buy a home had trouble doing so, even with good credit and a large down payment. (You guessed it: This compounded the real estate problems yet again.) Meanwhile, Wall Street investment banks and hedge funds had loaded up on real estate derivatives—fancy products like mortgage-backed securities whose value was somehow tied to the plunging real estate market. Like American homeowners, these institutions had borrowed heavily to make such investments, so they too faced creditors. Much of this debt was "insured" with the credit default swaps described in Chapter 7, wreaking havoc on firms with that exposure.

There was a stretch of time in the fall of 2008 when it looked like Wall Street—and therefore the global financial system—would implode. The most serious moment came when the investment bank Lehman Brothers recognized that it could not meet its short-term debt obligations—meaning that without some infusion of outside capital, the firm would have to declare bankruptcy. The U.S. Treasury and the Federal Reserve were unable, or unwilling, to save Lehman. (Earlier in the year they had saved Bear Stearns, another troubled investment bank, by arranging a takeover by JPMorgan Chase.) When Lehman declared bankruptcy, leaving all of its creditors high and dry, the global financial system essentially seized up. A Treasury official described the cascade of panic to *The New Yorker:* "Lehman Brothers begat the Reserve collapse [a money-market fund], which begat the money-market run, so the money-market funds wouldn't buy commercial paper [short-term loans to corporations like GE]. The commercial-paper market was on the brink of destruction. At this point, the banking system stops functioning."[12]

Sensible people started talking about surviving by raising goats in the backyard. (Okay, that was me.) My college roommate, who has gone on to become the CEO of a major company, admitted later that he had hidden $10,000 in a cowboy boot in his closet. (I was left wondering primarily why he owns cowboy boots.) We were not alone. James Stewart has described the Lehman collapse and all its attendant damage in a brilliant piece for *The New Yorker.* Here is one sample:

> Geithner [then president of the Federal Reserve Bank of New York] said, "It's hard to describe how bad it was and how bad it felt." He got a call from a "titan of the financial system," who said he was worried but he was doing fine. His voice was quavering. After hanging up, Geithner immediately called the man back. "Don't call anyone else," Geithner said. "If anyone hears your voice, you'll scare the shit out of them."

You don't have to like investment bankers to care about all of this (and to appreciate why the federal government needed to stop the panic on Wall Street). Once the financial system seizes up, no one gets credit. At that point, healthy companies become less healthy because they don't have access to loans that allow them to do things that are necessary for business, such as buying inventory. The damage of the financial crisis spread to every corner of American society. In 2009, pre-order sales for Girl Scout cookies plunged 19 percent from the year before.[13] Meanwhile, the number of adult films produced in Southern California fell from five or six thousand films a year to three or four thousand. *The Economist* reported on the macroeconomic effects of less porn: "Some firms have shut down, others are consolidating or scraping by. For the 1,200 active performers in the [San Fernando] Valley this means less action and more hardship . . . For every performer, there are several people in support, from sound-tech to catering and (yes) wardrobe, says Ms. Duke [a spokesperson for the adult film industry], so the overall effect on the Valley economy is large."[14]

Recessions can spread quickly across international borders. If the U.S. economy weakens, then we buy fewer goods from abroad. Pretty soon Mexico, which sends more than 80 percent of its exports to the United States, is reeling. In business as in sports, your competitor's misfortune is your gain. At the global level, the opposite is true. *If other powerful economies fall into recession, they stop buying our goods and services—and vice versa.* Think about it: If unemployment doubles in Japan or Germany, how exactly is that going to make you better off? During the financial crisis, the problems on Wall Street quickly spread to other countries. Americans—who are collectively the biggest consumers in the world—bought fewer imported goods, which harmed exporting economies around the globe. America's GDP contracted at an annual rate of 5.4 percent in the fourth quarter of 2008. You thought we had it bad? Singapore's economy fell in the same quarter at an annual rate of 16 percent, and Japan's by 12 percent.[15]

How do things get better? There are often underlying issues that need to work themselves out. In the case of the "tech wreck," we massively overinvested in Internet businesses and related technology. Some firms went bust; other firms cut back their IT spending. Resources were reallocated, at which point there were more U-Hauls going out of Silicon Valley than in. Or, in the case of higher energy prices, we reorganize our economy to deal with a world in which oil is $100 a barrel instead of $10. In the run-up to the financial crisis, consumers and firms borrowed too much; speculators built houses that never should have been built; Wall Street grew fat dealing in products with limited economic value. These things are now (painfully) fixing themselves. Recessions may actually be good for long-term growth because they purge the economy of less productive ventures, just as a harsh winter may be good for the long-term health of a species (if not necessarily for those animals that freeze to death).

The business cycle takes a human toll, as the layoffs splashed across the headlines attest. Policymakers are increasingly expected to smooth this business cycle; economists are supposed to tell them how to do it. Government has two tools at its disposal: fiscal policy and monetary policy. The objective of each is the same: to encourage consumers and businesses to begin spending and investing again so that the economy's capacity no longer sits idle.

Fiscal policy uses the government's capacity to tax and spend as a lever for prying the economy from reverse into forward. If nervous consumers won't spend, then the government will do it for them—and that can create a virtuous circle. While consumers are sitting at home with their wallets tucked firmly under the mattress, the government can start to build highways and bridges. Construction workers go back to work; their firms place orders for materials. Cement plants call idled workers back. As the world starts to look like a better place, we feel comfortable making major purchases again. The cycle we described earlier begins to work in reverse. This is the logic of the American Recovery and Reinvestment Act of 2009—the stimulus bill that was the first major piece of legislation under the Obama administration. The Act authorized more than $500 billion in federal spending on things ranging from expanded unemployment benefits to resurfacing the main highway near my house. (There is a big sign on the side of the road telling me that's where the money came from.)

The government can also stimulate the economy by cutting taxes. The American Recovery and Reinvestment Act did that, too. The final bill had nearly $300 billion in assorted tax cuts and credits. The economic logic is that consumers, finding more money in their paychecks at the end of the month, will decide to spend some of it. Again, this spending can help to break the back of the recession. Purchases generated by the tax cut put workers back on the job, which inspires more spending and confidence, and so on.

The notion that the government can use fiscal policy—spending, tax cuts, or both—to "fine-tune" the economy was the central insight of John Maynard Keynes. There is nothing wrong with the idea. Most economists would concede that, in theory, government has the tools to smooth the business cycle. The problem is that fiscal policy is not made in theory; it's made in Congress. For fiscal policy to be a successful antidote to recession, three things must happen: (1) Congress and the president must agree to a plan that contains an appropriate remedy; (2) they must pass their plan in a timely manner; and (3) the prescribed remedy must kick in fast. The likelihood of nailing all three of these requirements is slim. *Remarkably, in most postwar recessions, Congress did not pass legislation in response to the downturn until after it had ended.* In one particularly egregious example, Congress was still passing legislation in May 1977 to deal with the recession that ended in March 1975.[16] At the end of the relatively mild 2001–2002 recession, the *New York Times* ran the following headline: "Fed Chief Sees Decline Over; House Passes Recovery Bill." I'm not making this stuff up.

What about the Obama stimulus? The American Recovery and Reinvestment Act was seemingly timely, but most of the money was not spent immediately (though there still can be a psychological benefit, and therefore an economic benefit, to simply announcing that lots of spending is coming). Critics of this huge economic intervention argue that it lavished borrowed government money on all kinds of unimaginable projects, some of them quite silly, and will add huge sums to the national debt. Proponents of the stimulus, such as Obama's chair of the Council of Economic Advisers, Christina Romer, make the case that the $787 billion stimulus raised real GDP growth by 2 to 3 percentage points and saved a million jobs.[17] As far as I can tell, they're both right. I was a congressional candidate at the time, so my views are a matter of public record (for the small number of people who paid attention to them). The economy was caught in dangerous negative feedback loops—foreclosures were causing banking problems which were causing layoffs which were causing foreclosures, and so on. I was fond of saying, "A bad stimulus is better than no stimulus, and a bad stimulus is what we got." The government needed to do something to break the cycle (in part because monetary policy was not working, as will be explained in a moment). I would have preferred that the government target more of the spending toward infrastructure and human capital investments to improve the long-term productive capacity of the nation. I agree that rising government indebtedness is a problem, as will be discussed in Chapter 11. That said, given the financial panic described earlier in the chapter and the capacity for bad economic events to beget more bad economic events, there is a reasonable argument to be made that even paying people to dig holes and then fill them in would have been a better policy choice than doing nothing.

The second tool at the government's disposal is monetary policy, which has the potential to affect the economy faster than you can read this paragraph. The chairman of the Federal Reserve can raise or lower short-term interest rates with one phone call. No haggling with Congress; no waiting years for tax cuts. As a result, there is now a consensus among economists that normal business cycles are best managed with monetary policy. The whole next chapter is devoted to the mysterious workings of the Federal Reserve. For now, suffice it to say that cutting interest rates makes it cheaper for consumers to buy houses, cars, and other big-ticket items as well as for firms to invest in new plants and machinery. Cheap money from the Fed pries wallets open again.

During the depths of the "Great Recession" of 2007, however, the Fed couldn't make money any cheaper. The Fed pushed short-term interest rates all the way down to zero, for all intents and purposes, but consumers and businesses still weren't willing to borrow and spend (and unhealthy banks were in a poor position to lend). At that point, monetary policy can't do anything more; it becomes like "pushing on a wet noodle," as Keynes originally described it. This is the economic rationale for turning to a fiscal stimulus as well.

I conceded earlier in this chapter that GDP is not the only measure of economic progress. Our economy consists of hundreds of millions of people living in various states of happiness or unhappiness. Any president recovering from a horseshoe accident would demand a handful of other economic indicators, just as emergency room physicians ask for a patient's vital signs (or at least that is what they do on *Grey's Anatomy*). If you were to take the vital signs of any economy on the planet, here are the economic indicators, along with GDP, that policymakers would ask for first.

Unemployment. My mother does not have a job, but she is not unemployed. How could that be? This is not one of those strange logic riddles. The unemployment rate is the fraction of workers who would like to work but cannot find jobs. (My mother is retired and has no interest in working.) America's unemployment rate fell below 4 percent during the peak of the boom in the 1990s; it has since climbed over 10 percent. Even that may understate the number of people out of work. When Americans without jobs give up on finding one, they no longer count as unemployed and instead become "discouraged workers."

Anyone who cares about unemployment should care about economic growth, too. The general rule of thumb, based on research done by economist Arthur Okun and known thereafter as Okun's law, is that GDP growth of 3 percent a year will leave the unemployment rate unchanged. Faster or slower growth will move the unemployment rate up or down by one-half a percentage point for each percentage point change in GDP. Thus, GDP growth of 4 percent would lower unemployment by half a percentage point, and GDP growth of only 2 percent would cause unemployment to rise by half a percentage point. This relationship is not an iron law; rather, it describes the relationship in America between GDP growth and unemployment over the five-decade period studied by Mr. Okun, roughly 1930 to 1980.

Poverty. Even in the best of times, a drive through Chicago's housing projects is ample evidence that not everybody has been invited to the party. But how many Americans are poor? Indeed, what exactly constitutes "poor"? In the 1960s, the U.S. government created the poverty line as a (somewhat arbitrary) definition of the amount of income necessary to buy the basic necessities. Having been adjusted for inflation, the poverty level remains as the statistical threshold for who is poor in America and who is not. For example, the current poverty line for a single adult is $10,830; the poverty line for a family of two adults and two children is $22,050.

The poverty rate is simply the fraction of Americans whose incomes fall below the poverty line. Roughly 13 percent of Americans are poor, which is no better than we were doing in the 1970s. The poverty rate rose steadily throughout the 1980s and then drifted down in the 1990s. The overall poverty rate disguises some figures that would otherwise leap off the page: Roughly one in five American children is poor as are nearly 35 percent of black children. Our only resounding success is poverty among the elderly, which has fallen from 30 percent in the 1960s to below 10 percent, largely as the result of Social Security.

Income inequality. We care about the size of the pie; we also care about how it is sliced. Economists have a tool that collapses income inequality into a single number, the Gini index.* On this scale, a score of zero represents total equality—a state in which every worker earns exactly the same. At the other end, a score of 100 represents total inequality—a state in which all income is earned by one individual. The countries of the world can be arrayed along this continuum. In 2007, the United States had a Gini index of 45, compared to 28 for France, 23 for Sweden, and 57 for Brazil. By this measure, the United States has grown more unequal over the past several decades. America's Gini coefficient was 36.5 in 1980 and 37.9 in 1950.

Size of government. If we are going to complain about "big government," we ought to at least know how big that government is. One relatively simple measure of the size of government is the ratio of all government spending (local, state, and federal) to GDP. Government spending in America has historically been around 30 percent of GDP, which is low by the standards of the developed world. It's climbing right now, both because the stimulus is driving up government spending (the numerator) and because GDP has been shrinking (the denominator). Government spending in Britain is roughly 40 percent of GDP. In Japan, it is over 45 percent; in France and Sweden it is more than 50 percent. On the other hand, America is the only developed country in which the government does not pay for the bulk of health care services. Our government is smaller, but we get less, too.

Budget deficit/surplus. The concept is simple enough; a budget deficit occurs when the government spends more than it collects in rev-

---

* To derive the Gini index, the personal incomes in a country are arranged in ascending order. A line, the Lorenz curve, plots the cumulative share of personal income against the cumulative share of population. Total equality would be a 45-degree line. The Gini coefficient is the ratio of the area between the diagonal and the Lorenz curve to the total area under the diagonal.

enues and a surplus is the opposite. The more interesting question is whether either one of these things is good or bad. Unlike accountants, economists are not sticklers for balanced budgets. Rather, the prescription is more likely to be that governments should run modest surpluses in good times and modest deficits in tough times; the budget need only balance in the long run.

Here is why: If the economy slips into recession, then tax revenues will fall and spending on programs such as unemployment insurance will rise. This is likely to lead to a deficit; it is also likely to help the economy recover. Raising taxes or cutting spending during a recession will almost certainly make it worse. Herbert Hoover's insistence on balancing the budget in the face of the Great Depression is considered to be one of the great fiscal follies of all time. In good times, the opposite is true: Tax revenues will rise and some kinds of spending will fall, leading to a surplus, as we saw in the late 1990s. (We also saw how quickly it disappeared when the economy turned south.) Anyway, there is nothing wrong with modest deficits and surpluses as long as they coincide with the business cycle.

Let me offer two caveats, however. First, if a government runs a deficit, then it must make up the difference by borrowing money. In the case of the United States, we issue treasury bonds. The national debt is the accumulation of deficits. Beginning around 2001, the United States has been consistently spending more than we take in. It adds up. The U.S. national debt has climbed from a recent low of 33 percent of GDP in 2001 to a projected 68 percent of GDP by 2019. If the debt becomes large enough, investors may begin to balk at the prospect of lending the government more money.

Second, there is a finite amount of capital in the world; the more the government borrows, the less that leaves for the rest of us. Large budget deficits can "crowd out" private investment by raising real interest rates. As America's large budget deficits began to disappear (temporarily) during the 1990s, one profoundly beneficial effect was a fall in long-term real interest rates, making it cheaper for all of us to borrow.

Current account surplus/deficit. The U.S. current account deficit in 2008 was around $700 billion. Is it time to rush to the supermarket to stock up on canned goods and bottled water? Maybe. The current account balance, which can be in surplus or deficit, reflects the difference between the income that we earn from the rest of the world and the income that they earn from us. The bulk of that income comes from trade in goods and services. Thus, our balance of trade, which again can be in surplus or deficit, is the largest component of the current account. If we are running a trade deficit with the rest of the world, then we will almost always be running a current account deficit, too. (For the purists, the U.S. current account would also include dividends paid to Americans who own foreign stocks, remittances sent home by Americans working overseas, and other sources of income earned abroad.)

When the current account is in deficit, as ours is now, it is usually because a country is not exporting enough to "pay" for all of its imports. In other words, if we export $50 billion of goods and import $100 billion, our trading partners are going to want something in exchange for that other $50 billion worth of stuff. We can pay them out of our savings, we can borrow from them to finance the gap, or we can sell them some of our assets, such as stocks and bonds. As a nation, we are consuming more than we are producing, and we have to pay for the difference somehow.

Oddly, this can be a good thing, a bad thing—or somewhere in between. For the first century of America's existence, we ran large current account deficits. We borrowed heavily from abroad so that we could import goods and services to build up our industrial capacity. That was a good thing. Indeed, a current account deficit can be a sign of strength as money pours into countries that show a promising potential for future growth. If, on the other hand, a country is simply importing more than it exports without making investments that will raise future output, then there is a problem, just as you might have a problem if you squandered $100,000 in student loans without getting a degree. You now have to pay back what you borrowed, plus interest, but you have done nothing to raise your future income. The only way to pay back your debt will be to cut back on your future consumption, which is a painful process. Countries that run large current account deficits are not necessarily in financial trouble; on the other hand, countries that have gotten themselves into financial trouble are usually running large current account deficits.

National savings. We all tuck money away for our individual needs: college, retirement, etc. Businesses save money, too, by retaining profits rather than paying them out to the owners of the firm. Those private savings decisions, along with the government's decision to run a deficit or surplus, have a profound impact on our economy. The simple reason is that savings are necessary to finance investment, and investment is what makes us more productive as a society. If you put 10 percent of your income in the bank, then somewhere else in the country that money will end up building a plant or financing a college education. If Americans do not collectively put savings in the bank, then we must either forgo important investments or borrow from abroad. Again, this assumes that foreign investors are willing to lend at a reasonable rate, which may not be the case for an economy in a precarious state. Over time, countries' investment rates show a striking correlation with their domestic savings rates.

The U.S. national savings rate tells a cautionary tale. Personal saving fell steadily from over 9 percent in the 1960s and 1970s to 6 percent in the 1980s to below 5 percent in the mid-1990s to roughly zero by the end of the 1990s.[18] When the recession hit in 2007, the personal savings rate started to climb again. Governments (Washington, D.C., and the states) have been running deficits, or "dissaving." (U.S. businesses were the only ones setting any money aside until households were shocked into saving by the recession.) We can and have borrowed from abroad to finance our national investment—at a cost. Nobody lends money for nothing; borrowing from abroad means that we must pay some of our investment returns to our foreign lenders. Any country with significant exposure to foreign lenders must always worry that when times get tough, the herd of international investors will get spooked and flee with their capital.

Demographics. Americans are getting older, literally. As economist Paul Krugman has noted, the age distribution in America will eventually begin to look as it does in Florida. That is good for the companies that manufacture shuffleboard equipment. It is not so good for government finances. The bulk of government benefits, notably Social Security and Medicare, are bestowed on Americans who are retired. These programs are financed with payroll taxes imposed on younger Americans who are still working. If the ratio of young Americans to older Americans begins to change, then the financial health of programs like Social Security and Medicare begins to change, too.

Indeed, we can explain the importance of demographics *and* fix Social Security all in the next two paragraphs. Social Security is a "pay-as-you-go" program. When American workers pay into Social Security (that large FICA deduction on your paycheck), the money does not get invested somewhere so that you can draw on it twenty or thirty years later, as it would in a private pension fund. Rather, that money is used to pay current retirees. Straight from young Peter to old Paul. The program is one big pyramid scheme, and, like any good pyramid scheme, it works fine as long as there are enough workers on the bottom to continue paying the retirees at the top.

Therein lies the problem. Americans are having fewer children and living longer. This shift means that there are fewer workers to pay for every retiree—a lot fewer. In 1960, there were five workers for every retiree. Now there are three workers for every retiree. By

2032, there will be only two. Imagine Social Security (or Medicare) as a seesaw in which payments made by workers are on one side and benefits collected by retirees are on the other. The program is solvent as long as the seesaw balances. As the number of workers on one side shrinks while the number of retirees on the other side grows, the seesaw begins to tip. In theory, fixing the problem is easy. We can take more from current workers, either by increasing the payroll tax or by making them more productive and raising their incomes (so that the same tax generates more revenues). Or we can give less to retirees, either by cutting their benefits or by raising the retirement age. That is the very simple economic crux of the problem. Of course, if you think any of these solutions would be politically palatable, please go back and read Chapter 8 again.

Total national happiness. You decide. We don't have a number for that one yet.

An autoworker in Detroit who has spent his career getting laid off for months at a time and then called back to work is going to ask a simple question: Are we getting any better at all of this? Yes, we are. The United States has gone through eleven recessions since World War II.[19] None, including the recession that began in 2007, is even of the same order of magnitude as the Great Depression. From 1929 to 1933, real GDP fell by 30 percent while unemployment climbed from 3 percent to 25 percent. Prior to the Great Depression, the United States regularly experienced deep recessions, including financial panics, far worse than what we're going through now.[20] We haven't made the economic bumps go away, but they are smaller bumps.

One can also argue that what we've learned from past economic downturns, and the Great Depression in particular, has helped with policies this time around. Fed chairman (and former Princeton professor) Ben Bernanke is a scholar of the Great Depression. So is Obama's chair of the Council of Economic Advisers (and former UC Berkeley professor) Christina Romer. I can promise you that economists will still be arguing fifty years from now about what should or shouldn't have been done in response to the recession and subsequent financial crisis. However, even the toughest critics should concede that officials at the end of the Bush administration and the beginning of the Obama administration avoided the worst mistakes of the 1930s, when the Federal Reserve raised interest rates in the face of the Great Depression and Congress raised taxes—thrusting both monetary and fiscal policy in the wrong direction.

There is something to be said for not doing exactly the wrong thing. I suspect history will judge that policymakers did even better than that.

CHAPTER 10

The Federal Reserve:

Why that dollar in your pocket is more than just a piece of paper

Sometimes simple statements speak loudly. On September 11, 2001, hours after the terrorist attacks on the United States, the Federal Reserve issued the following statement: "The Federal Reserve System is open and operating. The discount window is available to meet liquidity needs."

Those terse and technical two sentences had a calming effect on global markets. The following Monday, as America's markets opened for their first trading sessions after the attack, the Federal Reserve cut interest rates by 0.5 percent, another act that moderated the financial and economic impact of the terrorist assaults.

How exactly does an inelegant two-sentence statement have such a profound effect on the world's largest economy—indeed, on the whole global economy?

The Federal Reserve has tools with more direct impact on the global economy than any other institution in the world, public or private. During the economic crisis that began to unfold in 2007, the Federal Reserve used everything in that toolkit—and then acquired some new gadgets—to wrestle the financial system back from the brink of panic. Since then, some have criticized the Fed and its chairman, Ben Bernanke, for doing too much; some have criticized the Fed for doing too little. Everyone agrees that what the Fed does matters enormously.

From where does the Federal Reserve, an institution that is not directly accountable to the voting public, derive such power? And how does that power affect the lives of everyday Americans? The answer to all those questions is the same: The Federal Reserve controls the money supply and therefore the credit tap for the economy. When that tap is open wide, interest rates fall and we spend more freely on things that require borrowed money—everything from new cars to new manufacturing plants. Thus, the Fed can use monetary policy to counteract economic downturns (or prevent them in the first place). And it can inject money into the financial system after sudden shocks, such as the 1987 stock market crash or the terrorist attacks of September 11 or the bursting of the American real estate bubble, when consumers and firms might otherwise freeze in place and stop spending. Or the Fed can tighten the tap by raising interest rates. When the cost of borrowed funds goes up, our spending slows. It is an awesome power. Paul Krugman once wrote, "If you want a simple model for predicting the unemployment rate in the United States over the next few years, here it is: It will be what Greenspan wants it to be, plus or minus a random error reflecting the fact that he is not quite God." The same is now true of Ben Bernanke.

God does not have to manage by committee; Ben Bernanke does. The Federal Reserve System is made up of twelve Reserve Banks spread across the country and a seven-person board of governors based in Washington. Ben Bernanke is chairman of the board of governors—he's the "Fed chairman." The Federal Reserve regulates commercial banks, supports the banking infrastructure, and generally makes the plumbing of the financial system work. Those jobs require competence, not genius or great foresight. Monetary policy, the Federal Reserve's other responsibility, is different. It might reasonably be described as the economic equivalent of brain surgery. Economists do not agree on how the Federal Reserve ought to manage our money supply. Nor do they even agree on exactly how or why changes in the money supply have the effects that they do. Yet economists do agree that effective monetary policy matters; the Fed must feed just the right amount of credit to the economy to keep it growing steadily. Getting it wrong can have disastrous consequences. Robert Mundell, winner of the 1999 Nobel Prize in Economics, has argued that bungled monetary policy in the 1920s and 1930s caused chronic deflation that destabilized the world. He has argued, "Had the price of gold been raised in the late 1920s, or, alternatively, had the major central banks pursued policies of price stability instead of adhering to the gold standard, there would have been no Great Depression, no Nazi revolution, and no World War II."[1]

The job would not appear to be that complicated. If the Fed can make the economy grow faster by lowering interest rates, then presumably lower interest rates are always better. Indeed, why should there be any limit to the rate at which the economy can grow? If we begin to spend more freely when rates are cut from 7 percent to 5 percent, why stop there? If there are still people without jobs and others without new cars, then let's press on to 3 percent, or even 1 percent. New money for everyone! Sadly, there *are* limits to how fast any economy can grow. If low interest rates, or "easy money," causes consumers to demand 5 percent more new PT Cruisers than they purchased last year, then Chrysler must expand production by 5 percent. That means hiring more workers and buying more steel, glass, electrical components, etc. At some point, it becomes difficult or impossible for Chrysler to find these new inputs, particularly qualified workers. At that point, the company simply cannot make enough PT Cruisers to satisfy consumer demand; instead, the company begins to raise prices. Meanwhile, autoworkers recognize that Chrysler is desperate for labor, and the union demands higher wages.

The story does not stop there. The same thing would be happening throughout the economy, not just at Chrysler. If interest rates are exceptionally low, firms will borrow to invest in new computer systems and software; consumers will break out their VISA cards for big-screen televisions and Caribbean cruises—all up to a point. When the cruise ships are full and Dell is selling every computer it can produce, then those firms will raise their prices, too. (When demand exceeds supply, firms can charge more and still fill every boat or sell every computer.) In short, an "easy money" policy at the Fed can cause consumers to demand more than the economy can produce. The only way to ration that excess demand is with higher prices. The result is inflation.

The sticker price on the PT Cruiser goes up, and no one is better off for it. True, Chrysler is taking in more money, but it is also paying more to its suppliers and workers. Those workers are seeing higher wages, but they are also paying higher prices for their basic needs. Numbers are changing everywhere, but the productive capacity of our economy and the measure of our well-being, real GDP, has hit the wall. Once started, the inflationary cycle is hard to break. Firms and workers everywhere begin to expect continually rising prices (which, in turn, causes continually rising prices). Welcome to the 1970s.

The pace at which the economy can grow without causing inflation might reasonably be considered a "speed limit." After all, there are only a handful of ways to increase the amount that we as a nation can produce. We can work longer hours. We can add new workers, through falling unemployment or immigration (recognizing that the workers available may not have the skills in demand). We can add machines and other kinds of capital that help us to produce things. Or we can become more productive—produce more with what we already have, perhaps because of an innovation or a technological change. Each of these sources of growth has natural constraints. Workers are scarce; capital is scarce; technological change proceeds at a finite and unpredictable pace. In the late 1990s, American autoworkers threatened to go on strike because they were being forced to work too much overtime. (Don't we wish we had that problem now . . .) Meanwhile, fast-food restaurants were offering signing bonuses to new employees. We were at the wall. Economists reckon that the speed limit of the

American economy is somewhere in the range of 3 percent growth per year.

The phrase "somewhere in the range" gives you the first inkling of how hard the Fed's job is. The Federal Reserve must strike a delicate balance. If the economy grows more slowly than it is capable of, then we are wasting economic potential. Plants that make PT Cruisers sit idle; the workers who might have jobs there are unemployed instead. An economy that has the capacity to grow at 3 percent instead limps along at 1.5 percent, or even slips into recession. Thus, the Fed must feed enough credit to the economy to create jobs and prosperity but not so much that the economy begins to overheat. William McChesney Martin, Jr., Federal Reserve chairman during the 1950s and 1960s, once noted that the Fed's job is to take away the punch bowl just as the party gets going.

Or sometimes the Fed must rein in the party long after it has gone out of control. The Federal Reserve has deliberately engineered a number of recessions in order to squeeze inflation out of the system. Most notably, Fed chairman Paul Volcker was the ogre who ended the inflationary party of the 1970s. At that point, naked people were dancing wildly on the tables. Inflation had climbed from 3 percent in 1972 to 13.5 percent in 1980. Mr. Volcker hit the monetary brakes, meaning that he cranked up interest rates to slow the economy down. Short-term interest rates peaked at over 16 percent in 1981. The result was a painful unwinding of the inflationary cycle. With interest rates in double digits, there were plenty of unsold Chrysler K cars sitting on the lot. Dealers were forced to cut prices (or stop raising them). The auto companies idled plants and laid off workers. The autoworkers who still had jobs decided that it would be a bad time to ask for more money.

The same thing, of course, was going on in every other sector of the economy. Slowly, and at great human cost, the expectation that prices would steadily rise was purged from the system. The result was the recession of 1981–1982, during which GDP shrank by 3 percent and unemployment climbed to nearly 10 percent. In the end, Mr.

Volcker did clear the dancers off the tables. By 1983, inflation had fallen to 3 percent. Obviously it would have been easier and less painful if the party had never gone out of control in the first place.

Where does the Fed derive this extraordinary power over interest rates? After all, commercial banks are private entities. The Federal Reserve cannot force Citibank to raise or lower the rates it charges consumers for auto loans and home mortgages. Rather, the process is indirect. Recall from Chapter 7 that the interest rate is really just a rental rate for capital, or the "price of money." The Fed controls America's money supply. We'll get to the mechanics of that process in a moment. For now, recognize that capital is no different from apartments: The greater the supply, the cheaper the rent. The Fed moves interest rates by making changes in the quantity of funds available to commercial banks. If banks are awash with money, then interest rates must be relatively low to attract borrowers for all the available funds. When capital is scarce, the opposite will be true: Banks can charge higher interest rates and still attract enough borrowers for all available funds. It's supply and demand, with the Fed controlling the supply.

These monetary decisions—the determination whether interest rates need to go up, down, or stay the same—are made by a committee within the Fed called the Federal Open Market Committee (FOMC), which consists of the board of governors, the president of the Federal Reserve Bank of New York, and the presidents of four other Federal Reserve Banks on a rotating basis. The Fed chairman is also the chairman of the FOMC. Ben Bernanke derives his power from the fact that he is sitting at the head of the table when the FOMC makes interest rate decisions.

If the FOMC wants to stimulate the economy by lowering the cost of borrowing, the committee has two primary tools at its disposal. The first is the discount rate, which is the interest rate at which commercial banks can borrow funds directly from the Federal Reserve. The relationship between the discount rate and the cost of borrowing at

Citibank is straightforward; when the discount rate falls, banks can borrow more cheaply from the Fed and therefore lend more cheaply to their customers. There is one complication. Borrowing directly from the Fed carries a certain stigma; it implies that a bank was not able to raise funds privately. Thus, turning to the Fed for a loan is similar to borrowing from your parents after about age twenty-five: You'll get the money, but it's better to look somewhere else first.

Instead, banks generally borrow from other banks. The second important tool in the Fed's money supply kit is the federal funds rate, the rate that banks charge other banks for short-term loans. The Fed cannot stipulate the rate at which Wells Fargo lends money to Citigroup. Rather, the FOMC sets a target for the federal funds rate, say 4.5 percent, and then manipulates the money supply to accomplish its objective. If the supply of funds goes up, then banks will have to drop their prices—lower interest rates—to find borrowers for the new funds. One can think of the money supply as a furnace with the federal funds rate as its thermostat. If the FOMC cuts the target fed funds rate from 4.5 percent to 4.25 percent, then the Federal Reserve will pump money into the banking system until the rate Wells Fargo charges Citigroup for an overnight loan falls to something very close to 4.25 percent.

All of which brings us to our final conundrum: How does the Federal Reserve inject money into a private banking system? Does Ben Bernanke print $100 million of new money, load it into a heavily armored truck, and drive it to a Citibank branch? Not exactly—though that image is not a bad way to understand what does happen.

Ben Bernanke and the FOMC do create new money. In the United States, they alone have that power. (The Treasury merely mints new currency and coins to replace money that already exists.) The Federal Reserve does deliver new money to banks like Citibank. But the Fed does not give funds to the bank; it trades the new money for government bonds that the banks currently own. In our metaphorical example, the Citibank branch manager meets Ben Bernanke's armored truck outside the bank, loads $100 million of new money into the bank's vault, and then hands the Fed chairman $100 million in government bonds from the bank's portfolio in return. Note that Citibank has not been made richer by the transaction. The bank has merely swapped $100 million of one kind of asset (bonds) for $100 million of a different kind of asset (cash, or, more accurately, its electronic equivalent).

Banks hold bonds for the same reason individual investors do; bonds are a safe place to park funds that aren't needed for something else. Specifically, banks buy bonds with depositors' funds that are not being loaned out. To the economy, the fact that Citibank has swapped bonds for cash makes all the difference. When a bank has $100 million of deposits parked in bonds, those funds are not being loaned out. They are not financing houses, or businesses, or new plants. But after Ben Bernanke's metaphorical armored truck pulls away, Citibank is left holding funds that can be loaned out. That means new loans for all the kinds of things that generate economic activity. Indeed, money injected into the banking system has a cascading effect. A bank that swaps bonds for money from the Fed keeps some fraction of the funds in reserves, as required by law, and then loans out the rest. Whoever receives those loans will spend them somewhere, perhaps at a car dealership or a department store. That money eventually ends up in other banks, which will keep some funds in reserve and then make loans of their own. A move by the Fed to inject $100 million of new funds into the banking system may ultimately increase the money supply by 10 times as much.

Of course, the Fed chairman does not actually drive a truck to a Citibank branch to swap cash for bonds. The FOMC can accomplish the same thing using the bond market (which works just like the stock market, except that bonds are bought and sold). Bond traders working on behalf of the Fed buy bonds from commercial banks and pay for them with newly created money—funds that simply did not exist twenty minutes earlier. (Presumably the banks selling their bonds will be those with the most opportunities to make new loans.) The Fed will continue to buy bonds with new money, a process called open market operations, until the target federal funds rate has been reached.

Obviously what the Fed giveth, the Fed can take away. The Federal Reserve can raise interest rates by doing the opposite of everything we've just discussed. The FOMC would vote to raise the discount rate and/or the target fed funds rate and issue an order to sell bonds from its portfolio to commercial banks. As banks give up lendable funds in exchange for bonds, the money supply shrinks. Money that might have been loaned out to consumers and businesses is parked in bonds instead. Interest rates go up, and anything purchased with borrowed capital becomes more expensive. The cumulative effect is slower economic growth.

The mechanics of the Fed's handiwork should not obscure the big picture. The Federal Reserve's mandate is to facilitate a sustainable pace of economic growth. But let's clarify how difficult that job really is. First, we are only guessing at the rate at which the economy can expand without igniting inflation. One debate among economists is over whether or not computers and other kinds of information technology have made Americans significantly more productive. If so, as Mr. Greenspan suggested during his tenure, then the economy's potential growth rate may have gone up. If not, as other economists have argued convincingly, then the old speed limit still applies. Obviously it is hard to abide by a speed limit that is not clearly posted.

But that is only the first challenge. The Fed must also reckon what kind of impact a change in interest rates will have and how long it will take. Will a quarter-point rate cut cause twelve people to buy new PT Cruisers in Des Moines or 421? When? Next week or six months from now? Meanwhile, the Fed has the most control over short-term interest rates, which may or may not move in the same direction as long-term rates. Why can't Ben Bernanke work his magic on long-term rates, too? Because long-term rates do not depend on the money supply today; they depend on what the markets predict money supply (relative to demand) will be ten, twenty, or even thirty years from now. Ben Bernanke has no control over the money supply in 2015. Also remember that while the

Fed is trying to use monetary policy to hit a particular economic target, Congress may be doing things with fiscal policy—government decisions on taxes and spending—that have a different effect entirely (or have the same effect, causing Fed policy to overshoot).

So let's stick with our speed limit analogy and recap what exactly the Fed is charged with doing. The Fed must facilitate a rate of economic growth that is neither too fast nor too slow. Bear in mind: (1) We do not know the economy's exact speed limit. (2) Both the accelerator and the brake operate with a lag, meaning that neither works immediately when we press on it. Instead, we have to wait a while for a response—anywhere from a few weeks to a few years, but not with any predictable pattern. An inexperienced driver might press progressively harder on the gas, wondering why nothing is happening (and enduring all kinds of public assaults on his pathetically slow driving), only to find the car screaming out of control nine months later. (3) Monetary and fiscal policy affect the economy independently, so while the Fed is gently applying the brake, Congress and the president may be jumping up and down on the accelerator. Or the Fed may tap on the accelerator ever so slightly only to have Congress weigh it down with a brick. (4) Last, there is the obstacle course of world events—a financial collapse here, a spike in the price of oil there. Think of the Fed as always driving in unfamiliar terrain with a map that's at least ten years out of date.

Bob Woodward's biography of Alan Greenspan was titled *Maestro*. In the 1990s, as the American economy roared through its longest expansion in economic history, Mr. Greenspan was given credit for his "Goldilocks" approach to monetary policy—doing everything just right. That reputation has since come partially unraveled. Mr. Greenspan is now criticized for abetting the housing and stock market bubbles by keeping interest rates too low for too long. "Cheap money" didn't cause inflation by sending everyone to buy PT Cruisers and Caribbean cruises. Instead we bought stocks and real estate, and those rising asset prices didn't show up in the consumer price index. Add one new challenge to monetary policy: We were speeding even though the gauges we're used to looking at said we weren't.

It's a hard job. Still, that conclusion is a long way from Nobel laureate Robert Mundell's dire claim that bad monetary policy laid the groundwork for World War II. To understand why irresponsible monetary policy can have cataclysmic effects, we must first make a short digression on the nature of money. To economists, money is quite distinct from wealth. Wealth consists of all things that have value—houses, cars, commodities, human capital. Money, a tiny subset of that wealth, is merely a medium of exchange, something that facilitates trade and commerce. In theory, money is not even necessary. A simple economy could get along through barter alone. In a basic agricultural society, it's easy enough to swap five chickens for a new dress or to pay a schoolteacher with a goat and three sacks of rice. Barter works less well in a more advanced economy. The logistical challenges of using chickens to buy books at Amazon would be formidable.

In nearly every society, some kind of money has evolved to make trade easier. (The word "salary" comes from the wages paid to Roman soldiers, who were paid in sacks of *sal*—salt.) Any medium of exchange—whether it is a gold coin, a whale tooth, or an American dollar—serves the same basic purposes. First, it serves as a means of exchange, so that I might enjoy pork chops for dinner tonight even though the butcher has no interest in buying this book. Second, it serves as a unit of account, so that the cost of all kinds of goods and services can be measured and compared using one scale. (Imagine life without a unit of account: The Gap is selling jeans for three chickens a pair while Tommy Hilfiger has similar pants on sale for eleven beaver pelts. Which pants cost more?) Third, money must be portable and durable. Neither bowling balls nor rose petals would serve the purpose. Last, money must be relatively scarce so that it can serve as a store of value.

Clever people will always find a medium of exchange that works. Cigarettes long served as the medium of exchange in prisons, where cash is banned. (It doesn't matter whether you smoke; cigarettes have value as long as enough other inmates smoke.) So what happened when smoking was banned in U.S. federal prisons? Inmates turned to another portable, durable store of value: cans of mackerel. According to the *Wall Street Journal*, a single can of mackerel, or "the mack" is the standard unit of currency behind bars. (Some prisons have moved from cans to plastic pouches, because the cans can be fashioned into weapons.) In a can or pouch, mackerel doesn't spoil, it can be bought on account in the commissary, and it costs about a dollar, making the accounting easy. A haircut costs two macks in the Lompoc Federal Correctional Complex.[2]

For much of American history, commerce was conducted with paper currency backed by precious metals. Prior to the twentieth century, private banks issued their own money. In 1913, the U.S. government banned private money and became the sole provider of currency. The basic idea did not change. Whether money was public or private, paper currency derived its value from the fact that it could be redeemed for a set quantity of gold or silver, either from a bank or from the government. Then something strange happened. In 1971, the United States permanently went off the gold standard. At that point, every paper dollar became redeemable for . . . nothing.

Examine that wad of $100 bills in your wallet. (If necessary, $1 bills can be substituted instead.) Those bills are just paper. You can't eat them, you can't drink them, you can't smoke them, and, most important, you can't take them to the government and demand anything in return. They have no intrinsic value. And that is true of nearly all the world's currencies. Left alone on a deserted island with $100 million, you would quickly perish. On the other hand, life would be good if you were rescued and could take the cash with you. Therein lies the value of modern currency: It has purchasing power. Dollars have value because people peddling real things—food, books, pedicures—will accept them. And people peddling real things will accept dollars because they are confident that other people peddling other real things will accept them, too. A dollar is a piece of paper whose value derives solely from our confidence that we will be able to use it to buy something we need in the future.

To give you some sense of how modern money is a confidence game, consider a bizarre phenomenon in India. Most Indians involved in commerce—shopkeepers, taxi drivers, etc.—will not accept a torn, crumpled, or overly soiled rupee note. Since other Indians know that many of their countrymen will not accept torn notes, they will not accept them either. Finally, when tourists arrive in the country, they quickly learn to accept only intact bills, lest they be stuck with the torn ones. The whole process is utterly irrational, since the Indian Central Bank considers any note with a serial number—torn, dirty, crumpled, or otherwise—to be legal tender. Any bank will exchange torn rupees for crisp new ones. That doesn't matter; rational people refuse legal tender because they believe that it might not be accepted by someone else. The whole bizarre phenomenon underscores the fact that our faith in paper currency is predicated on the faith that others place in the same paper.

Since paper currency has no inherent worth, its value depends on its purchasing power—something that can change gradually over time, or even stunningly fast. In the summer of 1997, I spent a few days driving across Iowa "taking the pulse of the American farmer" for *The Economist*. Somewhere outside of Des Moines, I began chatting with a corn, soybean, and cattle farmer. As he gave me a tour of his farm, he pointed to an old tractor parked outside the barn. "That tractor cost $7,500 new in 1970," he said. "Now look at this," he said angrily, pointing to a shiny new tractor right next to the old one. "Cost me $40,000. Can you explain that?"*

I could explain that, though that's not what I told the farmer, who was already suspicious of the fact that I was young, from the city, wearing a tie, and driving a Honda Civic. (The following year, when

---

* I can't remember the exact numbers, but they were something along these lines.

I was asked to write a similar story on Kentucky tobacco farmers, I had the good sense to rent a pickup truck.) My answer would have been one word: inflation. The new tractor probably wasn't any more expensive than the old tractor in real terms, meaning that he had to do the same amount of work, or less, in order to buy it. The sticker price on his tractor had gone up, but so had the prices at which he could sell his crops and cattle.

Inflation means, quite simply, that average prices are rising. The inflation rate, or the change in the consumer price index, is the government's attempt to reflect changing prices with a single number, say 4.2 percent. The method of determining this figure is surprisingly low-tech; government officials periodically check the prices of thousands and thousands of goods—clothes, food, fuel, entertainment, housing—and then compile them into a number that reflects how the prices of a basket of goods purchased by the average consumer has changed.

The most instructive way to think about inflation is not that prices are going up, but rather that the purchasing power of the dollar is going down. A dollar buys less than it used to. Therein lies the link between the Federal Reserve, or any central bank, and economic devastation. A paper currency has value only because it is scarce. The central bank controls that scarcity. Therefore a corrupt or incompetent central bank can erode, or even completely destroy, the value of our money. Suppose prison officials, in a fit of goodwill, decided to give every inmate 500 cans of mackerel. What would happen to the price of a prison haircut in "macks"? And mackerel is better than paper, in that it at least has some intrinsic value.

In 1921, a German newspaper cost roughly a third of a mark; two years later, a newspaper cost 70 million marks. It was not the newspaper that changed during that spell; it was the German mark, which was rendered useless as the government printed new ones with reckless abandon. Indeed, the mark lost so much value that it became cheaper for households to burn them than to use them to buy firewood. Inflation was so bad in Latin America in the 1980s that there were countries whose largest import became paper currency.[3] In the late 1990s, the Belarussian ruble was known as the "bunny," not only for the hare engraved on the note but also for the currency's remarkable ability to propagate. In August 1998, the Belarussian ruble lost 10 percent of its purchasing power in one week.

Massive inflation distorts the economy massively. Workers rush to spend their cash before it becomes worthless. A culture emerges in which workers rush out to spend their paychecks at lunch because prices will have gone up by dinner. Fixed-rate loans become impossible because no financial institution will agree to be repaid a fixed quantity of money when that money is at risk of becoming worthless. Think about it: Anyone with a fixed-rate mortgage in Germany in 1921 could have paid off the whole loan in 1923 with fewer marks than it cost to buy a newspaper. Even today, it is not possible to get a thirty-year fixed mortgage in much of Latin America because of fears that inflation will come roaring back.

America has never suffered hyperinflation. We have had bouts of moderate inflation; the costs were smaller and more subtle but still significant. At the most basic level, inflation leads to misleading or inaccurate comparisons. Journalists rarely distinguish between real and nominal figures, as they ought to. Suppose that American incomes rose 5 percent last year. That is a meaningless figure until we know the inflation rate. If prices rose by 7 percent, then we have actually become worse off. Our paycheck may look bigger but it buys 2 percent fewer goods than it did last year. Hollywood is an egregious offender, proclaiming summer after summer that some mediocre film has set a new box office record. Comparing gross receipts in 2010 to gross receipts in 1970 or 1950 is a silly exercise unless they are adjusted for inflation. A ticket to *Gone with the Wind* cost 19 cents. A ticket to *Dude, Where's My Car?* cost $10. Of course the gross receipts are going to look big by comparison.

Even moderate inflation has the potential to eat away at our wealth if we do not manage our assets properly. Any wealth held in cash will lose value over time. Even savings accounts and certificates of deposit, which are considered "safe" investments because the principal is insured, are vulnerable to the less obvious risk that their low interest rates may not keep up with inflation. It is a sad irony that unsophisticated investors eschew the "risky" stock market only to have their principal whittled away through the back door. Inflation can be particularly pernicious for individuals who are retired or otherwise living on fixed incomes. If that income is not indexed for inflation, then its purchasing power will gradually fade away. A monthly check that made for a comfortable living in 1985 becomes inadequate to buy the basic necessities in 2010.

Inflation also redistributes wealth arbitrarily. Suppose I borrow $1,000 from you and promise to pay back the loan, plus interest of $100, next year. That seems a fair arrangement for both of us. Now suppose that a wildly irresponsible central banker allows inflation to explode to 100 percent a year. The $1,100 that I pay back to you next year will be worth much less than either of us had expected; its purchasing power will be cut in half. In real terms, I will borrow $1,100 from you and pay back $550. Unexpected bouts of inflation are good for debtors and bad for lenders—a crucial point that we will come back to.

As a side note, you should recognize the difference between real and nominal interest rates. The nominal rate is used to calculate what you have to pay back; it's the number you see posted on the bank window or on the front page of a loan document. If Wells Fargo is paying a rate of 2.3 percent on checking deposits, that's the nominal rate. This rate is different from the real interest rate, which takes inflation into account and therefore reflects the true cost of "renting" capital. The real interest rate is the nominal rate minus the rate of inflation. As a simple example, suppose you take out a bank loan for one year at a nominal rate of 5 percent, and that inflation is also 5 percent that year. In such a case, your real rate of interest is zero. You pay back 5 percent more than you borrowed, but the value of that money has depreciated 5 percent over the course of the year, so what you pay back has exactly the same purchasing power as what you borrowed. The true cost to you of using someone else's capital for a year is zero.

Inflation also distorts taxes. Take the capital gains tax, for example. Suppose you buy a stock and sell it a year later, earning a 10 percent return. If the inflation rate was also 10 percent over that period, then you have not actually made any money. Your return exactly offsets the fact that every dollar in your portfolio has lost 10 percent of its purchasing power—a point lost on Uncle Sam. You owe taxes on your 10 percent "gain." Taxes are unpleasant when you've made money; they really stink when you haven't.

Having said all that, moderate inflation, were it a constant or predictable rate, would have very little effect. Suppose, for example, that we knew the inflation rate would be 10 percent a year forever—no higher, no lower. We could deal with that easily. Any savings account would pay some real rate of interest plus 10 percent to compensate for inflation. Our salaries would go up 10 percent a year (plus, we would hope, some additional sum based on merit). All loan agreements would charge some real rental rate for capital plus a 10 percent annual premium to account for the fact that the dollars you are borrowing are not the same as the dollars you will be paying back. Government benefits would be indexed for inflation and so would taxes.

But inflation is not constant or predictable. Indeed, the aura of uncertainty is one of its most insidious costs. Individuals and firms are forced to guess about future prices when they make economic decisions. When the autoworkers and Ford negotiate a four-year contract, both sides must make some estimates about future inflation. A contract with annual raises of 4 percent is very generous when the inflation rate is 1 percent but a lousy deal for workers if the inflation rate climbs to 10 percent. Lenders must make a similar calculation. Lending someone money for thirty years at a fixed rate of interest carries a huge risk in an inflationary environment. So when lenders fear future inflation, they build in a buffer. The greater the fear of inflation, the bigger the buffer. On the other hand, if a central bank proves that it is serious about preventing inflation, then the buffer gets smaller. One of the most significant benefits of the persistent low inflation of the 1990s was that lenders became less fearful of future inflation. As a result, long-term interest rates dropped sharply, making homes and other big purchases more affordable. Robert Barro, a Harvard economist who has studied economic growth in nearly one hundred countries over several decades, has confirmed that significant inflation is associated with slower real GDP growth.

It seems obvious enough that governments and central banks would make fighting inflation a priority. Even if they made honest mistakes trying to drive their economies at the "speed limit," we would expect small bursts of inflation, not prolonged periods of rising prices, let alone hyperinflation. Yet that is not what we observe. Governments, rich and poor alike, have driven their economies not just faster than the speed limit, but at engine-smoking, wheels-screeching kinds of speeds. Why? Because shortsighted, corrupt, or desperate governments can buy themselves some time by stoking inflation. We spoke about the power of incentives all the way back in Chapter 2. Still, see if you can piece this puzzle together: (1) Governments often owe large debts, and troubled governments owe even more; (2) inflation is good for debtors because it erodes the value of the money they must pay back; (3) governments control the inflation rate. Add it up: Governments can cut their own debts by pulling the inflation rip cord.

Of course, this creates all kinds of victims. Those who lent the government money are paid back the face value of the debt but in a currency that has lost value. Meanwhile, those holding currency are punished because their money now buys much less. And last, even future citizens are punished, because this government will find it difficult or impossible to borrow at reasonable interest rates again (though bankers do show an odd proclivity to make the same mistakes over and over again).

Governments can also benefit in the short run from what economists refer to as the "inflation tax." Suppose you are running a government that is unable to raise taxes through conventional means, either because the infrastructure necessary to collect taxes does not exist or because your citizens cannot or will not pay more. Yet you have government workers, perhaps even a large army, who demand to be paid. Here is a very simple solution. Buy some beer, order a pizza (or whatever an appropriate national dish might be), and begin running the printing presses at the national mint. As soon as the ink is dry on your new pesos, or rubles, or dollars, use them to pay your government workers and soldiers. *Alas, you have taxed the people of your country— indirectly.* You have not physically taken money from their wallets; instead, you've done it by devaluing the money that stays in their wallets. The Continental Congress did it during the Revolutionary War; both sides did it during the Civil War; the German government did it between the wars; countries like Zimbabwe are doing it now.

A government does not have to be on the brink of catastrophe to play the inflation card. Even in present-day America, clever politicians can use moderate inflation to their benefit. One feature of irresponsible monetary policy—like a party headed out of control—is that it can be fun for a while. In the short run, easy money makes everyone feel richer. When consumers flock to the Chrysler dealership in Des Moines, the owner's first reaction is that he is doing a really good job of selling cars. Or perhaps he thinks that Chrysler's new models are more attractive than the Fords and Toyotas. In either case, he raises prices, earns more income, and generally believes that his life is getting better. Only gradually does he realize that most other businesses are experiencing the same phenomenon. Since they are raising prices, too, his higher income will be lost to inflation.

By then, the politicians may have gotten what they wanted: reelection. A central bank that is not sufficiently insulated from politics can throw a wild party before the votes are cast. There will be lots of dancing on the tables; by the time voters become sick with an inflation-induced hangover, the election is over. Macroeconomic lore has it that Fed chairman Arthur Burns did such a favor for Richard Nixon in 1972 and that the Bush family is still angry with Alan Greenspan for not adding a little more alcohol to the punch before the 1992 election, when George H. W. Bush was turned out of office following a mild recession.

Political independence is crucial if monetary authorities are to do their jobs responsibly. Evidence shows that countries with independent central banks—those that can operate relatively free of political meddling—have lower average inflation rates over time. America's Federal Reserve is among those considered to be relatively independent. Members of its board of governors are appointed to fourteen-year terms by the president. That does not give them the same lifetime tenure as Supreme Court justices, but it does make it unlikely that any new president could pack the Federal Reserve with cronies. It is notable—and even a source of criticism—that the most important economic post in a democratic government is appointed, not elected. We designed it that way; we have made a democratic decision to create a relatively undemocratic institution. A central bank's effectiveness depends on its independence and credibility, almost to the point that a reputation can become self-fulfilling. If firms believe that a central bank will not tolerate inflation, then they will not feel compelled to raise prices. And if firms do not raise prices, then there will not be an inflation problem.

Fed officials are prickly about political meddling. In the spring of 1993, I had dinner with Paul Volcker, former chairman of the Federal Reserve. Mr. Volcker was teaching at Princeton, and he was kind enough to take his students to dinner. President Clinton had just given a major address to a joint session of Congress and Fed chairman Alan Greenspan, Volcker's successor, had been seated next to Hillary Clinton. What I remember most about the dinner was Mr. Volcker grumbling that it was inappropriate for Alan Greenspan to have been seated next to the president's wife. He felt that it sent the wrong message about the Federal Reserve's independence from the executive branch. That is how seriously central bankers take their political independence.

Inflation is bad; deflation, or steadily falling prices, is much worse. Even modest deflation can be economically devastating, as Japan has learned over the past two decades. It may seem counterintuitive that falling prices could make consumers worse off (especially if rising prices make them worse off, too), but deflation begets a dangerous economic cycle. To begin with, falling prices cause consumers to postpone purchases. Why buy a refrigerator today when it will cost less next week? Meanwhile, asset prices also are falling, so consumers feel poorer and less inclined to spend. This is why the bursting of a real estate bubble causes so much economic damage. Consumers watch the value of their homes drop sharply while their mortgage payments stay the same. They feel poorer (because they are). As we know from the last chapter, when consumers spend less, the economy grows less. Firms respond to this slowdown by cutting prices further still. The result is an economic death spiral, as Paul Krugman has noted:

> Prices are falling because the economy is depressed; now we've just learned that the economy is depressed because prices are falling. That sets the stage for the return of another monster we haven't seen since the 1930s, a "deflationary spiral," in which falling prices and a slumping economy feed on each other, plunging the economy into the abyss.[4]

This spiral can poison the financial system, even when bankers are not doing irresponsible things. Banks and other financial institutions get weaker as loans go bad and the value of the real estate and other assets used as collateral for those loans falls. Some banks begin to have solvency problems; others just have less capital for making new loans, which deprives otherwise healthy firms of credit and spreads the economic distress. The purpose of the Troubled Asset Relief

Program (TARP) intervention at the end of the George W. Bush administration—the so-called Wall Street bailout—was to "recapitalize" America's banks and put them back in a position to provide capital to the economy. The design of the program had its flaws. Communication about what the administration was doing and why they were doing it was abysmal. But the underlying concept made a lot of sense in the face of the financial crisis.

Monetary policy alone may not be able to break a deflationary spiral. In Japan, the central bank cut nominal interest rates to near zero a long time ago, which means that they can't go any lower. (Nominal interest rates can't be negative. Any bank that loaned out $100 and asked for only $98 back would be better off just keeping the $100 in the first place.)* Yet even with nominal rates near zero, the rental rate on capital—the real interest rate—might actually be quite high. Here is why. If prices are falling, then borrowing $100 today and paying back $100 next year is not costless. The $100 you pay back has *more* purchasing power than the $100 you borrowed, perhaps much more. The faster prices are falling, the higher your real cost of borrowing. If the nominal interest rate is zero, but prices are falling 5 percent a year, then the real interest rate is 5 percent—a cost of borrowing that is too steep when the economy is stagnant. Economists have long been convinced that what Japan needs is a stiff dose of inflation to fix all this. One very prominent economist went so far as to encourage the Bank of Japan to do "anything short of dropping bank notes out of helicopters."[5] To hark back to the politics of organized interests covered in

---

* Okay, that's not exactly true. At the height of the financial crisis, right around the time that Lehman Brothers declared bankruptcy, the yield on three-month U.S. Treasury notes fell below zero, which means that the nominal interest rate had turned negative. Remarkably, investors were paying more for something than it promised to pay them back in three months. For policymakers, this was a sign of panic. Keith Hennessey, director of the National Economic Council in the White House, told James Stewart of *The New Yorker*, "Treasury rates went negative! People were locking in a loss just to protect their money."

Chapter 8, one theory for why Japanese officials have not done more to fight falling prices is that Japan's aging population, many of whom live on fixed incomes or savings, see deflation as a good thing despite its dire consequences for the economy as a whole.

The United States has had its own encounters with deflation. There is a consensus among economists that botched monetary policy was at the heart of the Great Depression. From 1929 to 1933, America's money supply fell by 28 percent.[6] The Fed did not deliberately turn off the credit tap; rather, it stood idly by as the money supply fell of its own volition. The process by which money is circulated throughout the economy had become unhitched. Because of widespread bank failures in 1930, both banks and individuals began to hoard cash. Money that was stuffed under a mattress or locked in a bank vault could not be loaned back into the economy. The Fed did nothing while America's credit dried up (and actually raised interest rates sharply in 1931 to defend the gold standard). Fed officials should have been doing just the opposite: pumping money into the system.

In September 2009, the one-year anniversary of the collapse of Lehman Brothers, the chair of the Council of Economic Advisers, Christina Romer, gave a talk ominously entitled "Back from the Brink," which laid much of the credit for our escape from economic disaster at the door of the Federal Reserve. She explained, "The policy response in the current episode, in contrast [to the 1930s], has been swift and bold. The Federal Reserve's creative and aggressive actions last fall to maintain lending will go down as a high point in central bank history. As credit market after credit market froze or evaporated, the Federal Reserve created many new programs to fill the gap and maintain the flow of credit."

Did we drop cash out of helicopters? Almost. It turns out that the Princeton professor who advocated this strategy (not literally) a decade ago for Japan was none other than Ben Bernanke (earning him the nickname "Helicopter Ben" in some quarters).

Beginning with the first glimmers of trouble in 2007, the Fed used all its conventional tools aggressively, cutting the target federal funds rate seven times between September 2007 and April 2008. When that began to feel like pushing on a wet noodle, the Fed started to do things that one recent economic paper described as "not in the current textbook descriptions of monetary policy." The Fed is America's "lender of last resort," making it responsible for the smooth functioning of the financial system, particularly when that system is at risk of seizing up for lack of credit and liquidity. In that capacity, the Fed is vested with awesome powers. Article 13(3) of the Federal Reserve Act gives the Fed authority to make loans "to any individual, partnership, or corporation provided that the borrower is unable to obtain credit from a banking institution." Ben Bernanke can create $500 and loan it to your grandmother to fix the roof, if the local bank has said no and he decides that it might do some good for the rest of us.

Bernanke and crew pulled out the monetary policy equivalent of duct tape. The Federal Reserve urged commercial banks to borrow directly from the Fed via the discount window, gave banks the ability to borrow anonymously (so that it would not send signals of weakness to the market), and offered longer term loans. The Fed also loaned funds directly to an investment bank (Bear Stearns) for the first time ever; when Bear Stearns ultimately faced insolvency, the Fed loaned JPMorgan Chase $30 billion to take over Bear Stearns, sparing the market from the chaos that later followed the Lehman bankruptcy. In cases where institutions already had access to Fed capital, the rules for collateral were changed so that the borrowers could pledge illiquid assets like mortgage-backed securities—meaning that when grandma asked for her $500 loan, she could pledge all that stuff in the attic as collateral, even if it was not obvious who would want to buy it or at what price. That gets money to your grandma to fix the roof, which was the point of all this.[7]

Monetary policy is tricky business. Done right, it facilitates economic growth and cushions the economy from shocks that might otherwise wreak havoc. Done wrong, it can cause pain and misery. Is it possible that all the recent unconventional actions at the Federal Reserve have merely set the stage for another set of problems? Absolutely. It's more likely, at least based on evidence so far, that the Fed averted a more serious crisis and spared a great deal of human suffering as a result. President Barack Obama appointed Federal Reserve chairman Ben Bernanke to a second four-year term beginning in 2010. At the ceremony, the president said, "As an expert on the causes of the Great Depression, I'm sure Ben never imagined that he would be part of a team responsible for preventing another. But because of his background, his temperament, his courage, and his creativity, that's exactly what he has helped to achieve."[8] That's high praise. For now, it seems largely accurate.

CHAPTER 11

International Economics:

How did a nice country like Iceland go bust?

n 1992, George Soros made nearly $1 billion in a single day for the investment funds he managed. Most people need several weeks to make a billion dollars, or even a month. Soros made his billion on a single day in October by making a huge bet on the future value of the British pound relative to other currencies. He was right, making him arguably the most famous "currency speculator" ever.

How did he do it? In 1992, Britain was part of the European Exchange Rate Mechanism, or ERM. This agreement was designed to manage large fluctuations in the exchange rates between European nations. Firms found it more difficult to do business across the continent when they could not predict what the future exchange rates would likely be among Europe's multiple currencies. (A single currency, the euro, would come roughly a decade later.) The ERM created targets for the exchange rates among the participating countries. Each government was obligated to pursue policies that kept its currency trading on international currency markets within a narrow band around this target. For example, the British pound was pegged to 2.95 German marks and could not fall below a floor of 2.778 marks.

Britain was in the midst of a recession, and its currency was falling in value as international investors sold the pound and looked for more profitable opportunities elsewhere in the world. Currencies are no different than any other good; the exchange rate, or the "price" of one currency relative to another, is determined by supply relative to demand. As the demand for pounds fell, so did the value of the pound on currency markets. The British government vowed that it would "defend the pound" to keep it from falling below its designated value in the ERM. Soros didn't believe it—and that was what motivated his big bet.

The British government had two tools for propping up the value of the pound in the face of market pressure pushing it down: (1) The government could use its reserves of other foreign currencies to buy pounds—directly boosting demand for the currency; or (2) the government could use monetary policy to raise real interest rates, which, all else equal, makes British bonds (and the pounds necessary to buy them) more lucrative to global investors and attracts capital (or keeps it from leaving).

But the Brits had problems. The government had already spent huge sums of money buying pounds; the Bank of England (the British central bank) risked squandering additional foreign currency reserves to no better effect. Raising interest rates was not an attractive option for the government either. The British economy was in bad shape; raising interest rates during a recession slows the economy even further, which makes for bad economics and even worse politics. *Forbes* explained in a postmortem of the Soros strategy, "As Britain and Italy [with similar problems] struggled to make their currencies attractive, they were forced to maintain high interest rates to attract foreign investment dollars. But this crimped their ability to stimulate their sagging economies."[1]

Nonetheless, Prime Minister John Major declared emphatically that his "over-riding objective" was to defend the pound's targeted value in the ERM, even as that task seemed ever more difficult. Soros called the government's bluff. He bet that the Brits would eventually give up trying to defend the pound, at which point its value would fall sharply. The mechanics of his billion-dollar day are complex,* but the essence is straightforward: Soros bet heavily that the value of the pound would fall, and he was right.[2] On September 16, 1992—"Black Wednesday"—Britain withdrew from the ERM and the pound immediately lost more than 10 percent of its value. The pound's loss was Soros's gain—big time.

International economics shouldn't be any different than economics within countries. National borders are political demarcations, not economic ones. Transactions across national borders must still make all parties better off, or else we wouldn't do them. You buy a Toyota because you think it is a good car at a good price; Toyota sells it to you because they can make a profit. Capital flows across international borders for the same reason it flows anywhere else: Investors are seeking the highest possible return (for any given level of risk). Individuals, firms, and governments borrow funds from abroad because it is the

---

* Soros borrowed a huge sum in British pounds and immediately traded them for stronger currencies, such as the German deutsche mark. When the Brits eventually dropped out of the ERM and devalued the pound, he swapped his currency holdings back for more pounds than he had originally borrowed. He paid back his loans and kept the difference. Numbers make this all more intuitive. Suppose Soros borrowed 10 billion pounds and swapped them immediately for 10 billion deutsche marks. (The exchange rates and amounts are contrived to make the numbers easier.) When the pound was devalued, its value fell by more than 10 percent, so that 10 billion deutsche marks subsequently bought 11 billion pounds. Soros swapped his 10 billion deutsche marks for 11 billion pounds. He paid back his 10-billion-pound loan and kept the tidy balance for himself (or, more accurately, for his investment funds). Soros supplemented his currency gains with ancillary bets related to how the devaluation would affect European stocks and bonds.

cheapest way to "rent" capital that is necessary to make important investments or to pay the bills.

Everything I've just described could be Illinois and Indiana, rather than China and the United States. However, international transactions have an added layer of complexity. Different countries have different currencies; they also have different institutions for creating and managing those currencies. The Fed can create American dollars; it can't do much with Mexican pesos. You buy your Toyota in dollars. Toyota must pay its Japanese workers and executives in yen. And that is where things begin to get interesting.

The American dollar is just a piece of paper. It is not backed by gold, or rice, or tennis balls, or anything else with intrinsic value. The Japanese yen is exactly the same. So are the euro, the peso, the rupee, and every other modern currency. When individuals and firms begin trading across national borders, currencies must be exchanged at some rate. If the American dollar is just a piece of paper, and the Japanese yen is just a piece of paper, then how much American paper should we swap for Japanese paper?

The rate at which one currency can be exchanged for another is the exchange rate. We have a logical starting point for evaluating the relative value of different currencies. A Japanese yen has value because it can be used to purchase things; a dollar has value for the same reason. So, in theory, we ought to be willing to exchange $1 for however many yen or pesos or rubles would purchase roughly the same amount of stuff in the relevant country. If a bundle of everyday goods costs $25 in the United States, and a comparable bundle of goods costs 750 rubles in Russia, then we would expect $25 to be worth roughly 750 rubles (and $1 should be worth roughly 30 rubles). This is the theory of purchasing power parity, or PPP.

By the same logic, if the value of the ruble is losing 10 percent of its purchasing power within Russia every year while the U.S. dollar is holding its value, we would expect the ruble to lose value relative to the U.S. dollar (or depreciate) at the same rate. This isn't advanced math; if one currency buys less stuff than it used to, then anyone trading for that currency is going to demand more of it to compensate for the diminished purchasing power.*

I learned this lesson once—the hard way. I arrived in Guangzhou, China, in the spring of 1989 by train from Hong Kong. At the time, the Chinese government demanded that tourists exchange dollars for renminbi at ridiculous "official" rates that had no connection to the relative purchasing powers of the two currencies. For a better deal, backpackers typically exchanged money on the black market. I had studied my guide book, so when I arrived at the station in Guangzhou I knew roughly what the black market rate for dollars ought to be, subject to the usual bargaining. I found a currency trader right away and made an opening hardball offer—which the trader accepted immediately. He didn't even quibble, let alone bargain.

It turned out that my guide book was old; the Chinese currency had been steadily losing value ever since publication. I had swapped my $100 for the Chinese equivalent of about $13.50.

Purchasing power parity is a helpful concept. It is the tool used

---

* Economists make a distinction between the nominal exchange rate, which is the official rate at which one currency can be exchanged for another (the numbers posted on the board at the currency exchange), and the real exchange rate, which takes inflation into account in both countries and is therefore a better indicator of changes in purchasing power of one currency relative to another. For example, assume that the U.S. dollar can be exchanged at your local bank for 10 pesos. Further assume that (1) inflation is zero in the United States and 10 percent annually in Mexico; and (2) a year later your local bank will exchange $1 for 11 pesos. In nominal terms, the U.S. dollar has appreciated 10 percent relative to the peso (each dollar buys 10 percent more pesos). But the real exchange rate hasn't changed at all. You will get 10 percent more pesos at the currency exchange window than you did last year, but because of inflation over the course of the year, each peso now buys 10 percent less than it used to. As a result, the total purchasing power of the pesos that you get from the bank teller this year for your $100 is exactly the same as the purchasing power of the (fewer) pesos you got for your $100 last year. Any reference to exchange rates in the balance of this chapter refers to real exchange rates.

by official agencies to make comparisons across countries. For example, when the CIA or the United Nations gathers data on per capita income in other countries and converts that figure into dollars, they often use PPP, as it presents the most accurate snapshot of a nation's standard of living. If someone earns 10,000 Jordanian dinars a year, how many dollars would a person need in the United States to achieve a comparable standard of living?

In the long run, basic economic logic suggests that exchange rates should roughly align with purchasing power parity. If $100 can be exchanged for enough pesos to buy significantly more stuff in Mexico, who would want the $100? Many of us would trade our dollars for pesos so that we could buy extra goods and services in Mexico and live better. (Or, more likely, clever entrepreneurs would take advantage of the exchange rate to buy cheap goods in Mexico and import them to the United States at a profit.) In either case, the demand for pesos would increase relative to dollars and so would their "price"—which is the exchange rate. (The prices of Mexican goods might rise, too.) In theory, rational people would continue to sell dollars for pesos until there was no longer any economic advantage in doing so; at that point, $100 in the United States would buy roughly the same goods and services as $100 worth of pesos in Mexico—which is also the point at which the exchange rate would reach purchasing power parity.

Here is the strange thing: Official exchange rates—the rate at which you can actually trade one currency for another—deviate widely and for long stretches from what PPP would predict. If purchasing power parity makes economic sense, why is it often a poor predictor of exchange rates in practice? The answer lies in the crucial distinction between goods and services that are tradable, meaning that they can be traded internationally, and those that are not tradable, which are (logically enough) called nontradable. Televisions and cars are tradable goods; haircuts and child care are not.

In that light, let's revisit our dollar-peso example. Suppose that at the official peso-dollar exchange rate, a Sony television costs half as much in Tijuana as it does in San Diego. A clever entrepreneur can swap dollars for pesos, buy cheap Sony televisions in Mexico, and then sell them for a profit back in the United States. If he did this on a big enough scale, the value of the peso would climb (and probably the price of televisions in Mexico), moving the official exchange rate in the direction that PPP predicts. *Our clever entrepreneur would have a hard time doing the same thing with haircuts.* Or trash removal. Or babysitting. Or rental housing. In a modern economy, more than three-quarters of goods and services are nontradable.

A typical basket of goods—the source of comparison for purchasing power parity—contains both tradable and nontradable goods. If the official exchange rate makes a nontradable good or service particularly cheap in some country (e.g., you can buy a meal in Mumbai for $5 that would cost $50 in Manhattan), there is nothing an entrepreneur can do to exploit this price difference—so it will persist.

Using the same Mumbai meal example, you should recognize why PPP is the most accurate mechanism for comparing incomes across countries. At official exchange rates, a Mumbai salary may look very low when converted to dollars, but because many nontradable goods and services are much less expensive in Mumbai than in the United States, a seemingly low salary may buy a much higher standard of living than the official exchange rate would suggest.

Currencies that buy more than PPP would predict are said to be "overvalued"; currencies that buy less are "undervalued." *The Economist* created a tongue-in-cheek tool called the Big Mac Index for evaluating official exchange rates relative to what PPP would predict. The McDonald's Big Mac is sold around the world. It contains some tradable components (beef and the condiments) and lots of nontradables (local labor, rent, taxes, etc.). *The Economist* explains, "In the long run, countries' exchange rates should move towards rates that would equalize the prices of an identical basket of goods and services. Our basket is a McDonald's Big Mac, produced in 120 countries. The Big Mac PPP is the exchange rate that would leave hamburgers costing the same in America as elsewhere. Comparing these with actual rates signals if a currency is under- or overvalued."[3]

In July 2009, a Big Mac cost an average of $3.57 in the United States and 12.5 renminbi in China, suggesting that $3.57 should be worth roughly 12.5 renminbi (and $1 worth 3.5 renminbi). But that was not even close to the official exchange rate. At the bank, $1 bought 6.83 renminbi—making the renminbi massively undervalued relative to what "burgernomics" would predict. (Conversely, the dollar is overvalued by the same measure.) This is not a freak occurrence; the Chinese government has promoted economic policies that rely heavily on a "cheap" currency. Of late, the value of the renminbi relative to the dollar has been a significant source of tension between the United States and China—a topic we'll come back to later in this chapter.

Exchange rates can deviate quite sharply from what PPP would predict. That invites two additional questions: Why? And so what?

Let's deal with the second question first. Imagine checking into your favorite hotel in Paris, only to discover that the rooms are nearly twice as expensive as they were when you last visited. When you protest to the manager, he replies that the room rates have not changed in several years. And he's telling the truth. What has changed is the exchange rate between the euro and the dollar. The dollar has "weakened" or "depreciated" against the euro, meaning that each of your dollars buys fewer euros than it did the last time you were in France. (The euro, on the other hand, has "appreciated.") To you, that makes the hotel more expensive. To someone visiting Paris from elsewhere in France, the hotel is the same price as it has always been. A change in the exchange rate makes foreign goods cheaper or more expensive, depending on the direction of the change.

That is the crucial point here. If the U.S. dollar is weak, meaning that it can be exchanged for fewer yen or euros than normal, then foreign goods become more expensive. What is true for the Paris hotel is also true for Gucci handbags and Toyota trucks. The price in euros or yen hasn't changed, but that price costs Americans more dollars, which is what they care about.

At the same time, a weak dollar makes American goods less expensive for the rest of the world. Suppose Ford decides to price the Taurus at $25,000 in the United States and at the local currency equivalent (at official exchange rates) in foreign markets. If the euro has grown stronger relative to the dollar, meaning that every euro buys more dollars than it used to, then the Taurus becomes cheaper for Parisian car buyers—but Ford still brings home $25,000. It's the best of all worlds for American exporters: cheaper prices but not lower profits!

The good news for Ford does not end there. A weak dollar makes imports more expensive for Americans. A car priced at 25,000 euros used to cost $25,000 in the United States; now it costs $31,000—not because the price of the car has gone up, but because the value of the dollar has fallen. In Toledo, the sticker price jumps on every Toyota and Mercedes, making Fords cheaper by comparison. Or Toyota and Mercedes can hold their prices steady in dollars (avoiding the hassle of restickering every car on the lot) but take fewer yen and euros back to Japan and Germany. Either way, Ford gets a competitive boost.

In general, a weak currency is good for exporters and punishing for importers. In 1992, when the U.S. dollar was relatively weak, a *New York Times* story began, "The declining dollar has turned the world's wealthiest economy into the Filene's basement of industrial countries."[4] A strong dollar has the opposite effect. In 2001, when the dollar was strong by historical standards, a *Wall Street Journal* headline proclaimed, "G.M. Official Says Dollar Is Too Strong for U.S. Companies." When the Japanese yen appreciates against the dollar by a single yen, a seemingly tiny amount given that the current exchange rate is one dollar to 90 yen, Toyota's annual operating earnings fall by $450 million.[5]

There is nothing inherently good or bad about a "strong" or "weak" currency relative to what PPP would predict. An undervalued currency promotes exports (and therefore the industries that produce them). At the same time, a cheap currency raises the costs of imports, which is bad for consumers. (Ironically, a weak currency can also harm exporters by making any imported inputs more expensive.) A government that deliberately keeps its currency undervalued is essentially taxing consumers of imports and subsidizing producers of exports. An overvalued currency does the opposite—making imports artificially cheap and exports less competitive with the rest of the world. Currency manipulation is like any other kind of government intervention: It may serve some constructive economic purpose—or it may divert an economy's resources from their most efficient use. Would you support a tax that collected a significant fee on every imported good you bought and used the revenue to mail checks to firms that produce exports?

How do governments affect the strength of their currencies? At bottom, currency markets are like any other market: The exchange rate is the function of the demand for some currency relative to the supply. The most important factors affecting the relative demand for currencies are global economic forces. A country with a booming economy will often have a currency that is appreciating. Strong growth presents investment opportunities that attract capital from the rest of the world. To make these local investments (e.g., to build a manufacturing plant in Costa Rica or buy Russian stocks), foreign investors must buy the local currency first. The opposite happens when an economy is flagging. Investors take their capital somewhere else, selling the local currency on their way out.

All else equal, great demand for a country's exports will cause its currency to appreciate. When global oil prices spike, for example, the Middle East oil producers accumulate huge quantities of dollars. (International oil sales are denominated in dollars.) When these profits are repatriated to local currency, say back to Saudi Arabia, they cause the Saudi riyal to appreciate relative to the dollar.

Higher interest rates, which can be affected in the short run by the Federal Reserve in the United States or the equivalent central bank in other countries, make a currency more valuable. All else equal, higher interest rates provide investors with a greater return on capital, which draws funds into a country. Suppose a British pound can be exchanged for a $1.50 and the real return on government bonds in both the United Kingdom and the United States is 3 percent. If the British government uses monetary policy to raise their short-term interest rates to 4 percent, American investors would be enticed to sell U.S. treasury bonds and buy British bonds. To do so, of course, they have to use the foreign exchange market to sell dollars and buy pounds. If nothing else changes in the global economy (an unlikely scenario), the increased demand for British pounds would cause the pound to appreciate relative to the dollar.

Of course, "all else equal" is a phrase that never actually applies to the global economy. Economists have an extremely poor record of predicting movements in exchange rates, in part because so many complex global phenomena are affecting the foreign exchange markets at once. For example, the U.S. economy was ground zero for the global recession that began in 2007. With the U.S. economy in such a poor state, one would have expected the dollar to depreciate relative to other major global currencies. In fact, U.S. treasury bonds are a safe place to park capital during economic turmoil. So as the financial crisis unfolded, investors from around the world "fled to safety" in U.S. treasuries, causing the U.S. dollar to appreciate despite the floundering American economy.

Countries can also enter the foreign exchange market directly, buying or selling their currencies in an effort to change their relative value, as the British government tried to do while fighting off the 1992 devaluation. Given the enormous size of the foreign exchange market—with literally trillions of dollars in currencies changing hands every day—most governments don't have deep enough pockets to make much of a difference. As the British government and many others have learned, a currency intervention can feel like trying to warm up a cold bathtub with one spoonful of hot water at a time, particularly while speculators are doing the opposite. As the British government was buying pounds, Soros and others were selling them—effectively dumping cold water in the same tub.

We still haven't really answered the basic question at the beginning of the chapter: How many yen should a dollar be worth? Or rubles? Or krona? There are a lot of possible answers to that question, depending in large part on the exchange rate mechanism that a particular country adopts. An array of mechanisms can be used to value currencies against one another:

The gold standard. The simplest system to get your mind around is the gold standard. No modern industrialized country uses gold any longer (other than for overpriced commemorative coins), but in the decades following World War II the gold standard provided a straightforward mechanism for coordinating exchange rates. Countries pegged their currencies to a fixed quantity of gold and therefore, implicitly, to each other. It's like one of those grade-school math problems: If an ounce of gold is worth $35 in America and 350 francs in France, what is the exchange rate between the dollar and the franc?

One advantage of the gold standard is that it provides predictable exchange ranges. It also protects against inflation; a government cannot print new money unless it has sufficient gold reserves to back the new currency. Under this system, the paper in your wallet *does* have intrinsic value; you can take your $35 and demand an ounce of gold instead. The "gold standard" has a nice ring to it; however, the system made for catastrophic monetary policy during the Great Depression and can seriously impair monetary policy even during normal circumstances. When a currency backed by gold comes under pressure (e.g., because of a weakening economy), foreigners start to demand gold instead of paper. In order to defend the nation's gold reserves, the central bank must raise interest rates—even though a weakening economy needs the opposite. Economist Paul Krugman, who earned a Nobel Prize in 2008 for his work on international trade, explained recently, "In the early 1930s this mentality led governments to raise interest rates and slash spending, despite mass unemployment, in an attempt to defend their gold reserves. And even when countries went off gold, the prevailing mentality made them reluctant to cut rates and create jobs."[6] If the United States had been on the gold standard in 2007, the Fed would have been largely powerless to ward off the crisis. Under the gold standard, a central bank can always devalue the currency (e.g., declare that an ounce of gold buys more dollars than it used to), but that essentially defeats the purpose of having a gold standard in the first place.

In 1933, Franklin Roosevelt ended the right of individual Americans to exchange cash for gold, but nations retained that right when making international settlements. In 1971, Richard Nixon ended that, too. Inflation in the United States was making the dollar less desirable; given a choice between $35 and an ounce of gold, foreign governments were increasingly demanding the gold. After a weekend of deliberation at Camp David, Nixon unilaterally "closed the gold window." Foreign governments could redeem gold for dollars on Friday—but not on Monday. Since then, the United States (and all other industrialized nations) have operated with "fiat money," which is a fancy way of saying that those dollars are just paper.

Floating exchange rates. The gold standard fixes currencies against one another; floating rates allow them to fluctuate as economic conditions dictate, even minute by minute. Most developed economies have floating exchange rates; currencies are traded on foreign exchange markets, just like a stock exchange or eBay. At any given time, the exchange rate between the dollar and yen reflects the price at which parties are willing to voluntarily trade one for the other—just like the market price of anything else. When Toyota makes loads of dollars selling cars in the United States, they trade them for yen with some party that is looking to do the opposite. (Or Toyota can use the dollars to pay American workers, make investments inside the United States, or buy American inputs.)

With floating exchange rates, governments have no obligation to maintain a certain value of their currency, as they do under the gold standard. The primary drawback of this system is that currency fluctuations create an added layer of uncertainty for firms doing international business. Ford may make huge profits in Europe only to lose money in the foreign exchange markets when it tries to bring the euros back home. So far, exchange rate volatility has proven to be a drawback of floating rates, though not a fatal flaw. International companies can use the financial markets to hedge their currency risk. For example, an American firm doing business in Europe can enter into a futures contract that locks in some euro-dollar exchange rate at a specified future date—just as Southwest Airlines might lock in future fuel prices or Starbucks might use the futures market to protect against an unexpected surge in the price of coffee beans.

Fixed exchange rates (or currency bands). Fixed or "pegged" exchange rates are a lot like the gold standard, except that there is no gold. (This may seem like a problem—and it often is.) Countries pledge to maintain their exchange rates at some predetermined rate with a group of other countries—such as the nations of Europe. The relevant currencies trade freely on markets, but each participating government agrees to implement policies to keep its currency trading within the predetermined range. The European Exchange Rate Mechanism described at the beginning of this chapter was such a system.

The primary problem with a "peg" is that countries can't credibly commit to defending their currencies. When a currency begins to look weak, as the pound did, then speculators pounce, hoping to make millions (or billions) if the currency is devalued. Of course, when speculators (and others concerned about devaluation) aggressively sell the local currency—as Soros did—then devaluation becomes all the more likely.

Borrowing someone else's strong reputation. At the end of 1990, inflation in Argentina was more than 1,000 percent a year, to no one's great surprise given the country's history of hyperinflation. Is that a currency you want to own? Argentina had long been the world's inflation bad boy—the monetary equivalent of someone who stands you up for three straight dates and then tries to tell you that the fourth time will be different. It won't be, and everyone knows it. So when Argentina finally got serious about fighting inflation, the central bank had to do something radical. Basically, it hired the United States as a chaperon. In 1991, Argentina declared that it was relinquishing control over its own monetary policy. No more printing money. Instead, the government created a currency board with strict rules to ensure that henceforth every Argentine peso would be worth one U.S. dollar. To make that possible (and credible to the world), the currency board would guarantee that every peso in circulation would be backed by one U.S. dollar held in reserve. Thus, the currency board would be allowed to issue new pesos only if it had new dollars in its vaults to back them up. Moreover, every Argentine peso would be convertible on demand for a U.S. dollar. In effect, Argentina created a gold standard with the U.S. dollar substituting for the gold.

It worked for a while. Inflation plummeted to double digits and then to single digits. Alas, there was a huge cost. Remember all those wonderful things the Fed chairman can do to fine-tune the economy? The Argentine government could not do any of them; it had abdicated control over the money supply in the name of fighting inflation. Nor did Argentina have any independent control over its exchange rate; the peso was fixed against the dollar. If the dollar was strong, the peso was strong. If the dollar was weak, the peso was weak.

This lack of control over the money supply and exchange rate ultimately took a steep toll. Beginning in the late 1990s, the Argentine economy slipped into a deep recession; authorities did not have the usual tools to fight it. To make matters worse, the U.S. dollar was strong because of America's economic boom, making the Argentine peso strong. That punished Argentine exporters and did further harm to the economy. In contrast, Brazil's currency, the real, fell more than

50 percent between 1999 and the end of 2001. To the rest of the world, Brazil had thrown a giant half-price sale and Argentina could do nothing but stand by and watch. As the Argentine economy limped along, economists debated the wisdom of the currency board. The proponents argued that it was an important source of macroeconomic stability; the skeptics said that it would cause more harm than good. In 1995, Maurice Obstfeld and Kenneth Rogoff, economists at UC Berkeley and Princeton, respectively, had published a paper warning that most attempts to maintain a fixed exchange rate, such as the Argentine currency board, were likely to end in failure.[7]

Time proved the skeptics right. In December 2001, the long-suffering Argentine economy unraveled completely. Street protests turned violent, the president resigned, and the government announced that it could no longer pay its debts, creating the largest sovereign default in history. (Ironically, Ken Rogoff had by then made his way from Princeton University to the International Monetary Fund, where, as chief economist, he had to deal with the economic wreckage that he had warned against years earlier.) The Argentine government scrapped its currency board and ended the guaranteed one-for-one exchange between the peso and the dollar. The peso immediately plunged some 30 percent in value relative to the dollar.

Funny money. Some currencies have no international value at all. In 1986, I crossed through the Berlin Wall into East Berlin, behind the Iron Curtain. When we crossed into East Germany at "Checkpoint Charlie," we were required to change a certain amount of "hard currency" (dollars or West German marks) for a certain amount of East German currency. How was that exchange rate determined? Make believe. The East German mark was a "soft" currency, meaning that it did not trade anywhere outside of the communist world and therefore had no purchasing power anywhere else. The exchange rate was more or less arbitrary, though I'm fairly certain that the purchasing power of what we got was worth less than the purchasing power of what we gave up. In fact, we weren't even allowed to take our East German money out of the country when we left. Instead, the East German border guards took what we had left and "put it on account" (that's really what they said) for our next visit. Somewhere in the now unified Germany, there is an account with my name on it that contains a small amount of worthless East German currency. So I've got that going for me.

Soft currencies were a more serious problem for the few U.S. companies doing business in communist countries with soft currencies. In 1974, Pepsi struck a deal to sell its products in the Soviet Union. Communists drink cola, too. But what the heck was Pepsi going to do with millions of rubles? Instead, Pepsi and the Soviet government opted for old-fashioned barter. Pepsi swapped its soft-drink syrup to the Soviet government in exchange for Stolichnaya vodka, which did have real value in the West.[8]

That all sounds so orderly, except for the riots in the streets in Argentina. In fact, the Argentina-type currency meltdown is surprisingly frequent. Let's revisit a line from a few pages ago: "Investors take their capital somewhere else, selling the local currency on their way out." Only now, let's dress that statement up to more closely approximate reality: "Investors panic, weeping and screaming as they sell assets and ditch the local currency—as much as possible, for whatever price is possible—in hopes of getting out the door before the market completely collapses!"

Argentina, Mexico, Russia, Turkey, South Korea, Thailand, and the country for which we've named the chapter, Iceland. What do they have in common? Not geography. Not culture. Certainly not climate. They are all countries that have suffered currency crises. No two crises are exactly the same. They do have a pattern, usually a play in three acts: (1) A country attracts significant foreign capital. (2) Something bad happens: a government borrows too heavily and stands at risk of default; a property bubble bursts; a country with a pegged exchange rate faces devaluation; a banking system is exposed as rife with bad loans—or some combination of all of these things. (3)

Foreign investors try to move their capital somewhere else—preferably before everyone else does. Asset prices fall (as foreigners sell) and the currency plunges. Both of these things make the underlying economic problems worse, which causes asset prices and the currency to plunge further. The country pleads with the rest of the world to help stop the downward economic spiral.

To get a sense of how this all plays out, let's look at the most recent victim: Iceland. Iceland is not a poor, developing country. In fact, Iceland was at the top of the UN Human Development Index rankings in 2008. Here are Iceland's three acts, as best I can figure them out:

Act I. In the first decade of the twenty-first century, Iceland's currency, the Icelandic krona, was extremely strong, and real interest rates were high by global standards. Iceland's relatively unregulated banks were attracting capital from all over the world as investors sought high real returns. At the peak, Iceland's banks had assets 10 times the size of the country's entire GDP. The banks were using this huge pool of capital to make the kinds of investments that seemed very smart in 2006. Meanwhile, the high domestic interest rates induced Icelanders to borrow in other currencies, even for relatively small purchases. An economist at the University of Iceland told CNN Money, "When you bought a car, you'd be asked, 'How do you want the financing? Half in yen and half in euros?'"[9]

Act II. The global financial crisis was bad for the world and disastrous for Iceland. Iceland's banks suffered huge losses from bad investments and nonperforming loans. By the fall of 2008, the country's three major banks were defunct; the central bank, which had taken control of the largest private banks, was technically in default as well. The *New York Times* reported a story in November 2008 that began, "People go bankrupt all the time. Companies do, too. But countries?"

As the krona plummeted, the cost of all those consumer loans in foreign currencies skyrocketed. Think about it: If you borrow in euros, and the krona loses half its value relative to the euro, the monthly payment in krona on your loan *doubles*. Of course, many of the assets that Icelanders had purchased with those loans, such as homes and property, were simultaneously plummeting in value.

Act III. The Icelandic krona lost half its value. The stock market fell by 90 percent; GDP fell 10 percent; unemployment hit a forty-year high. People were angry—just like in Argentina. One woman told *The Economist*, "If I met a banker, I'd kick his ass so hard my shoes would be stuck inside." And she was a preschool teacher.[10]

Even the Big Mac Index had a sad postscript in Iceland. In October 2009, Iceland's three McDonald's restaurants closed after becoming victims of the financial crisis. McDonald's required that its Iceland franchises buy their food inputs and packaging from Germany. Because the krona had plummeted in value relative to the euro and because the government had imposed high import tariffs, the cost of these inputs from Germany roughly doubled. The owner of the Iceland franchises said that to make a "decent profit," a Big Mac would have had to sell for the equivalent of more than six dollars—higher than anywhere else in the world and an untenable price for a country in the midst of a deep recession. McDonald's closed its doors in Iceland instead.[11]

The economic wreckage that results time after time as investors flee a country suggests an obvious fix: Maybe it should be harder to flee. Some countries have experimented with capital controls, which place various kinds of limits on the free flow of capital. Like many obvious fixes, this one has less obvious problems. If foreign investors can't leave a country with their capital, they are less likely to show up in the first place. It's a bit like trying to improve revenues at a department store by banning all returns. A group of economists studied fifty-two poor countries between 1980 and 2001 to examine the relationship between financial liberalization (making it easier to move capital in and out of the country) and economic performance. There is a trade-off: Countries that impose some kind of capital controls also grow more slowly. *The Economist* summarized the study's findings: "An occasional crisis may be a price worth paying for faster growth."[12]

Okay, what if we all had the same currency? Wouldn't that help avoid currency-related headaches? After all, Iowa has never had a financial meltdown because Illinois investors took their capital back across the Mississippi River. There are benefits to broadening a currency zone; this was the logic of the euro, which replaced most of the individual currencies in Europe. A single currency across Europe (and in the fifty U.S. states) reduces transaction costs and promotes price transparency (meaning that it's easier to spot and exploit price discrepancies when goods are all priced in the same currency). But here, too, there is a trade-off. Remember, monetary policy is the primary tool that any government possesses to control the "speed" of its economy. A central bank raises or lowers interest rates by making its currency more or less scarce. Countries that share a currency with other nations, such as the European countries that adopted the euro, must give up control over their own monetary policy. The European Central Bank now controls monetary policy for the whole euro zone. (Obviously Louisiana and California do not have their own monetary policy either.) This can be a problem if one part of the currency zone is in an economic slump and would benefit from lower interest rates while another region at the same time is growing quickly and must raise rates to ward off inflation.

We don't really care about currencies per se; what we really care about is the underlying flow of goods and services. These trades across international borders are what make us better off; currencies are merely a tool for facilitating mutually beneficial transactions. In the long run, we would expect the value of the goods and services that we send to other countries to be more or less equal to the value of what they send to us. If not, someone is getting a really bad deal. Even little kids trading snacks in the lunchroom recognize that what you give up should be worth what you get back.

Except for the United States. We're the guys in the lunchroom giving up liverwurst sandwiches and getting a turkey sandwich, plus chips, cookies, juice, and a peanut-free snack. The United States has been running large and persistent current account deficits with the rest of the world, meaning that year after year we are getting more goods and services from the rest of the world than we sell to them. (The current account measures income earned abroad from trade in goods and services, plus some other sources of foreign income, such as dividends and interest on overseas investments as well as remittances sent home by Americans working abroad.) How are we getting away with that? Might it be a problem in the long run? The answer to the second question is yes. The first question is more complicated.

As noted in Chapter 9, there is nothing inherently bad about a current account deficit, nor anything inherently good about a current account surplus; countries like Algeria and Equatorial Guinea were running current account surpluses in 2007, but that does not make them economic powerhouses. Still, there is an unavoidable economic reality lurking here: A country running a current account deficit is earning less income from the rest of the world than it is paying out. Consider a simple example: If we buy $100 million in cars from Japan and sell them $50 million in planes, then we've got a $50 million current account deficit. The Japanese are not sending us an extra $50 million in merchandise because we're friendly and good looking; they expect us to make up the difference. To do that, we have only a couple of options. One option is to sell our Japanese trading partners assets instead—stocks, bonds, real estate, and so on.

For example, we might sell Japanese firms $25 million in Manhattan real estate and $25 million of equity in American firms (stocks). Now the ledger makes sense. Americans get $100 million of goods and services from Japan; in exchange, we send over $50 million in goods (the planes), and another $50 million in assets. That's an even deal. It comes with a price, however; the assets that we're giving up (real estate and stocks) would have generated income for us in the future (rents and dividends). Now that income will go to our trading partner instead. We're buying cars now by giving up future income.

That's not our only choice. We can buy our merchandise on credit. We can ask some willing party in the global financial community to loan us $50 million. In that case, we "pay for" our $100 million in Japanese cars with $50 million in planes and $50 million in borrowed capital. That, too, has obvious future costs. We have to pay back the loans, with interest. Again, we are paying for current consumption by borrowing against the future—literally in this case.

Why is the United States running chronic current account deficits? It has virtually nothing to do with the quality of our goods and services or the competitiveness of our labor force, as conventional wisdom would have it. (To my earlier point, do you think Algeria and Equatorial Guinea are running current account surpluses because they are producing better stuff with more productive workers?) The United States is running chronic current account deficits because year after year we are consuming more than we produce. In other words, we are doing the opposite of saving (in which you produce more than you consume and set the extra aside). As a nation, we are literally doing what economists call "dissaving."

The connection between the current account balance and a nation's savings rate is crucial. Any country that is consuming more than it produces must by definition be running a current account deficit because (1) the stuff you are consuming beyond what you produce must come from somewhere else in the world; and (2) you can't trade goods and services for the extra stuff that you're getting from the rest of the world because you've consumed everything you have.

As usual, a farming analogy will help. Suppose Farmer America grows corn. He is a highly productive farmer, handsome and smart, who uses only the most modern farming techniques. (These details are irrelevant here, just as they are when describing whether a national economy runs a current account surplus or deficit.) There are only four broad things that Farmer America can do with what he grows: He can eat it (consumption); he can plant it for next year's crop (investment); he can send it to the government to pay for services (government spending); or he can trade it for other stuff (exports traded for imports). That's it. So let's imagine that Farmer America's year looks like the following:

He grows 100 bushels of corn. He eats 70. He sends 30 to the government. He needs 20 to plant next year. But if you do the math, you'll see that Farmer America is using 120 bushels a year but growing only 100. He must be a net borrower of corn—20 bushels in this case. That is the equivalent of a current account deficit, and it's just math—if he uses more corn than he grows, the rest has to come from somewhere else.

Farmer China works across the way. He grows only 65 bushels of corn, because he is new to farming and uses relatively primitive methods. Farmer China consumes 20 bushels, sends 10 to the government, and sets 15 aside to plant next year. Again, some quick math suggests that Farmer China is not using everything he grows. He has an extra 20 bushels. As convenience would have it, these bushels can be traded to Farmer America, who has come up short. Of course, Farmer America doesn't have any crops to trade, so he offers an IOU instead. Farmer China gives Farmer America the corn (an "export")—and loans him the money to buy it.

Let's jump from farm analogies to reality: So far, the United States owes China about a trillion dollars.

Normally these kinds of global imbalances have self-correcting mechanisms. The currency of a country with a large current account deficit will usually begin to depreciate. Assume that New Zealand is running a current account deficit. The rest of the world is steadily accumulating New Zealand dollars because they are selling more goods to New Zealand than they are buying from it; foreign firms will want to trade their accumulated New Zealand dollars for their home currency. On the foreign exchange market, the supply of New Zealand dollars for sale will exceed the demand for them, pushing the value of the New Zealand dollar down relative to the currencies of its trading partners. The falling New Zealand dollar helps to correct the trade imbalance by making New Zealand's exports more competitive and imports more expensive. For example, if the New Zealand dollar depreciates relative to the yen, then Toyotas become more expensive in New Zealand while New Zealand's farm products (kiwis?) look cheaper in Japan. Meanwhile, the same thing happens with other countries; New Zealand will begin to import less and export more, narrowing the current account deficit.

The current situation involving China and the United States is different. The two countries are arguably locked in an unhealthy symbiotic relationship that has the potential to come unglued at any time. China has created a very successful development strategy built upon "export-led growth," meaning that the bulk of job growth and prosperity has been generated by firms making products for export. Many of those exports come to the United States.

China's export-oriented development strategy depends on keeping the renminbi relatively cheap. To accomplish that, the Chinese government recycles accumulated dollars primarily into U.S. treasury bonds, which are loans to the U.S. federal government. Both parties get what they want (or need), at least in the short run. The Chinese government has used exports to generate jobs and growth. America has funded its dissavings with enormous loans from China. The situation really isn't much different than Farmer China and Farmer America: The United States gets loans from China to buy its exports.

In the long run, the situation poses serious risks for both parties. The United States has become a large debtor nation. Debtors are always vulnerable to the whims and demands of their creditors. America has a borrowing habit; China feeds it. James Fallows has noted, "Without China's billion dollars a day, the United States could not keep its economy stable or spare the dollar from collapse."[13] Worse, China could threaten to dump its huge hoard of dollar-denominated assets. That would be a ruinous thing to do. As Fallows points out, "Their years of national savings are held in the same dollars that would be ruined; in a panic, they'd get only a small share out before the value fell." Still, that's an awfully powerful weapon to give a nation with which we often disagree.

The Chinese have it worse. Suppose America's debt burden grows beyond what U.S. taxpayers can (or are willing) to pay back. The U.S. government could default—simply refuse to honor its debts. That is highly unlikely, mostly because there is another irresponsible option that is more subtle: America can "inflate away" much of its debt to China (and other creditors) by printing money. If we recklessly print dollars, the currency will lose value—and so will our dollar-denominated debts. If inflation climbs to 20 percent, then the real value of what we have to pay back will fall by 20 percent. If inflation is 50 percent, then half of our debt to China effectively goes away. Is this a likely outcome? No. But if someone owed me a trillion dollars and also had the authority to print those dollars, I would spend a lot of time worrying about inflation.

This dysfunctional economic relationship will end. The crucial questions are when, why, and how. James Fallows has summarized where we stand now: "In effect, every person in the (rich) United States has over the past 10 years or so borrowed about $4,000 from someone in the (poor) People's Republic of China. Like so many imbalances in economics, this one can't go on indefinitely, and therefore won't. But the way it ends—suddenly versus gradually, for predictable reasons versus during a panic—will make an enormous difference to the U.S. and Chinese economies over the next few years, to say nothing of bystanders in Europe and elsewhere."[14]

Given the stakes involved, are any adults supervising all of this? Yes, but they are getting long in the tooth. In the waning days of World War II, representatives of the Allied nations gathered at the Mt. Washington Hotel in Bretton Woods, New Hampshire. (It's a delightful place in both summer and winter, if you are looking for a New England getaway.) Their mission was to create a stable financial infrastructure for the postwar world. They created two international institutions, or "the two sisters."

The institution at the center of the global fight against poverty is the Washington-based World Bank. (The first $250 million loan was to France in 1947 for postwar reconstruction.) The World Bank, which is owned by its 183 member countries, raises capital from its members and by borrowing in the capital markets. Those funds are loaned to developing nations for projects likely to promote economic development. The World Bank is at the center of many of the international development issues covered in Chapter 13.

If the World Bank is the world's welfare agency, then its sister organization, the International Monetary Fund (IMF), is the fire department responsible for dousing international financial crises. Iceland called the IMF. So did Argentina, Mexico, and all the others. The IMF was also conceived at Bretton Woods as a cooperative global institution. Members pay funds into the IMF; in exchange they can borrow in times of difficulty "on condition that they undertake economic reforms to eliminate these difficulties for their own good and that of the entire membership." No country is ever required to accept loans or advice from either the IMF or the World Bank. Both organizations derive power and influence from the carrots they wield.

Few institutions have attracted as much criticism as the World Bank and the IMF from such a broad swath of the political spectrum. *The Economist* once commented, "If the developing countries had a dollar for every proposal to change the 'international financial architecture,' the problem of third-world poverty would be solved."[15] Conservatives charge that the World Bank and the IMF are bureaucratic organizations that squander money on projects that have failed to lead nations out of poverty. They also argue that IMF bailouts make financial crises more likely in the first place; investors make imprudent international loans because they believe the IMF will come to the rescue when a country gets into trouble. In 2000, the Republican-led Congress convened a commission that recommended shrinking and overhauling both the World Bank and the International Monetary Fund.[16]

At the other end of the political spectrum, the antiglobalization coalition accuses the World Bank and IMF of acting as capitalist lackeys, forcing globalization on the developing world and leaving poor countries saddled with large debts in the process. The organizations' meetings have become an occasion for violent protest. When the two institutions held their fall meeting in Prague in 2000, the local Kentucky Fried Chicken and Pizza Hut both ordered replacement glass ahead of time.

As the global recession of 2007 unfolded, the United States criticized several European nations for not doing more to stimulate their economies. The specific criticism is debatable, but it makes a crucial point nonetheless. For the American economy to recover, the European economies needed to recover, too. And Japan. And China. And every other major economy. Nations are not competitors in the traditional sense of the word. After all, the Red Sox would never complain that the Yankees were not doing enough in the off-season to improve their team. Baseball is a zero-sum game. Only one team can win the World Series. International economics is the opposite. All countries can become richer over time, even as individual firms within those countries compete for profits and resources. Global GDP has grown steadily for centuries. We're richer collectively than we were in 1500. Who got poorer to make that possible? No one. The goal of global economic policy should be to make it easier for nations to cooperate with one another. The better we do it, the richer and more secure we will all be.

CHAPTER 12

Trade and Globalization:

The good news about Asian sweatshops

Imagine a spectacular invention: a machine that can convert corn into stereo equipment. When running at full capacity, this machine can turn fifty bushels of corn into a DVD player. Or with one switch of the dial, it will convert fifteen hundred bushels of soybeans into a four-door sedan. But this machine is even more versatile than that; when properly programmed, it can turn Windows software into the finest French wines. Or a Boeing 777 into enough fresh fruits and vegetables to feed a city for months. Indeed, the most amazing thing about this invention is that it can be set up anywhere in the world and programmed to turn whatever is grown or produced there into things that are usually much harder to come by.

Remarkably, it works for poor countries, too. Developing nations can put the things they manage to produce—commodities, cheap textiles, basic manufactured goods—into the machine and obtain goods that might otherwise be denied them: food, medicine, more advanced manufactured goods. Obviously, poor countries that have access to this machine would grow faster than countries that did not. We would expect that making this machine accessible to poor countries would be part of our strategy for lifting billions of people around the globe out of dire poverty.

Amazingly, this invention already exists. It is called trade.

If I write books for a living and use my income to buy a car made in Detroit, there is nothing particularly controversial about the transaction. It makes me better off, and it makes the car company better off, too. That's Chapter 1 kind of stuff. A modern economy is built on trade. We pay others to do or make things that we can't—everything from manufacturing a car to removing an appendix. As significant, we pay people to do all kinds of things that we could do but choose not to, usually because we have something better to do with our time. We pay others to brew coffee, make sandwiches, change the oil, clean the house, even walk the dog. Starbucks was not built on any great technological breakthrough. The company simply recognized that busy people will regularly pay several dollars for a cup of coffee rather than make their own or drink the lousy stuff that has been sitting around the office for six hours.

The easiest way to appreciate the gains from trade is to imagine life without it. You would wake up early in a small, drafty house that you had built yourself. You would put on clothes that you wove yourself after shearing the two sheep that graze in your backyard. Then you would pluck a few coffee beans off the scraggly tree that does not grow particularly well in Minneapolis—all the while hoping that your chicken had laid an egg overnight so that you might have something to eat for breakfast. The bottom line is that our standard of living is high because we are able to focus on the tasks that we do best and trade for everything else.

Why would these kinds of transactions be different if a product or service originated in Germany or India? They're not, really. We've crossed a political boundary, but the economics have not changed in any significant way. Individuals and firms do business with one another because it makes them both better off. That is true for a worker at a Nike factory in Vietnam, an autoworker in Detroit, a Frenchman eating a McDonald's hamburger in Bordeaux, or an American drinking a fine Burgundy in Chicago. Any rational discussion of trade must begin with the idea that people in Chad or Togo or South Korea are no different from you or me; they do things that they hope will make their lives better. Trade is one of those things. Paul Krugman has noted, "You could say—and I would—that globalization, driven not by human goodness but by the profit motive, has done far more good for far more people than all the foreign aid and soft loans ever provided by well-intentioned governments and international agencies." Then he adds wistfully, "But in saying this, I know from experience that I have guaranteed myself a barrage of hate mail."[1]

Such is the nature of "globalization," the term that has come to represent the increase in the international flow of goods and services. Americans and most others on the planet are more likely than ever to buy goods or services from another nation and to sell goods and services abroad in return. In the late 1980s, I was traveling through Asia while writing a series of articles for a daily newspaper in New Hampshire. In a relatively remote part of Bali, I was so surprised to find a Kentucky Fried Chicken that I wrote a story about it. "Colonel Sanders has succeeded in putting fast-food restaurants in the most remote areas of the world," I wrote. Had I realized that the idea of "cultural homogenization" would become a flashpoint for civil unrest a decade later, I might have become rich and famous as one of the earliest commentators on globalization. Instead, I merely noted, "In this relatively undisturbed environment, Kentucky Fried Chicken seems out of place."[2]

That KFC restaurant was more than the curiosity that I made it out to be. It was a tangible sign of what the statistics clearly show: The world is growing more economically interdependent. The world's exports as a share of global GDP have climbed from 8 percent in 1950 to around 25 percent today.[3] U.S. exports as a fraction of GDP grew from 5 percent to nearly 10 percent over the same stretch. It is worth noting that the bulk of the American economy still consists of goods and services produced for domestic consumption. At the same time, because of the sheer size of that economy, America is one of the world's largest exporters, behind only China and Germany in total value. The United States has much to gain from an open, international trading system. Then again, so does the rest of the world.

Having made that case in many different venues, now I get hate mail, too. Sometimes it's actually kind of clever. My favorite is an e-mail that came in response to a column arguing that a richer, rapidly growing India is good for the United States. After the usual introduction arguing that my job should be outsourced to some low wage country as soon as possible, the e-mail concluded, "Why don't you and Tom Friedman [author of the pro-globalization book *The World Is Flat*] get a room together? The world isn't flat, it's just your head!" Others tend to be less subtle, such as the e-mail with the subject line: YOU SUCK!!!!!!!!!!!!!!!!!!!!!!!!!! (Yes, that is the exact number of exclamation points.)

All those exclamation points notwithstanding, nearly all theory and evidence suggest that the benefits of international trade far exceed the costs. The topic is worthy of an entire book; some good ones wade into everything from the administrative structure of the WTO to the fate of sea turtles caught in shrimp nets. Yet the basic ideas underlying the costs and benefits of globalization are simple and straightforward. Indeed, no modern issue has elicited so much sloppy thinking. The case for international trade is built on the most basic ideas in economics.

Trade makes us richer. Trade has the distinction of being one of the most important ideas in economics and also one of the least intuitive. Abraham Lincoln was once advised to buy cheap iron rails from Britain to finish the transcontinental railroad. He replied, "It seems to me that if we buy the rails from England, then we've got the rails and they've got the money. But if we build the rails here, we've got our rails and we've got our money."[4] To understand the benefits of trade, we must find the fallacy in Mr. Lincoln's economics. Let me paraphrase his point and see if the logical flaw becomes clear: If I buy meat from the butcher, then I get the meat and he gets my money. But if I raise a cow in my backyard for three years and slaughter it myself, then I've got the meat and I've got my money. Why don't I keep a cow in my backyard? Because it would be a tremendous waste of time—time that I could have used to do something else far more productive. *We trade with others because it frees up time and resources to do things that we are better at.*

Saudi Arabia can produce oil more cheaply than the United States can. In turn, the United States can produce corn and soybeans more cheaply than Saudi Arabia. The corn-for-oil trade is an example of absolute advantage. When different countries are better at producing different things, they can both consume more by specializing at what they do best and then trading. People in Seattle should not grow their own rice. Instead, they should build airplanes (Boeing), write software (Microsoft), and sell books (Amazon)—and leave the rice-growing to farmers in Thailand or Indonesia. Meanwhile, those farmers can enjoy the benefits of Microsoft Word even though they do not have the technology or skills necessary to produce such software. Countries, like individuals, have different natural advantages. It does not make any more sense for Saudi Arabia to grow vegetables that it does for Tiger Woods to do his own auto repairs.

Okay, but what about countries that don't do anything particularly well? After all, countries are poor because they are not productive. What can Bangladesh offer to the United States? A great deal, it turns out, because of a concept called comparative advantage. Workers in Bangladesh do not have to be better than American workers at producing anything for there to be gains from trade. Rather, they provide goods to us so that we can spend our time specializing at whatever we do best. Here is an example. Many engineers live in Seattle. These men and women have doctorates in mechanical engineering and probably know more about manufacturing shoes and shirts than nearly anyone in Bangladesh. So why would we buy imported shirts and shoes made by poorly educated workers in Bangladesh? Because our Seattle engineers also know how to design and manufacture commercial airplanes. Indeed, that is what they do *best*, meaning that making jets creates the most value for their time. Importing shirts from Bangladesh frees them up to do this, and the world is better off for it.

Productivity is what makes us rich. Specialization is what makes us productive. Trade allows us to specialize. Our Seattle engineers are more productive at making planes than they are at sewing shirts; *and* the textile workers in Bangladesh are more productive at making shirts and shoes than they are at whatever else they might do (or else they would not be willing to work in a textile factory). I am writing at the moment. My wife is running a software consulting firm. A wonderful woman named Clementine is looking after our children. We do not employ Clemen because she is better than we are at raising our children (though there are moments when I believe that to be true). We employ Clemen because she enables us to work during the day at the jobs we do well, and that is the best possible arrangement for our family—not to mention for Clemen, for the readers of this book, and for my wife's clients.

Trade makes the most efficient use of the world's scarce resources.

Trade creates losers. If trade transports the benefits of competition to the far corners of the earth, then the wreckage of creative destruction cannot be far behind. Try explaining the benefits of globalization to shoe workers in Maine who have lost jobs because their plant moved to Vietnam. (Remember, I was the speechwriter for the governor of Maine; *I have tried to explain that.*) Trade, like technology, can destroy jobs, particularly low-skilled jobs. If a worker in Maine earns $14 an hour for something that can be done in Vietnam for $1 an hour, then he had better be 14 times as productive. If not, a profit-maximizing firm will choose Vietnam. Poor countries lose jobs, too. Industries that have been shielded from international competition for decades, and have therefore adopted all the bad habits that come from not having to compete, can be crushed by ruthlessly efficient competition from abroad. How would you like to have been the producer of Thumbs-Up Cola in India when Coca-Cola entered the market in 1994?

In the long run, trade facilitates growth and a growing economy can absorb displaced workers. Exports rise and consumers are made richer by cheap imports; both of those things create demand for new workers elsewhere in the economy. Trade-related job losses in America tend to be small relative to the economy's capacity to produce new jobs. One post-NAFTA study concluded that an average of 37,000 jobs per year were lost from 1990 to 1997 because of free trade with Mexico, while over the same period the economy was creating 200,000 jobs per month.[5] Still, "in the long run" is one of those heartless phrases—along with "transition costs" or "short-term displacement"—that overly minimize the human pain and disruption.

Maine shoe workers are expected to pay their mortgages *in the short run*. The sad reality is that they may not be better off in the long run, either. Displaced workers often have a skills problem. (Far more workers are made redundant by new technology than by trade.) If an industry is concentrated in a geographic area, as they often are, laid-off workers may watch their communities and way of life fade away.

The *New York Times* documented the case of Newton Falls, a community in upstate New York that grew up around a paper mill that opened in 1894. A century later, that mill closed, in part because of growing foreign competition. It's not pretty:

> Since October—after a last-ditch effort to save the mill fell through— Newton Falls has edged closer to becoming a case study of doleful rural sociology: a dying town, where the few people left give mournful testament to having their community wind down like an untended clock, ticking inexorably toward a final tock.[6]

Yes, the economic gains from trade outweigh the losses, but the winners rarely write checks to the losers. And the losers often lose badly. What consolation is it to a Maine shoe worker that trade with Vietnam will make the country as a whole richer? *He's poorer and probably always will be.* I've gotten those e-mails, too.

Indeed, we're back to the same discussion about capitalism that we had at the beginning of the book and again in Chapter 8. Markets create a new, more efficient order by destroying the old one. There is nothing pleasant about that, particularly for individuals and firms equipped for the old order. International trade makes markets bigger, more competitive, and more disruptive. Mark Twain anticipated the fundamental dilemma: "I'm all for progress; it's change I don't like."

Marvin Zonis, an international consultant and a University of Chicago Booth School of Business professor, has called the potential benefits of globalization "immense," particularly for the poorest of the poor. He has also noted, "Globalization disrupts everything, everywhere. It disrupts established patterns of life—between husband and wife, parents and children; between men and women, young and old; between boss and worker, governor and governed."[7] We can do things to soften those blows. We can retrain or even relocate workers. We can provide development assistance to communities harmed by the loss of a major industry. We can ensure that our schools teach the kinds of skills that make workers adaptable to whatever the economy may throw at them. In short, we can make sure that the winners do write checks (if indirectly) to the losers, sharing at least part of their gains. It's good politics and it's the right thing to do.

Kenneth Scheve, a Yale political science professor, and Matthew Slaughter, an economist at the Tuck School of Business at Dartmouth, wrote a provocative piece in *Foreign Affairs* arguing that the United States should adopt a "fundamentally more progressive federal tax system" (e.g., tax the rich more) as the best way of saving globalization from a protectionist backlash. What's interesting is that these guys are not left-wing radicals wearing tie-dye shirts; Matt Slaughter served in the George W. Bush administration. Rather, they argue that the huge benefits for the U.S. economy as a whole are being put at risk by the fact that too many Americans aren't seeing their paychecks get bigger. Scheve and Slaughter explain:

[U.S.] policy is becoming more protectionist because the public is becoming more protectionist, and the public is becoming more protectionist because incomes are stagnating or falling. The integration of the world economy has boosted productivity and wealth creation in the United States and much of the rest of the world. But within many countries, and certainly within the United States, the benefits of this integration have been unevenly distributed—and this fact is increasingly being recognized. Individuals are asking themselves, "Is globalization good for me?" and, in a growing number of cases, arriving at the conclusion that it is not.

The authors propose "a New Deal for globalization—one that links engagement with the world economy to a substantial redistribution of income." Remember, this isn't hippy talk. These are the capitalists who see angry workers with pitchforks loitering outside the gates of a very profitable factory, and they are making a very pragmatic calculation: Throw these people some food (and maybe some movie tickets and beer) before we all end up worse off.[8]

Protectionism saves jobs in the short run and slows economic growth in the long run. We can save the jobs of those Maine shoe workers. We can protect places like Newton Falls. We can make the steel mills in Gary, Indiana, profitable. We need only get rid of their foreign competition. We can erect trade barriers that stop the creative destruction at the border. So why don't we? The benefits of protectionism are obvious; we can point to the jobs that will be saved. Alas, the costs of protectionism are more subtle; it is difficult to point to jobs that are never created or higher incomes that are never earned.

To understand the costs of trade barriers, let's ponder a strange question: Would the United States be better off if we were to forbid trade across the Mississippi River? The logic of protectionism suggests that we would. For those of us on the east side of the Mississippi, new jobs would be created, since we would no longer have access to things like Boeing airplanes or Northern California wines. *But nearly every skilled worker east of the Mississippi is already working, and we are doing things that we are better at than making airplanes or wine.*

Meanwhile, workers in the West, who are now very good at making airplanes or wine, would have to quit their jobs in order to make the goods normally produced in the East. They would not be as good at those jobs as the people who are doing them now. Preventing trade across the Mississippi would turn the specialization clock backward. We would be denied superior products and forced to do jobs that we're not particularly good at. In short, we would be poorer because we would be collectively less productive. This is why economists favor trade not just across the Mississippi, but also across the Atlantic and the Pacific. Global trade turns the specialization clock forward; protectionism stops that from happening.

America punishes rogue nations by imposing economic sanctions. In the case of severe sanctions, we forbid nearly all imports and exports. A recent *New York Times* article commented on the devastating impact of sanctions in Gaza. Since Hamas came to power and refused to renounce violence, Israel has limited what can go in and out of the territory, leaving Gaza "almost entirely shut off from normal trade and travel with the world." Prior to the Iraq War, our (unsuccessful) sanctions on Iraq were responsible for the deaths of somewhere between 100,000 and 500,000 children, depending on whom you believe.[9] More recently, the United Nations has imposed several rounds of increasingly harsh sanctions on Iran for not suspending its clandestine nuclear program. The *Christian Science Monitor* explained the economic logic: Tougher sanctions "would hit the ruling mullahs hard by raising Iran's already high unemployment, and perhaps force trickle-up regime change."

Civil War buffs should remember that one key strategy of the North was imposing a naval blockade on the South. Why? Because then the South couldn't trade what it produced well (cotton) to Europe for what it needed most (manufactured goods).

So here's a question: Why would we want to impose trade sanctions on ourselves—which is exactly what any kind of protectionism does? Can the antiglobalization protesters explain how poor countries will get richer if they trade less with rest of the world—like Gaza?

Cutting off trade leaves a country poorer and less productive—which is why we tend to do it to our enemies.

Trade lowers the cost of goods for consumers, which is the same as raising their incomes. Forget about shoe workers for a moment and think about shoes. Why does Nike make shoes in Vietnam? Because it is cheaper than making them in the United States, and that means less expensive shoes for the rest of us. One paradox of the trade debate is that individuals who claim to have the downtrodden at heart neglect the fact that cheap imports are good for low-income consumers (and for the rest of us). Cheaper goods have the same impact on our lives as higher incomes. We can afford to buy more. The same thing is true, obviously, in other countries.

Trade barriers are a tax—albeit a hidden tax. Suppose the U.S. government tacked a 30-cent tax on every gallon of orange juice sold in America. The conservative antigovernment forces would be up in arms. So would liberals, who generally take issue with taxes on food and clothing, since such taxes are regressive, meaning that they are most costly (as a percentage of income) for the disadvantaged. *Well, the government does add 30 cents to the cost of every gallon of orange juice, though not in a way that is nearly as transparent as a tax.* The American government slaps tariffs on Brazilian oranges and orange juice that can be as high as 63 percent. Parts of Brazil are nearly ideal for growing citrus, which is exactly what has American growers concerned. So the government protects them. Economists reckon that the tariffs on Brazilian oranges and juice limit the supply of imports and therefore add about 30 cents to the price of a gallon of orange juice. Most consumers have no idea that the government is taking money out of their pockets and sending it to orange growers in Florida.[10] That does not show up on the receipt.

Lowering trade barriers has the same impact on consumers as cutting taxes. The precursor to the World Trade Organization was the General Agreement on Tariffs and Trade (GATT). Following World War II, GATT was the mechanism by which countries negotiated to bring down global tariffs and open the way for more trade. In the eight rounds of GATT negotiations between 1948 and 1995, average tariffs in industrial countries fell from 40 percent to 4 percent. That is a massive reduction in the "tax" paid on all imported goods. It has also forced domestic producers to make their goods cheaper and better in order to stay competitive. If you walk into a car dealership today, you are better off than you were in 1970 for two reasons. First, there is a wider choice of excellent imports. Second, Detroit has responded (slowly, belatedly, and incompletely) by making better cars, too. The Honda Accord makes you better off, and so does the Ford Taurus, which is better than it would have been without the competition.

Trade is good for poor countries, too. If we had patiently explained the benefits of trade to the protesters in Seattle or Washington or Davos or Genoa, then perhaps they would have laid down their Molotov cocktails. Okay, maybe not. The thrust of the antiglobalization protests has been that world trade is something imposed by rich countries on the developing world. If trade is mostly good for America, then it must be mostly bad for somewhere else. At this point in the book, we should recognize that zero-sum thinking is usually wrong when it comes to economics. So it is in this case. Representatives from developing nations were the ones who complained most bitterly about the disruption of the WTO talks in Seattle. Some believed that the Clinton administration secretly organized the protests to scuttle the talks and protect American interest groups, such as organized labor. Indeed, after the failure of the WTO talks in Seattle, UN chief Kofi Annan blamed the developed countries for erecting trade barriers that exclude developing nations from the benefits of global trade and called for a "Global New Deal."[11] The WTO's current round of talks to reduce global trade barriers, the Doha Round, has stalled in large part because a bloc of developing nations is demanding that the United States and Europe reduce their agricultural subsidies and trade barriers; so far the rich countries have refused.

Trade gives poor countries access to markets in the developed world. That is where most of the world's consumers are (or at least the ones with money to spend). Consider the impact of the African Growth and Opportunity Act, a law passed in 2000 that allowed Africa's poorest countries to export textiles to the United States with little or no tariff. Within a year, Madagascar's textile exports to the United States were up 120 percent, Malawi's were up 1,000 percent, Nigeria's were up 1,000 percent, and South Africa's were up 47 percent. As one commentator noted, "Real jobs for real people."[12]

Trade paves the way for poor countries to get richer. Export industries often pay higher wages than jobs elsewhere in the economy. But that is only the beginning. New export jobs create more competition for workers, which raises wages everywhere else. Even rural incomes can go up; as workers leave rural areas for better opportunities, there are fewer mouths to be fed from what can be grown on the land they leave behind. Other important things are going on, too. Foreign companies introduce capital, technology, and new skills. Not only does that make export workers more productive; it spills over into other areas of the economy. Workers "learn by doing" and then take their knowledge with them.

In his excellent book *The Elusive Quest for Growth*, William Easterly tells the story of the advent of the Bangladeshi garment industry, an industry that was founded almost by accident. The Daewoo Corporation of South Korea was a major textile producer in the 1970s. America and Europe had slapped import quotas on South Korean textiles, so Daewoo, ever the profit-maximizing firm, skirted the trade restrictions by moving some operations to Bangladesh. In 1979, Daewoo signed a collaborative agreement to produce shirts with the Bangladeshi company Desh Garments. Most significant, Daewoo took 130 Desh workers to South Korea for training. In other words, Daewoo invested in the human capital of its Bangladeshi workers. The intriguing thing about human capital, as opposed to machines or financial capital, is that it can never be taken away. Once those

Bangladeshi workers knew how to make shirts, they could never be forced to forget. And they didn't.

Daewoo later severed the relationship with its Bangladeshi partner, but the seeds for a booming export industry were already planted. Of the 130 workers trained by Daewoo, 115 left during the 1980s to start their own garment-exporting firms. Mr. Easterly argues convincingly that the Daewoo investment was an essential building block for what became a $3 billion garment export industry. Lest anyone believe that trade barriers are built to help the poorest of the poor, or that Republicans are more averse to protecting special interests than Democrats, it should be noted that the Reagan administration slapped import quotas on Bangladeshi textiles in the 1980s. I would be hard pressed to explain the economic rationale for limiting the export opportunities of a country that has a per capita GDP of $1,500.

Most famously, cheap exports were the path to prosperity for the Asian "tigers"—Singapore, South Korea, Hong Kong, and Taiwan (and for Japan before that). India was strikingly insular during the four decades after achieving independence from Britain in 1947; it was one of the world's great economic underachievers during that stretch. (Alas, Gandhi, like Lincoln, was a great leader and a bad economist; Gandhi proposed that the Indian flag have a spinning wheel on it to represent economic self-sufficiency.) India reversed course in the 1990s, deregulating its domestic economy and opening up to the world. The result is an ongoing economic success story. China, too, has used exports as a launching pad for growth. Indeed, if China's thirty provinces were counted as individual countries, the twenty fastest-growing countries in the world between 1978 and 1995 would all have been Chinese. To put that development accomplishment in perspective, it took fifty-eight years for GDP per capita to double in Britain after the launch of the Industrial Revolution. In China, GDP per capita has been doubling every ten years. In the cases of India and China, we're talking about hundreds of millions of people being lifted out of poverty and, increasingly, into the middle class. Nicholas

Kristof and Sheryl WuDunn, Asian correspondents for the *New York Times* for over a decade, have written:

> We and other journalists wrote about the problems of child labor and oppressive conditions in both China and South Korea. But, looking back, our worries were excessive. Those sweatshops tended to generate the wealth to solve the problems they created. If Americans had reacted to the horror stories in the 1980s by curbing imports of those sweatshop products, then neither southern China nor South Korea would have registered as much progress as they have today.[13]

China and Southeast Asia are not unique. The consultancy AT Kearney conducted a study of how globalization has affected thirty-four developed and developing countries. They found that the fastest-globalizing countries had rates of growth that were 30 to 50 percent higher over the past twenty years than countries less integrated into the world economy. Those countries also enjoyed greater political freedom and received higher scores on the UN Human Development Index. The authors reckon that some 1.4 billion people escaped absolute poverty as a result of the economic growth associated with globalization. There was bad news, too. Higher rates of globalization were associated with higher rates of income inequality, corruption, and environmental degradation. More on that later.

But there is an easier way to make the case for globalization. If not more trade and economic integration, then what instead? Those who oppose more global trade must answer one question, based on a point made by Harvard economist Jeffrey Sachs: Is there an example in modern history of a single country successfully developing without trading and integrating with the global economy?[14]

No, there is not.

Which is why Tom Friedman has suggested that the antiglobalization coalition ought to be known as "The Coalition to Keep the World's Poor People Poor."

Trade is based on voluntary exchange. Individuals do things that make themselves better off. That obvious point is often lost in the globalization debate. McDonald's does not build a restaurant in Bangkok and then force people at gunpoint to eat there. People eat there because they want to. And if they don't want to, they don't have to. And if no one eats there, the restaurant will lose money and close. Does McDonald's change local cultures? Yes. That was what caught my attention a decade ago when I wrote about Kentucky Fried Chicken arriving in Bali. I wrote, "Indonesians have their own version of fast food that is more practical than the Colonel's cardboard boxes and Styrofoam plates. A meal bought at a food stall is wrapped in a banana leaf and newspaper. The large green leaf retains heat, is impermeable to grease, and can be folded into a neat package."

By and large, the banana leaves of the world appear to be losing to cardboard. Not long ago I attended a business gathering with my wife in Puerta Vallarta, Mexico. Puerto Vallarta is a lovely city that spills down from the hills to the Pacific Ocean. The focal point of the city is a promenade that runs along the ocean. Near the middle of that promenade is a point that juts out into the ocean, and at the end of that point, on what I would reckon is one of the most valuable pieces of real estate in the city, is a Hooters restaurant. When our group spotted this infamous American export, one man grumbled, "That is just wrong."

A Hooters in all the world's great cities is probably not what Adam Smith had in mind. University of Chicago professor Marvin Zonis has noted, "Certain aspects of American popular culture—the depravity and the coarseness, the violence and the sexuality—are eminently worth resenting."[15] The threat of "cultural homogenization"—the worst of it coming from America—is a common knock against globalization. But it is an issue that leads us back to a crucial point from Chapter 1: Who decides? I was not happy to see a Hooters in Puerto

Vallarta, but, as I pointed out many pages ago, I don't run the world. More important, I don't live or vote in Puerto Vallarta. Neither do the rock-throwing thugs in Seattle or Genoa or Pittsburgh (or wherever else they tend to show up).

Are there legitimate reasons to limit the proliferation of fast-food restaurants and the like? Yes, they present classic externalities. Fast-food restaurants cause traffic and litter; they are ugly and can contribute to sprawl. (Before my valuable work opposing a new train station on Fullerton Avenue, I was part of a group trying to prevent a McDonald's from moving in across the street.) These are local decisions that ought to be made by the people affected—those who might eat in the safe, clean environment of a McDonald's restaurant as well as those who may have fast-food wrappers blown in their gutters. Free trade is consistent with one of our most fundamental liberal values: the right to make our own private decisions.

There is now a McDonald's in Moscow and a Starbucks in the Forbidden City in Beijing. Stalin never would have allowed the former; Mao would not have allowed the latter. Which is a point worth pondering.

The cultural homogenization argument may not be true anyway. Culture is transmitted in all directions. I can now rent Iranian movies from Netflix. National Public Radio recently ran a segment on craftsmen and artists in remote regions of the world who are selling their work via the Internet. One can log on to Novica.com and find a virtual global marketplace for arts and crafts. Katherine Ryan, who works for Novica, explains, "There's a community in Peru where most of the artists had gone to work in the coal mines. And now, because of the success of one artist in Novica, he has been able to hire many of his family members and neighbors back into the weaving business, and they're no longer coal miners. They're now doing what for many generations their family did, and that's weave incredible tapestries."[16] John Micklethwait and Adrian Wooldridge, authors of the globalization tract *A Future Perfect*, point out that in the realm of business, a previously obscure Finnish company like Nokia has been able to thump American behemoths like Motorola.

We're still just warming up when it comes to the side effects of globalization. A Hooters in Puerto Vallarta is a mild headache relative to the horrors of Asian sweatshops. Yet the same principles apply. Nike does not use forced labor in its Vietnamese factories. Why are workers willing to accept a dollar or two a day? *Because it is better than any other option they have.* According to the Institute for International Economics, the average wage paid by foreign companies in low-income countries is twice the average domestic manufacturing wage.

Nicholas Kristof and Sheryl WuDunn described a visit with Mongkol Latlakorn, a Thai laborer whose fifteen-year-old daughter was working in a Bangkok factory making clothes for export to America.

> She is paid $2 a day for a nine-hour shift, six days a week. On several occasions, needles have gone through her hands, and managers have bandaged her up so that she could go back to work.
>
> "How terrible," we murmured sympathetically.
>
> Mongkol looked up, puzzled. "It's good pay," he said. "I hope she can keep that job. There's all this talk about factories closing now, and she said there are rumors that her factory might close. I hope that doesn't happen. I don't know what she would do then."[17]

The implicit message of the antiglobalization protests is that we in the developed world somehow know what is best for people in poor countries—where they ought to work and even what kind of restaurants they ought to eat in. As *The Economist* has noted, "The skeptics distrust governments, politicians, international bureaucrats and markets alike. So they end up appointing themselves as judges, overruling not just governments and markets but also the voluntary preferences of the workers most directly concerned. That seems a great deal to take on."[18]

The comparative advantage of workers in poor countries is cheap labor. That is all they have to offer. They are not more productive than American workers; they are not better educated; they do not have access to better technology. They are paid very little by Western standards because they accomplish very little by Western standards. If foreign companies are forced to raise wages significantly, then there is no longer any advantage to having plants in the developing world. Firms will replace workers with machines, or they will move someplace where higher productivity justifies higher wages. *If sweatshops paid decent wages by Western standards, they would not exist.* There is nothing pretty about people willing to work long hours in bad conditions for a few dollars a day, but let's not confuse cause and effect. Sweatshops do not cause low wages in poor countries; rather, they pay low wages because those countries offer workers so few other alternatives. Protesters might as well hurl rocks and bottles at hospitals because so many sick people are suffering there.

Nor does it make sense that we can make sweatshop workers better off by refusing to buy the products that they make. Industrialization, however primitive, sets in motion a process that can make poor countries richer. Mr. Kristof and Ms. WuDunn arrived in Asia in the 1980s. "Like most Westerners, we arrived in the region outraged at sweatshops," they recalled fourteen years later. "In time, though, we came to accept the view supported by most Asians: that the campaign against sweatshops risks harming the very people it is intended to help. For beneath their grime, sweatshops are a clear sign of the industrial revolution that is beginning to reshape Asia." After describing the horrific conditions—workers denied bathroom breaks, exposed to dangerous chemicals, forced to work seven days a week—they conclude, "Asian workers would be aghast at the idea of American consumers boycotting certain toys or clothing in protest.

The simplest way to help the poorest Asians would be to buy more from sweatshops, not less."[19]

You're not convinced? Paul Krugman offers a sad example of good intentions gone awry:

In 1993, child workers in Bangladesh were found to be producing clothing for Wal-Mart and Senator Tom Harkin proposed legislation banning imports from countries employing underage workers. The direct result was that Bangladeshi textile factories stopped employing children. But did the children go back to school? Did they return to happy homes? Not according to Oxfam, which found that the displaced child workers ended up in even worse jobs, or on the streets—and that a significant number were forced into prostitution.[20]

Oops.

Preferences change with income, particularly with regard to the environment. Poor people care about different things than rich people do. By global standards, poor does not mean settling for a Ford Fiesta when you really wanted the BMW. Poor is watching your children die of malaria because you could not afford a $5 mosquito net. In parts of the world, $5 is five days of income. By those same standards, anyone reading this book is rich. The fastest way to end any meaningful discussion of globalization is to wave the environment card. But let's do a simple exercise to illustrate why it may be terribly wrong to impose our environmental preferences on the rest of the world. Here is the task: Ask four friends to name the world's most pressing environmental problem.

It's a fair bet that at least two of them will say global warming and none will mention clean water. *Yet inadequate access to safe drinking water—a problem easily cured by rising living standards—kills two million people a year and makes another half billion seriously ill.* Is global warming a serious problem? Yes. Would it be your primary concern if children in your town routinely died from diarrhea? No. The first fallacy related to trade and the environment is that poor countries should be held to the same environmental standards as the developed world. (The debate over workplace safety is nearly identical.) Producing things causes waste. I remember the first day of an environmental economics course when visiting professor Paul Portney, former head of Resources for the Future, pointed out that the very act of staying alive requires that we produce waste. The challenge is to weigh the benefits of what we produce against the costs of producing it, including pollution. Someone living comfortably in Manhattan may view those costs and benefits differently from someone living on the brink of starvation in rural Nepal. Thus, trade decisions that affect the environment in Nepal ought to be made in Nepal, recognizing that environmental problems that cross political boundaries will be settled the same way they always are, which is through multilateral agreements and organizations.

The notion that economic development is inherently bad for the environment may be wrong anyway. In the short run, just about any economic activity generates waste. If we produce more, we will pollute more. Yet it is also true that as we get richer, we pay more attention to the environment. Here is another quiz. In what year did air quality in London (the city for which we have the best long-term pollution data) reach its worst level ever? To make it easier, let's narrow the choices: 1890; 1920; 1975; 2001. The answer is 1890. Indeed, the city's current air quality is better than at any time since 1585. (There is nothing particularly "clean" about cooking over an open fire.) Environmental quality is a luxury good in the technical sense of the word, which means that we place more value on it as we get richer. Therein lies one of the powerful benefits of globalization: Trade makes countries richer; richer countries care more about environmental quality and have more resources at their disposal to deal with pollution. Economists reckon that many kinds of pollution rise as a country gets richer (when every family buys a motorcycle) and then fall in the later stages of development (when we ban leaded gasoline and require more efficient engines).

Critics of trade have alleged that allowing individual countries to make their own environmental decisions will lead to a "race to the bottom" in which poor countries compete for business by despoiling their environments. It hasn't happened. The World Bank recently concluded after six years of study, "Pollution havens—developing countries that provide a permanent home to dirty industries—have failed to materialize. Instead, poorer nations and communities are acting to reduce pollution because they have decided that the benefits of abatement outweigh the costs."[21]

Climate change is a trickier case, in that carbon emissions are a zero-sum situation, at least in developing countries in the near term. Big, rapidly growing countries like China and India have a voracious appetite for energy; to meet that need, they turn mostly to carbon-based fuels. China is heavily dependent on coal, which is a particularly bad CO_2 offender. Trade makes these countries richer. As they get richer, they will use more energy. As they use more energy, their CO_2 emissions will rise. That's a problem. So what is the best remedy?

If you think it is to curtail trade, let me present a slightly different version of the same basic challenge. China and India are sending more and more of their citizens to university (while extending basic education more widely, too). Education is making China and India richer. As they get richer, they use more energy . . . Do you see where this is going? Should we ban education?

No. The answer to the CO_2 problem is to promote growth—in India, China, the United States, and everywhere else—in ways that minimize the environmental damage. The best way to do that is to discourage the use of dirty fuels by imposing some kind of carbon tax that is harmonized across countries—sooner rather than later, because India and China are making development decisions, such as building power plants, that are going to be with us for fifty years.

The case for keeping people poor because it's good for the planet is economically and morally bankrupt.

Poverty is a bitch. The principal of a high school near Chicago's Robert Taylor housing projects once told me that when I was writing a story on urban education. He was talking about the challenges of teaching kids who had grown up poor and deprived. He might as well have been talking about the state of the world. Many parts of the world—places we rarely think about, let alone visit—are desperately poor. We ought to make them richer; economics tells us that trade is an important way to do it. Paul Krugman has nicely summarized the anxiety over globalization with an old French saying: Anyone who is not a socialist before he is thirty has no heart; anyone who is still a socialist after he is thirty has no head. He writes:

> If you buy a product made in a third-world country, it was produced by workers who are paid incredibly little by Western standards and probably work under awful conditions. Anyone who is not bothered by those facts, at least some of the time, has no heart. But that doesn't mean the demonstrators are right. On the contrary, anyone who thinks that the answer to world poverty is simple outrage against global trade has no head—or chooses not to use it. The anti-globalization movement already has a remarkable track record of hurting the very people and causes it claims to champion.[22]

The trend toward more global trade is often described as an unstoppable force. It is not. We've been down this road before, only to have the world trading system torn apart by war and politics. One of the most rapid periods of globalization took place during the end of the nineteenth century and the beginning of the twentieth. John Micklethwait and Adrian Wooldridge, authors of *A Future Perfect*, have noted, "Look back 100 years and you discover a world that by many economic measures was more global than it is today: where you could travel without a passport, where the gold standard was an international currency, and where technology (cars, trains, ships, and telephones) was making the world enormously smaller." Alas, they point out, "That grand illusion was shot to pieces on the playing fields of the Somme."[23]

Political boundaries still matter. Governments can slam the door on globalization, as they have before. That would be a shame for rich countries and poor countries alike.

CHAPTER 13

Development Economics:

The wealth and poverty of nations

L et us briefly contemplate the life of Nashon Zimba, a twenty-five-year-old man who lives with his wife and baby daughter in Malawi. There is no question that Mr. Zimba is a hardworking man. He built his own home, as *The Economist* describes:

He digs up mud, shapes it into cuboids and then dries it in the sun to make bricks. He mixes his own cement, also from mud. He cuts branches to make beams, and thatches the roof with sisal or grass. His only industrial input is the metal blade on his axe. Working on his own, while at the same time growing food for his family, Mr. Zimba has erected a house that is dark, cramped, cold in the winter, steamy in summer and has running water only when tropical storms come through the roof.[1]

For all that work, Mr. Zimba is a poor man. His cash income in 2000 was roughly $40. He is hardly alone. Malawian GDP per capita was less than $200 at the time that story was written. Even today, the nation's entire annual economic output is only about $12 billion— or about half the size of Vermont's economy. Lest anyone naively believe that there is something pleasantly simple about this existence, it should be pointed out that 30 percent of young children in Malawi are malnourished; more than two of every ten children will die before they reach their fifth birthday.

According to the UN's Food and Agriculture Organization, there are a billion people in the world who don't get enough to eat. The vast majority are in the developing world; roughly half are in India and China. How is that possible? At a time when we can split the atom, land on the moon, and decode the human genome, why do 2 billion people live on less than $2 a day?[2]

The short answer is that their economies have failed them. At bottom, creating wealth is a process of taking inputs, including human talent, and producing things of value. Poor economies are not organized to do that. In his excellent book on economic development, *The Elusive Quest for Growth*, World Bank economist William Easterly describes a street scene in Lahore, Pakistan:

> People throng the markets in the old city, where the lanes are so narrow that the crowds swallow the car. People buying, people selling, people eating, people cooking. Every street, every lane crammed with shops, each shop crammed with people. This is a private economy with a lot of dynamism.[3]

It is also, he notes, a country that is largely illiterate, ill housed, and ill fed. The Pakistani government has built nuclear weapons but is unable to conduct an immunization program against measles. "Wonderful people," writes Mr. Easterly. "Terrible government." And it is a terrible government that has become increasingly dangerous for the rest of the world. We can (probably) safely ignore Malawi. Not Pakistan.

Every country has resources, if only the wits and hard work of the people who inhabit it. Most countries, including some of the poorest nations on earth, have far more resources than that. Let me get the bad news out of the way: Economists do not have a recipe for making poor countries rich. True, there have been some fabulous success stories, such as the original Asian "tigers"—Hong Kong, Singapore, South Korea, and Taiwan—which saw their economies grow more than 8 percent a year for nearly three decades. China and India have had a terrific decade, much to the benefit of hundreds of millions of people. But we do not have a proven formula for growth that can be rolled out in country after country like some kind of development franchise. Just think about China and India: One is the world's largest democracy; the other is not democratic at all.

On the other hand, we do have a good understanding of what makes rich countries rich. If we can catalog the kinds of policies that functional economies have in common, then we can turn our attention to Nobel laureate Douglass North's common-sense query "Why don't poor countries simply adopt policies that make for plenty?"[4]

The following is a sample of the kinds of policies and, in some cases, lucky geographical endowments that development economists have come to believe make the difference between the wealth and poverty of nations.

Effective government institutions. To grow and prosper, a country needs laws, law enforcement, courts, basic infrastructure, a government capable of collecting taxes—and a healthy respect among the citizenship for each of these things. These kinds of institutions are the tracks on which capitalism runs. They must be reasonably honest. Corruption is not merely an inconvenience, as it is sometimes treated; it is a cancer that misallocates resources, stifles innovation, and discourages foreign investment. While American attitudes toward government range from indifference to hostility, most other countries would love to have it so good, as *New York Times* foreign affairs columnist Tom Friedman has pointed out:

I took part in a seminar two weeks ago at Nanjing University in China, and I can still hear a young Chinese graduate student pleading for an answer to her question: "How do we get rid of all our corruption?" Do you know what your average Chinese would give to have a capital like Washington today, with its reasonably honest and efficient bureaucracy? Do you know how unusual we are in the world that we don't have to pay off bureaucrats to get the simplest permit issued?[5]

The relationship between government institutions and economic growth prompted a clever and intriguing study. Economists Daron Acemoglu, Simon Johnson, and James Robinson hypothesized that the economic success of developing countries that were formerly colonized has been affected by the quality of the institutions that their colonizers left behind.[6] The European powers adopted different colonization policies in different parts of the world, depending on how hospitable the area was to settlement. In places where Europeans could settle without serious hardship, such as the United States, the colonizers created institutions that have had a positive and long-lasting effect on economic growth. In places where Europeans could not easily settle because of a high mortality rate from disease, such as the Congo, the colonizers simply focused on taking as much wealth home as quickly as possible, creating what the authors refer to as "extractive states."

The study examined sixty-four ex-colonies and found that as much as three-quarters of the difference in their current wealth can be explained by differences in the quality of their government institutions. In turn, the quality of those government institutions is explained, at least in part, by the original settlement pattern. The legal origin of the colonizers—British, French, Belgian—had little influence (though the British come out looking good because they tended to colonize places more hospitable to settlement).

Basically, good governance matters. The World Bank rated 150 countries on six broad measures of governance, such as accountability, regulatory burden, rule of law, graft (corruption), etc. There was a clear and causal relationship between better governance and better development outcomes, such as higher per capita incomes, lower infant mortality, and higher literacy.[7] We don't have to love the Internal Revenue Service, but we ought to at least offer it some grudging respect.

Property rights. Private property may seem like a province of the rich; in fact, it can have a crucial impact on the poor. The developed world is full of examples of informal property rights—homes or businesses built on land that is communal or owned by the government and ignored (such as the shantytowns on the outskirts of many large cities). Families and entrepreneurs make significant investments in their "properties." But there is a crucial difference between those assets and their counterparts in the developed world: The owners have no legal title to the property. They cannot legally rent it, subdivide it, sell it, or pass it on to family. Perhaps most important, they cannot use it as collateral to raise capital.

Peruvian economist Hernando de Soto has argued convincingly that these kinds of informal property arrangements should not be ignored. He reckons that the total value of property held but not legally owned by poor people in the developing world is worth more than $9 trillion. That is a lot of collateral gone to waste, or "dead capital" as he calls it. To put that number in perspective, it is 93 times the amount of development assistance that the rich countries provided to the developing world over the past three decades.

The Economist tells a story of a Malawian couple who make a living slaughtering goats. Since business is good, they would like to expand. To do so, however, would require an investment of $250—or $50 more than the average annual income in Malawi. This couple "owns" a home worth more than that. Might they borrow against the value of their land and the bungalow they have built on it? No. The home is built on "customary" land that has no formal title. The couple has a contract signed by the local village chief, but it is not enforceable in a court of law. *The Economist* goes on to note:

About two-thirds of the land in Malawi is owned this way. People usually till the land their parents tilled. If there is a dispute about boundaries, the village chief adjudicates. If a family offends gravely against the rules of the tribe, the chief can take their land away and give it to someone else.[8]

Those informal property rights are like barter—they work fine in a simple agrarian society, but are woefully inadequate for a more complex economy. It is bad enough that poor countries are poor; it is all the worse that their most valuable assets are rendered less productive than they might be.

Property rights have another less obvious benefit: They enable people to spend less time defending their possessions, which frees them up to do more productive things. Between 1996 and 2003, the Peruvian government issued property rights to 1.2 million urban squatter households, giving them formal ownership to what they had previously informally claimed as their own. Harvard Economist Erica Field determined that property rights enabled residents to work more hours in the formal labor market. She surmises that property rights give more flexibility to people who previously had to stay home, or had to operate improvised businesses out of their home, in order to protect their property. She also makes another important point: Most programs designed to help the poor reduce their work effort. (This is the Samaritan's dilemma; if I ease your hardship, you have less incentive to help yourself.) Providing formal property rights does the opposite: It encourages work.[9]

No excessive regulation. Government has plenty to do—and even more that it should not do. Markets must do the heavy lifting. Let's talk about articles 575 and 615 of the Russian civil code. These regulations would be very important if you were a firm in Moscow doing something as simple as installing a vending machine. Article 575 forbids firms from giving anything away free, which includes the space that a firm "gives" to Coca-Cola when a vending machine is installed. Meanwhile, article 615 forbids subletting property without the landlord's consent; the square meter taken up by the vending machine can be construed as a sublease. In addition, the tax collector forbids commercial enterprises (e.g., vending machines) to operate without a cash register. And since selling soft drinks from a machine constitutes retail trade, there are assorted fire, health, and safety inspections.[10]

Excessive regulation goes hand in glove with corruption. Government bureaucrats throw up hurdles so that they can extort bribes from those who seek to get over or around them. Installing a vending machine in Moscow becomes much easier if you hire the right "security firm." What about opening a business elsewhere in the developed world? Again, Peruvian economist Hernando de Soto has done fascinating work. He and fellow team members documented their efforts to open a one-person clothing stall on the outskirts of Lima as a legally registered business. He and his researchers vowed that they would not pay bribes so that their efforts would reflect the full cost of complying with the law. (In the end, they were asked for bribes on ten occasions and paid them twice to prevent the project from stalling completely.) The team worked six hours a day for forty-two weeks in order to get eleven different permits from seven different government bodies. Their efforts, not including the time, cost $1,231, or 31 times the monthly minimum wage in Peru—all to open a one-person shop.[11]

Chapter 4 outlined all the reasons government should stick to the basics. Harvard economist Robert Barro's classic study of economic growth in roughly one hundred countries over three decades found that government consumption—total government spending excluding education and defense—was negatively correlated with per capita GDP growth. He concluded that such spending (and the required taxation) is not likely to increase productivity and will therefore do more harm than good. The Asian tigers, the all-star team in the economic development league, made their economic ascent with government spending in the range of 20 percent of GDP. Elsewhere in the world, high tax rates that are applied unevenly distort the economy and provide opportunities for graft and corruption. Many poor governments might actually collect more revenue if they implemented taxes that were low, simple, and easy to collect.

The Internet has a huge potential to improve transparency everywhere, but particularly in poor countries. Something as simple as posting on-line the amount of money allocated by the central government for a specific local project, such as a road or a health clinic, can enable citizens to compare what they were supposed to get to what actually showed up. "We got $5,000 for a community center? That doesn't look like a $5,000 community center. Let's go talk to the mayor."

Human capital. Human capital is what makes individuals productive, and productivity is what determines our standard of living. As University of Chicago economist and Nobel laureate Gary Becker has pointed out, all countries that have had persistent growth in income have also had large increases in the education and training of their labor forces. (We have strong reasons to believe that the education causes the growth, not the other way around.) He has written, "These so-called Asian tigers grew rapidly by relying on a well-trained, educated, hard-working, and conscientious labor force."[12]

In poor countries, human capital does all the good things we would expect, and then some. Education can improve public health (which is, in turn, a form of human capital). Some of the most pernicious public health problems in the developing world have relatively simple fixes (boiling water, digging latrines, using condoms, etc.). Higher rates of education for women in developing countries are associated with lower rates of infant mortality. Meanwhile, human capital facilitates the adoption of superior technologies from developed countries. One cause for optimism in the development field has always been that poor countries should, in theory, be able to narrow the gap with richer nations by borrowing their innovations. Once a technology is invented, it can be shared with poor countries at virtually no cost. The people of Ghana need not invent the personal computer in order to benefit from its existence; they do need to know how to use it.

Now for more bad news. In Chapter 6, I described an economy in which skilled workers generate economic growth by creating new jobs or doing old jobs better. Skills are what matter—for individuals and for the economy as a whole. That is still true, but there is a glitch when we get to the developing world: Skilled workers usually need other skilled workers in order to succeed. Someone who is trained as a heart surgeon can succeed only if there are well-equipped hospitals, trained nurses, firms that sell drugs and medical supplies, and a population with sufficient resources to pay for heart surgery. Poor countries can become caught in a human capital trap; if there are few skilled workers, then there is less incentive for others to invest in acquiring skills. Those who do become skilled find that their talents are more valuable in a region or country with a higher proportion of skilled workers, creating the familiar "brain drain." As World Bank economist William Easterly has written, the result can be a vicious cycle: "If a nation starts out skilled, it gets more skilled. If it starts out unskilled, it stays unskilled."[13]

As a side note, this phenomenon is relevant in rural America, too. Not long ago, I wrote a story for *The Economist* that we referred to internally as "The Incredible Shrinking Iowa."[14] As the working title would suggest, parts of Iowa, and other large swathes of the rural Midwest, are losing population relative to the rest of the country. Remarkably, forty-four of Iowa's ninety-nine counties had fewer people in 2000 than they had in 1900. Part of that depopulation stems from rising farm productivity; Iowa's farmers have literally grown themselves out of jobs. But something else is going on, too. Economists have found that individuals with similar skills and experience can earn significantly higher wages in urban areas than they can elsewhere. Why? One plausible explanation is that specialized skills are more valuable in metropolitan areas where there is a density of other workers with complementary skills. (Think Silicon Valley or a cardiac surgery center in Manhattan.) Rural America has a mild case of something that deeply afflicts the developing world. Unlike technology or infrastructure or pharmaceuticals, we cannot export huge quantities of human capital to poor countries. We cannot airlift ten thousand university degrees to a small African nation. Yet as long as individuals in poor countries face limited opportunities, they will have a diminished incentive to invest in human capital.

How does a country break out of the trap? Remember that question when we come to the importance of trade.

Geography. Here is a remarkable figure: Only two of thirty countries classified by the World Bank as rich—Hong Kong and Singapore—lie between the Tropic of Cancer (which runs through Mexico across North Africa and through India) and the Tropic of Capricorn (which runs through Brazil and across the northern tip of South Africa and through Australia). Geography may be a windfall that we in the developed world take for granted. Development expert Jeffrey Sachs wrote a seminal paper in which he posited that climate can explain much of the world's income distribution. He writes, "Given the varied political, economic, and social histories of regions around the world, it must be more than coincidence that almost all of the tropics remain underdeveloped at the start of the twenty-first century."[15] The United States and all of Europe lie outside the tropics; most of Central and South America, Africa, and Southeast Asia lie within.

Tropical weather is wonderful for vacation; why is it so bad for everything else? The answer, according to Mr. Sachs, is that high temperatures and heavy rainfall are bad for food production and conducive to the spread of disease. As a result, two of the major advances in rich countries—better food production and better health—cannot be replicated in the tropics. Why don't the residents of Chicago suffer from malaria? Because cold winters control mosquitoes—not because scientists have beaten the disease. So in the tropics, we find yet another poverty trap; most of the population is stuck in low-productivity farming. Their crops—and therefore their lives—are unlikely to get better in the face of poor soil, unreliable rainfall, and chronic pests.

Obviously countries cannot pick up and move to more favorable climates. Mr. Sachs proposes two solutions. First, we ought to encourage more technological innovation aimed at the unique ecology of the tropics. The sad fact is that scientists, like bank robbers, go where the money is. Pharmaceutical companies earn profits by developing blockbuster drugs for consumers in the developed world. Of the 1,233 new medicines granted patents between 1975 and 1997, only thirteen were for tropical diseases.[16] But even that overstates the attention paid to the region; nine of those drugs came from research done by the U.S. military for the Vietnam War or from research for the livestock and pet market.How do we make private companies care as much about sleeping sickness (on which no major company is doing research) as they do about canine Alzheimer's (for which Pfizer already has a drug)? Change the incentives. In 2005, British Prime Minister Gordon Brown embraced an idea that economists have long kicked around: Identify a disease that primarily afflicts a poor part of the world and then offer a large cash prize to the first firm that develops a vaccine that meets predetermined criteria (e.g., is effective, is safe for use in children, doesn't need refrigeration, etc.). Brown's plan was actually more sophisticated; he proposed that rich governments precommit to buying a certain number of doses of the "winning" vaccine at a certain price. Poor people would get lifesaving drugs. The pharmaceutical company would get what it needs to justify the vaccine research: a return on investment, just as it does when developing drugs that consumers in rich countries will buy. (The British government has been thinking this way for a long time. In 1714, after two thousand sailors drowned when a fleet got lost, crashed into the rocky coast, and sunk, the British government offered 20,000 pounds to anyone who developed an instrument for measuring longitude at sea. The prize led to the invention of the chronometer.)[17]

The other hope for poor countries in the tropics, says Mr. Sachs, is to step out of the trap of subsistence agriculture by opening their economies to the rest of the world. He notes, "If the country can escape to higher incomes via non-agricultural sectors (e.g., through a large expansion of manufactured exports), the burdens of the tropics can be lifted."[18] Which brings us once again to our old friend trade.

Openness to trade. We've had a whole chapter on the theoretical benefits of trade. Suffice it to say that those lessons have been lost on governments in many poor countries in recent decades. The fallacious logic of protectionism is alluring—the idea that keeping out foreign goods will make the country richer. Strategies such as "self-sufficiency" and "state leadership" were hallmarks of the postcolonial regimes, such as India and much of Africa. Trade barriers would "incubate" domestic industries so that they could grow strong enough to face international competition. Economics tells us that companies shielded from competition do not grow stronger; they grow fat and lazy. Politics tells us that once an industry is incubated, it will always be incubated. The result, in the words of one economist, has been a "largely self-imposed economic exile."[19]

At great cost, it turns out. The preponderance of evidence suggests that open economies grow faster than closed economies. In one of the most influential studies, Jeffrey Sachs, now director of The Earth Institute at Columbia University, and Andrew Warner, a researcher at the Harvard Center for International Development, compared the economic performance of closed economies, as defined by high tariffs and other restrictions on trade, to the performance of open economies. Among poor countries, the closed economies grew at 0.7 percent per capita annually during the 1970s and 1980s while the open economies grew at 4.5 percent annually. Most interesting, when a previously closed economy opened up, growth increased by more than a percentage point a year. To be fair, some prominent economists have taken issue with the study on the grounds (among other quibbles) that economies closed to trade often have a lot of other problems, too. Is it the lack of trade that makes these countries grow slowly, or is it general macroeconomic dysfunction? For that matter, does trade cause growth or is it something that just happens while economies are growing for other reasons? After all, the number of televisions sold rises sharply during extended spells of economic growth, but watching television does not make countries richer.

Conveniently for us, a recent paper in the *American Economic Review*, one of the most respected journals in the field, is entitled "Does Trade Cause Growth?" Yes, the authors answer. All else equal, countries that trade more have higher per capita incomes.[20] Jeffrey Frankel and David Romer, economists at Harvard and UC Berkeley, respectively, conclude, "Our results bolster the case for the importance of trade and trade-promoting policies."

Researchers have plenty left to quibble about. That is what researchers do. In the meantime, we have strong theoretical reasons to believe that trade makes countries better off and solid empirical evidence that trade is one thing that has separated winners from losers in recent decades. The rich countries must do their part by keeping their economies open to exports from poor countries. Mr. Sachs has called for a "New Compact for Africa." He writes, "The current pattern of rich countries—to provide financial aid to tropical Africa while blocking Africa's chances to export textiles, footwear, leather goods, and other labor-intensive products—may be worse than cynical. It may in fact fundamentally undermine Africa's chances for economic development."[21]

Responsible fiscal and monetary policy. Governments, like individuals, will get themselves in serious trouble if they consistently overspend on things that do not raise future productivity. At a minimum, large budget deficits require the government to borrow heavily, which takes capital out of the hands of private borrowers, who are likely to use it more efficiently. Chronic deficit spending can also signal other future problems: higher taxes (to pay back the debt), inflation (to erode the value of the debt), or even default (just giving up on the debt).

All of these problems are compounded if the government has borrowed heavily from abroad to finance its profligate spending. If foreign investors lose confidence and decide to take their money and go home—as skittish global investors are wont to do—then the capital that was financing the deficit dries up, or becomes prohibitively expensive. In short, the music stops. The government is left on the brink of default, which we have seen in countries ranging from Mexico to Turkey. (There is, by the way, some modest concern that this could happen to the United States.)

On the monetary side, Chapter 10 made clear the dangers of letting the money party get out of control. It happens often anyway. Argentina is the poster child for irresponsible monetary policy; from 1960 to 1994, the average Argentine inflation rate was 127 percent per year. To put that in perspective, an Argentine investor who had the equivalent of $1 billion in savings in 1960 and kept all of it in Argentine pesos until 1994 would have been left with the equivalent spending power of one-thirteenth of a penny. Economist William Easterly has noted, "Trying to have normal growth during high inflation is like trying to win an Olympic sprint hopping on one leg."

Natural resources matter less than you would think. Israel, which has no oil to speak of, is a far richer country than nearly all of its Middle Eastern neighbors that have large petroleum reserves. Israeli GDP per capita is $28,300 compared to $20,500 for Saudi Arabia and $12,800 for Iran. Meanwhile, resource-poor countries like Japan and Switzerland have fared much better than resource-rich Russia.[22] Or consider oil-rich Angola. The country takes in some $3.5 billion a year from its oil industry.[23] What has happened to the people who might benefit from this treasure in the ground? Much of the oil money goes to fund a never-ending civil war that has ravaged the country. Angola has the world's highest rate of citizens maimed by land mines (1 out of 133). One-third of Angola's children die before age five; life expectancy is forty-two. Large swathes of the capital have no electricity, no running water, no sewers, and no garbage pickup.[24]

These are not anecdotal examples carefully picked to make a point. Economists believe that a rich endowment of natural resources may actually be a detriment to development. All else equal, it is great to discover the world's largest zinc deposit. *But all else is not equal.* Commodity-rich countries are changed by the experience in ways that can do more harm than good. One study of economic performance in ninety-seven countries over two decades found that growth was higher in countries that were less endowed with natural resources. Of the top eighteen fastest-growing nations, only two were rich in things that can be taken out of the ground. Why?

Mineral riches change an economy. First, they divert resources away from other industries, such as manufacturing and trade, that can be more beneficial to long-term growth. For example, the Asian tigers were resource-poor; their path to prosperity began with labor-intensive exports and progressed into more technology-intensive exports. The countries grew steadily richer in the process. Second, resource-rich economies become far more vulnerable to wild swings in the price of commodities. A country built on oil will have a rough stretch when the barrel price drops from $90 to $15. Meanwhile, demand for a nation's currency rises as the rest of the world begins to buy its diamonds or bauxite or oil or natural gas. That will cause the currency to appreciate, which, we now know, makes the country's other exports, such as manufactured goods, more expensive.

Economists started referring to the perverse effects of abundant natural resources as "Dutch disease" after observing the economic effects of an enormous North Sea natural gas discovery by the Netherlands in the 1950s. The spike in natural gas exports drove up the value of the Dutch guilder (as the rest of the world demanded more guilders in order to buy Dutch natural gas), making life more difficult for other exporters. The government also used the gas revenues to expand social spending, which raised employers' social security contributions and therefore their production costs. The Dutch had long been a nation of traders, with exports making up more than 50 percent of GDP. By the 1970s, other export industries, the traditional lifeblood of the economy, had grown far less competitive. One business publication noted, "Gas so distended and distorted the workings of the economy that it became a mixed blessing for a trading nation."[25]

Last, and perhaps most important, countries could use the revenues from natural resources to make themselves better off—but they don't. Money that might be spent on public investments with huge returns—education, public health, sanitation, immunizations, infrastructure—is more often squandered. After the World Bank helped to build an oil pipeline that originates in Chad and runs through Cameroon to the ocean, Chad's president, Idriss Déby, used the first $4.5 million installment of oil money to buy weapons for fighting rebels.[26]

Democracy. Does making the trains run on time matter more to the economic growth of poor countries than niceties like freedom of expression and political representation? No; the opposite is true. Democracy is a check against the most egregious economic policies, such as outright expropriation of wealth and property. Amartya Sen, a professor of economics and philosophy at Harvard, was awarded the Nobel Prize in Economics in 1998 for several strands of work related to poverty and welfare, one of which is his study of famines. Mr. Sen's major finding is striking: The world's worst famines are not caused by crop failure; they are caused by faulty political systems that prevent the market from correcting itself. Relatively minor agricultural disturbances become catastrophes because imports are not allowed, or prices are not allowed to rise, or farmers are not allowed to grow alternative crops, or politics in some other way interferes with the market's normal ability to correct itself. He writes, "[Famines] have never materialized in any country that is independent, that goes to elections regularly, that has opposition parties to voice criticisms and that permits newspapers to report freely and question the wisdom of government policies without extensive censorship."[27] China had the largest recorded famine in history; thirty million people died as the result of the failed Great Leap Forward in 1958–1961. India has not had a famine since independence in 1947.

Economist Robert Barro's seminal study of economic growth

in some one hundred countries over many decades found that basic democracy is associated with higher economic growth. More advanced democracies, however, suffer slightly lower rates of growth. Such a finding is consistent with our understanding of how interest groups can promote policies that are not always good for the economy as a whole.

War is bad. Now there is a real shocker. Still, the data on the proportion of extremely poor countries involved in armed conflict are strikingly high. Paul Collier, head of the Oxford Center for the Study of African Economies and author of the book *The Bottom Billion,* points out that nearly three-quarters of the world's billion poorest people are caught in a civil war or have recently been through one. It's hard to run a business or get an education in the midst of a war. (Obviously the causality runs in both directions: War devastates countries; nations in a shambles are more likely to collapse into civil war.) Once again, natural resources can make things worse by financing weapons and giving the factions something to fight over. (Collier coined the sadly clever phrase "Diamonds are a guerilla's best friend.")[28] The important point is that security is a prerequisite for most of the other things that have to happen for an economy to flourish. In 2004, *The Economist* published a story about the challenges of doing business in Somalia, a country that had been in the throes of civil war for thirteen years. The story noted, "There are two ways to run a business in Somalia. You can pay off the local warlord, not always the most trustworthy of chaps, and hope he will stop his militiamen from murdering your staff. Or you can tell him to get stuffed and hire your own militia."[29]

Woman power. Imagine two farmers, each with a thousand acres. One of them cultivates all of his land every year; the other leaves half of his land fallow, year after year. Who will grow more? It's not a trick question. The guy who uses all of his land can grow more. What does this have to do with women? Bill Gates made the connection when speaking about technological progress to an audience segregated by sex in Saudi Arabia. A *New York Times Magazine* article on the role of women in economic development recounts the incident:

> Four-fifths of the listeners were men, on the left. The remaining one-fifth were women, all covered in black cloaks and veils, on the right. A partition separated the two groups. Toward the end, in the question-and-answer session, a member of the audience noted that Saudi Arabia aimed to be one of the Top 10 countries in the world in technology by 2010 and asked if that was realistic. "Well, if you're not fully utilizing half the talent in the country," Gates said, "you're not going to get close to the Top 10."[30]

The Saudis shouldn't have been surprised. The Arab Human Development Report came to the same basic conclusion (in a lot more pages) several years earlier. In the 2002 report, several prominent Arab scholars sought to explain the paltry rate of growth in the twenty-two countries that make up the Arab League. Over the previous two decades, real per capita income growth had been a paltry 0.5 percent a year, lower than any place in the world except sub-Saharan Africa. One of the three key problems identified by the authors was "women's status." (The other two were a lack of political freedoms and a dearth of human capital.) *The Economist* reported on the findings: "One in every two Arab women still can neither read nor write. Their participation in their countries' political and economic life is the lowest in the world."[31] Investing in girls and women can be like planting the other half of that 1,000 acre field. There is another subtle (and mildly amusing) part of "women power." Women in the developing world (and maybe elsewhere) do smarter things with their money. As women get wealthier, they spend more money on the family's nutrition, medicine, and housing. When men get wealthier, they spend more money on alcohol and tobacco. Really. There was an elegant little experiment on this point in the Ivory Coast, where men and women traditionally grow different crops. In some years the men's cash crops are bountiful; in other years the women's cash crops do particularly well. MIT economist Esther Duflo found that when the men have a banner year, the household spends more on drinking and smoking; when the women rake in the cash, the household spends more on food.[32] Development officials have learned that if they give cash to the female head of household, it will do more good.

Experts could tick off many other things that matter in the development process: savings and investment rates, fertility rates, ethnic strife, colonial history, cultural factors, etc. All of which raises a question: If we have a decent idea of what constitutes good policy, why is the path out of poverty so steep and treacherous? The answer lies in the difference between describing why Tiger Woods is a great golfer and actually playing like him. It is one thing to explain what makes rich countries work; it is quite another to develop a strategy for transforming the developing world. Consider some simple examples: Building effective government institutions is easier when the population is literate and educated, yet decent public education requires effective government institutions. Public health is crucial, but it's hard to build health clinics when huge amounts of money are lost to corrupt officials. And so on.

There is a broad continuum of expert opinion on what, if anything, rich countries can do to improve life elsewhere in the world. Jeffrey Sachs anchors one end of that continuum. As you may have inferred from some of the research in this chapter, Sachs believes that impoverished nations are caught in poverty traps, and only capital from the developed world will rescue them. If we were to care and spend more in the developed world, we could jump-start the development process in poor countries—like getting a big boulder moving at the top of a hill. For example, Sachs argues that the world's rich countries should undertake a comprehensive program to fight AIDS in Africa. He reckons that America's share of such a program would cost about $10 a person—the price of a movie and popcorn.[33] So far, U.S. contributions to such efforts have been far smaller. Indeed, America's total foreign aid budget comes to one-tenth of 1 percent of GDP—a fraction of what we are capable of and a third of what the Europeans give. Mr. Sachs warned long before September 11 that we ought to invest in the developing world, "not only for humanitarian reasons, but also because even remote countries in turmoil become outposts of disorder for the rest of the world."[34]

William Easterly, whose work has also been cited extensively here, anchors the other end of that continuum. He believes that the whole development aid process is broken. His views are best encapsulated by an old joke about the failed development strategies that have gone in and out of favor over the past half century:

A peasant discovers that many of his chickens are dying, so he seeks advice from a priest. The priest recommends that the peasant say prayers for his chickens, but the chickens continue to die. The priest then recommends music for the chicken coop, but the deaths continue unabated. Pondering again, the priest recommends repainting the chicken coop in bright colors. Finally, all the chickens die. "What a shame," the priest tells the peasant, "I had so many more good ideas."[35]

Easterly should know. He spent decades working at the World Bank, where he was the guy trying to save the dying chickens. He argues in *The White Man's Burden* and other works that traditional aid projects are inflexible and ineffective. The results are miserable, both at the micro level (aid agencies hand out mosquito nets that end up getting used as fishing nets or wedding veils) and at the macro level (we can't show that what we're doing is making countries better off). Instead, we focus on inputs—how generous are we?—which he compares to evaluating a Hollywood movie by the size of its budget.

Easterly says that traditional development aid has been a mistake— because we still haven't figured out how to do it.[36] He writes in the *American Economic Review:*

Economists are reasonably confident that some combination of free markets and good institutions has an excellent historical track record of achieving development (as opposed to, say, totalitarian control of the economy by kleptocrats). It is just that we don't know how to get from here to there; which specific actions contribute to free markets and good institutions; how all the little pieces fit together. That is, we don't know how to achieve development.[37]

Easterly doesn't think we should give up trying to help people in poor countries. Instead, we should do small, context-sensitive projects with measurable benefits. He writes, "[Aid] could seek to create more opportunities for poor individuals, rather than try to transform poor societies."

To be fair, the primary stumbling block to development in poor countries is not bad advice from rich countries. The best ideas for economic growth are quite simple, yet, as this chapter has pointed out, there are plenty of leaders in the developing world doing the economic equivalent of smoking, eating cheeseburgers, and driving without their seat belts. A study done by the Harvard Center for International Development of global growth patterns between 1965 and 1990 found that most of the difference between the huge success of East Asia and the relatively poor performance of South Asia, sub-Saharan Africa, and Latin America can be explained by government policy. In that respect, foreign aid presents the same kind of challenges as any other welfare policy. Poor countries, like poor people, often have very bad habits. Providing support can prolong behavior that needs to be changed. One study came to the unsurprising conclusion that foreign aid has a positive effect on growth when good policies are already in place, and has little impact on growth when they are not. The authors recommended that aid be predicated on good policy, which would make the aid more effective and provide an incentive for governments to implement better policies.[38] (Similar criteria have been proposed for relieving the debts of heavily indebted poor countries.) Of course, turning our backs on the neediest cases (and denying bailouts to countries in crisis) is easier in theory than it is in practice. In 2005, the World Bank published a document that might qualify as bureaucratic introspection—*Economic Growth in the 1990s: Learning from a Decade of Reform*. Policymakers were a lot more confident that they knew how to fix the world in 1990 than they are today. Harvard development economist Dani Rodrik describes the tone of the report, which seems to incorporate William Easterly's skepticism without abandoning Jeffrey Sach's resolve: "There are no confident assertions here of what works and what doesn't—and no blueprints for policymakers to adopt. The emphasis is on the need for humility, for policy diversity, for selective and modest reforms, and for experimentation."[39]

Last, much of the world is poor because the rich countries have not tried very hard to make it otherwise. I realize that pointing out the failure of development aid and then arguing for more of it is like Yogi Berra criticizing a restaurant for having bad food *and* small portions. Still, things become better when there is an overwhelming political will to make them better. That is bigger than economics.

Epilogue
Life in 2050: Seven Questions

Economics can help us to understand and improve an imperfect world. In the end, though, it is just a set of tools. We must decide how to use them. Economics does not foreordain the future any more than the laws of physics made it inevitable that we would explore the moon. Physics made it possible; humans chose to do it—in large part by devoting resources that might have been spent elsewhere. John F. Kennedy did not alter the laws of physics when he declared that the United States would put a man on the moon; he merely set a goal that required good science to get there. Economics is no different. If we are to make the best use of these tools, we ought to think about where we are trying to go. We must decide what our priorities are, what trade-offs we are willing to make, what outcomes we are or are not willing to accept. To paraphrase economic historian and Nobel laureate Robert Fogel, we must first define the "good life" before economics can help us get there. Here are seven questions worth pondering about life in 2050, not for the sake of predicting the future, but because the decisions that we make now will affect how we live then.

How many minutes of work will a loaf of bread cost? It's the productivity question. From a material standpoint, it's pretty much all that matters. Nearly everything else we've discussed—institutions, property rights, investment, human capital—is a means toward this end (and other ends, too). If productivity grows at 1 percent a year over the next four decades, our standard of living will be some 50 percent higher by 2050. If productivity grows at 2 percent a year, then our standard of living will more than double in the same time frame—assuming we continue to work as hard as we do now. Indeed, that leads to a subquestion that I find more interesting: How rich is rich enough?

Americans are richer than most of the developed world; we also work harder, take less vacation, and retire later. Will that change? There is something in labor economics called the "backward-bending labor supply curve." Thankfully, the idea is simpler and more interesting than the name would suggest. Economic theory predicts that as our wages go up, we will work longer hours—up to a point, and then we will begin to work less. Time becomes more important than money. Economists just aren't quite sure where that curve starts to bend backward, or how sharply it bends.

Productivity growth gives us choices. We can continue to work the same amount while producing more. Or we can produce the same amount by working less. Or we can strike some balance. Assuming Americans continue to grow steadily more productive, will we choose to work sixty hours a week in 2050 and live richly (in a material sense) as a result? Or will there come a time when we decide to work twenty-five hours a week and listen to classical music in the park for the balance? I had dinner not long ago with a portfolio manager for a large investment company who is convinced that Americans are going to wake up one day and decide that they work too hard. Ironically, he was not planning to work less hard himself; he was planning to invest in companies that make leisure goods.

How many people will be sleeping under Wacker Drive? This is the pie-slicing question. In 2000, I was assigned by *The Economist* to write a story on poverty in America. With the economy still booming, I sought some way to express the striking dichotomy between America's rich and poor. I found it right outside the front door of my office building:

A stroll down Wacker Drive, in Chicago, offers an instant snapshot of America's surging economy. Young professionals stride along, barking orders into mobile phones. Shoppers stream towards the smart shops on Michigan Avenue. Construction cranes tower over a massive new luxury condominium building going up on the horizon. All is bustle, glitter and boom.

But there is a less glamorous side to Wacker Drive, literally below the surface. Lower Wacker is the subterranean service road that runs directly beneath its sophisticated sister, allowing delivery trucks to make their way through the bowels of the city. It is also a favourite refuge for the city's homeless, many of whom sleep in cardboard encampments between the cement props. They are out of sight of all that gleams above, and largely out of mind. As Wacker Drive, so America.[1]

What are we willing to promise the most disadvantaged? The market economies of the developed world lie along a continuum, with America at one end and the relatively paternalistic European economies, such as France and Sweden, at the other. Europe offers the kinder, gentler version of a market economy—at some cost. In general, the European nations are more protective of workers and have a more substantial safety net. Generous benefits are mandated by law; health care is a birthright. This leads to a more compassionate society in many ways. European poverty rates, particularly for children, are far lower than those in the United States. Income inequality is lower, too.

It also leads to higher unemployment and a slower rate of innovation and job creation. Workers, bundled with lots of mandatory benefits, are expensive. Since employees cannot be fired easily, firms are slow to hire them in the first place. Meanwhile, generous unemployment and welfare benefits make workers slower to take jobs that might be offered.

The result is what economists refer to as a "sclerotic" labor market. During normal economic times, European unemployment rates tend to be significantly higher than the American rate, particularly for youth.

The American system is a richer, more dynamic, more entrepreneurial economy—and harsher and more unequal. It is conducive to creating a big pie in which the winners get huge slices. The European system is better at guaranteeing at least some pie for everybody. Capitalism comes in all kinds of flavors. Which one will we choose?

Will we use the market in imaginative ways to solve social problems? The easiest and most effective way to get something done is to give the people involved a reason to want it done. We all nod, as if this were the most obvious point in the world—and then we go out and design policies that do just the opposite. We have an entire public school system that still does not really reward teachers and principals when their students do well (or punish them when their students do poorly). We talk about how important education is, but we make it difficult and time-consuming for smart people to become teachers (despite evidence that this training has little impact). We don't pay good teachers more than bad ones.

We make it artificially cheap to travel by car, implicitly subsidizing everything from urban sprawl to global warming. We assess most of our taxes on productive activity, like work, savings, and investment, when we might raise revenue and conserve resources with more "green taxes."

If we get the incentives right, we can use markets to do all kinds of things. Consider the case of rare diseases. However bad it is to have a serious illness, it is worse to have a serious illness that is also rare. At one point, there were some five thousand diseases considered so rare that drug companies ignored them because they had no hope of recovering their research costs even if they found a cure.[2] In 1983, Congress passed the Orphan Drug Act, which provided incentives to make such work more profitable: research grants, tax credits, and exclusive rights to market and price drugs for rare diseases—so-called orphan drugs—for seven years. In the decade before the act, fewer than ten orphan drugs came to market. Since the act, roughly two hundred such drugs have come to market.

Or something as simple as deposits for cans and bottles. Not surprisingly, recycling rates are much higher in states with deposits than in states without. There is also less trash and litter. And if landfill space is at a premium—which it is in most places—shouldn't we be paying to dispose of our household trash based on the volume we generate? What effect do you think that would have on the quantity of consumer packaging?

Markets don't solve social problems on their own (or else they wouldn't be social problems). But if we design solutions with the proper incentives, it feels a lot more like rowing downstream.

Will we have strip malls in 2050? Nothing says that we must accept what the market tosses us. *New York Times* columnist Anthony Lewis paid homage to the beauty of Italy's Tuscany and Umbria regions ("The silvery olive groves, the fields of sunflowers, the vineyards, the stone houses and barns") and lamented that such small farms are not economical in a world of corporate agriculture but says they should be preserved anyway. He wrote, "Italy is evidence that there is more to life—a civilized life—than the unregulated competition of the market. There are values of humanity, culture, beauty, community that may require deviations from the cold logic of market theory."[3] There is nothing in economics that says he's wrong. We may well collectively decide that we would like to protect a way of life, or something that is aesthetically pleasing, even if it means higher taxes, more expensive food, or less economic growth. To an economist, and to Mr. Lewis, life is about maximizing utility, not income. Sometimes utility means preserving an olive grove or an old vineyard—just because we like the way it looks. As we grow wealthier, we are often more willing to put aesthetics above the pocketbook. We may invest resources in rural America because it's important to our identity as a nation. We may subsidize small farms in Vermont because they're beautiful, not because it will make milk cheaper. And so on.

That point comes with several heavy doses of caution. First, we must always make explicit the costs of fiddling with markets, whatever those costs may be. How is the outcome different than it would have been, and who pays? Second, we should take care that these costs fall most heavily on those who enjoy the benefits. Last and most important, we should make sure that one group (such as those of us who think that strip malls are hideously ugly) does not use the political and regulatory process to impose its aesthetic preferences on another group (those who own strip malls and the people who enjoy the cheap and convenient shopping there). That said, there is nothing to stop us from dreaming of a world without strip malls.

Do we really have monetary policy figured out? I asked that question in the first edition of this book, back in 2002. Here is part of the answer: "The Japanese economy—that miracle of the 1980s—remains stubbornly resistant to traditional monetary and fiscal fixes, prompting what the Wall Street Journal has called 'one of the great economic debates of the age.'"[4] Could something similar happen here?

It did, beginning in 2007. That doesn't make me a genius (as I've also predicted that the Cubs will win the World Series on multiple occasions). It does prove that we have not conquered the business cycle (the economic ebb and flow that leads to periodic recessions). We thought we had it tamed, and then the financial crisis nearly took us right off the rails. These swings in the economy take a lot of innocent victims with them.

Ben Bernanke and the Fed seem to have done a lot of things right. What have they done wrong that we don't know about yet? Remember, Alan Greenspan was a genius (keeping inflation in check) until he wasn't anymore (because loose money fueled the asset bubbles).

There is a regulatory challenge as well. (The discussions have started, but we're not anywhere near a solution.) How do we manage the "systemic risk" in an interdependent financial system? The iron law of capitalism is that firms that fail should fail. We did that with Lehman Brothers and it nearly took all of us with them. The global financial system does not look like a textbook model where strong firms thrive in a crisis and weak firms fail; it's more like a group of mountain climbers tethered together on the edge of a precipice. How do we allow the market to punish wrongdoers without sending all of us spilling down the mountain?

In forty years, will "African tigers" refer to wildlife or to development success stories? Here is an exercise: Find a young child, say age eight or nine, and try to explain to him or her why much of the world lives comfortably, even luxuriously, while millions of people elsewhere on the planet are starving to death and billions more are barely getting by. At some point, the explanation just starts to feel inadequate. Clearly we do not have a silver bullet for economic development. We don't have one for cancer either, but we haven't given up. Will the world be significantly less poor in 2050? That answer is not obvious. We can imagine an East Asian scenario in which countries transform themselves in a matter of decades. Or we can imagine a sub-Saharan Africa scenario in which countries stumble from decade to decade without any significant economic growth at all. One scenario will lift billions of people out of poverty and misery; the other won't.

When we ask whether poor countries will still be poor four decades from now, the question seems distant and abstract, almost as if the answer will be determined by some future alignment of the stars. But when we break that question into its component parts—when we ask about the things that we know will distinguish rich countries from poor countries—then global poverty seems more tractable. Will governments in developing countries create and sustain the kinds of institutions that support a market economy? Will they develop export industries that enable them to break out of the trap of subsistence agriculture—and will the United States open its huge market to those products? Will the rich countries use their technology and resources to fight the diseases that are ravaging the developing world, especially AIDS? Will the family of a baby girl born tomorrow in rural India have an incentive to invest in her human capital?

Can America get its fiscal house back in order? The United States is the world's largest debtor. We owe Chinese bondholders more than a trillion dollars. We've had to borrow heavily to pay our bills for the past decade. The sobering part is that some of our most significant government expenses lie ahead as the Baby Boomers retire and begin to claim Social Security and Medicare. The "peace dividend" at the end of the Cold War lasted about 45 minutes, so we seem stuck with large defense budgets for the foreseeable future. Math is math; every reasonable calculation I've seen shows that our fiscal trajectory is unsustainable.

So what will we do about it? U.S. society has developed not merely an aversion to higher taxes, but a palpable hostility. That would be fine if we were willing to trim government to a size that we could fund. But we haven't done that either.

Think about what that means. Going forward, somehow we have to raise enough revenue to (1) pay for whatever government we choose to have, which we aren't doing fully now; (2) pay the interest we've accumulated on past bills; and (3) pay for the new expenses associated with an aging population and expensive entitlement promises.

That's going to require serious political leadership and recognition by Americans that the status quo is not an option. Simon Johnson, who had plenty of experience with financial crises as the former chief economist for the International Monetary Fund, has noted, "Overborrowing always ends badly, whether for an individual, a company, or a country."[5] During the first decade of the new millennium, three parties borrowed heavily: consumers, financial firms, and the U.S. government. So far, two have paid a huge price for that leverage. Is there another shoe to drop?

Those are just my questions. My hope is that by now you have more of your own. The remarkable thing about economics is that once you've been exposed to the big ideas, they begin to show up everywhere. The sad irony of Econ 101 is that students too often suffer through dull, esoteric lectures while economics is going on all around them. Economics offers insight into wealth, poverty, gender relations, the environment, discrimination, politics—just to name a few of the things we've touched upon. How could that possibly not be interesting?

Notes

Introduction

1. Thomas Friedman, "Senseless in Seattle," *New York Times*, December 1, 1999.
2. Claudia Goldin and Cecilia Rouse, "Orchestrating Impartiality: The Impact of 'Blind' Auditions on Female Musicians," *American Economic Review*, September 2000.
3. Charles Himmelberg, Christopher Mayer, and Todd Sinai, "Assessing High House Prices: Bubbles, Fundamentals and Misperceptions," *Journal of Economic Perspectives*, vol. 19, no. 4 (Fall 2005).
4. David Brooks, "An Economy of Faith and Trust," *New York Times*, January 16, 2009.

CHAPTER 1. THE POWER OF MARKETS

1. M. Douglas Ivester, Remarks to the Economic Club of Chicago, February 25, 1999.
2. Stephen Moore and Julian Simon, *The Greatest Century That Ever Was: 25 Miraculous Trends of the Past 100 Years*, Cato Institute Policy Analysis, No. 364 (Washington, D.C.: Cato Institute, December 15, 1999).
3. Cara Buckley, "A Man Down, a Train Arriving, and a Stranger Makes a Choice," *New York Times*, January 3, 2007.
4. Michael Grossman, "Health Economics," *NBER Reporter*, Winter 1998/99.
5. "America Then and Now: It's All in the Numbers," *New York Times*, December 31, 2000.

6. "Relieving O'Hare," *The Economist*, January 10, 1998.

7. June 21, 2001, p. A1.

8. David Kushner, "The Latest Way to Get Cocaine Out of Colombia? Underwater," *New York Times Sunday Magazine*, April 26, 2009.

9. Michael Cooper, "Transit Use Hit Five-Decade High in 2008 as Gas Prices Rose," *New York Times*, March 9, 2009.

10. Fernando A. Wilson, Jim Stimpson, and Peter E. Hilsenrath, "Gasoline Prices and Their Relationship to Rising Motorcycle Fatalities, 1990–2007," *American Journal of Public Health*, vol. 99, no. 10 (October 2009).

11. Jaime Sneider, "Good Propaganda, Bad Economics," *New York Times*, May 16, 2000, p. A31.

12. Richard H. Thaler and Cass R. Sunstein, *Nudge: Improving Decisions about Health, Wealth, and Happiness* (New Haven, Conn.: Yale University Press, 2008).

13. Press release from The Royal Swedish Academy of Sciences, October 9, 2002.

14. Jonathan Gruber, "Smoking's 'Internalities,'" *Regulation*, vol. 25, no. 4 (Winter 2002/2003).

15. Annamaria Lusardi, "The Importance of Financial Literacy," *NBER Reporter: Research Summary*, no. 2 (2009).

16. Thomas Gilovich, Robert Vallone, and Amos Tversky, "The Hot Hand in Basketball: On the Misperception of Random Sequences," *Cognitive Psychology* 17 (1985).

CHAPTER 2. INCENTIVES MATTER

1. Costa Rican Embassy, Washington, D.C.

2. Ian Fisher, "Victims of War: The Jungle Gorillas, and Tourism," *New York Times*, March 31, 1999.

3. Daniel Yergin and Joseph Stanislaw, *The Commanding Heights* (New York: Simon & Schuster, 1998), pp. 216–17.

4. "Paying Teachers More," *The Economist*, August 24, 2000.

5. David Stout, "Child Safety Seats to Be Required for Commercial Planes," *New York Times*, December 16, 1999, p. A20.

6. Julia Preston, "Mexico's Political Inversion: The City That Can't Fix the Air," *New York Times*, February 4, 1996, Sect. 4, p. 4.

7. Ibid.; Lucas W. Davis, "The Effect of Driving Restrictions on Air Quality in Mexico City," *Journal of Political Economy*, vol. 116, no. 1 (February 2008).

8. "Avoiding Gridlock," *The Economist*, February 17, 2003.

9. "Ken's Coup," *The Economist*, March 20, 2003.

10. "How to Pay Bosses," *The Economist*, November 16, 2002.

11. Floyd Norris, "Stock Options: Do They Make Bosses Cheat?" *New York Times*, August 5, 2005.

12. Simon Johnson, "The Quiet Coup," *The Atlantic*, May 2009.

13. John Tierney, "A Tale of Two Fisheries," *New York Times Magazine*, August 27, 2000, p. 38.

14. "A Rising Tide," *The Economist*, September 20, 2008.

15. Dirk Johnson, "Leaving the Farm for the Other Real World," *New York Times*, November 7, 1999, p. 3.

16. Virginia Postrel, "The U.S. Tax System Is Discouraging Married Women from Working," *New York Times*, November 2, 2000, p. C2.

17. Friedrich Schneider and Dominik H. Enste, "Shadow Economies: Size, Causes, and Consequences," *Journal of Economic Literature*, March 2000.

CHAPTER 3. GOVERNMENT AND THE ECONOMY

1. Donald G. McNeil, Jr., "A Fouled City Puts Its Foot Down, but Carefully," *New York Times*, November 9, 1999.

2. "Mum's the Word," *The Economist*, December 5, 1998.

3. "Czechs Puff Away to the Benefit of State Coffers," United Press International, July 17, 2001.

4. Robert Frank, "Feeling Crash-Resistant in an SUV," *New York Times*, May 16, 2000.

5. Katharine Q. Seelye, "Utility Buys Town It Choked, Lock, Stock and Blue Plume," *New York Times*, May 13, 2002.

6. "Here's Hoping: A Survey of Nigeria," *The Economist*, January 15, 2000.

7. Blaine Harden, "Angolan Paradox: Oil Wealth Only Adds to Misery," *New York Times*, April 9, 2000.

8. Barbara Crossette, "U.N. Says Bad Government Is Often the Cause of Poverty," *New York Times*, April 5, 2000, p. A11.

9. John G. Fernald, "Roads to Prosperity? Assessing the Link Between Public Capital and Productivity," *American Economics Review*, vol. 89, no. 3 (June 1999), pp. 619–38.

10. Jerry L. Jordan, "How to Keep Growing 'New Economies,'" *Economic Commentary*, Federal Reserve Bank of Cleveland, August 15, 2000.

11. Barry Bearak, "In India, the Wheels of Justice Hardly Move," *New York Times*, June 1, 2000.

12. Thomas L. Friedman, "I Love D.C.," *New York Times*, November 7, 2000, p. A29.

13. Amartya Sen, *Development as Freedom* (New York: Alfred A. Knopf, 1999).

14. Giacomo Balbinotto Neto, Ana Katarina Campelo, and Everton Nunes

da Silva, "The Impact of Presumed Consent Law on Organ Donation: An Empirical Analysis from Quantile Regression for Longitudinal Data," Berkeley Program in Law & Economics, Paper 050107–2 (2007).

CHAPTER 4. GOVERNMENT AND THE ECONOMY II

1. John Markoff, "CIA Tries Foray into Capitalism," *New York Times*, September 29, 1999.
2. March 6, 2001.
3. Jackie Calmes and Louise Story, "In Washington, One Bank Chief Still Holds Sway," *New York Times*, January 19, 2009.
4. Milton Friedman, *Capitalism and Freedom* (Chicago: University of Chicago Press, 1982).
5. Celia W. Dugger, "A Cruel Choice in New Delhi: Jobs vs. a Safer Environment," *New York Times*, November 24, 2000.
6. "A Useful Poison," *The Economist*, December 14, 2000.
7. "Fighting Malaria," *The Economist*, May 1, 2003.
8. "A Useful Poison," *The Economist*, December 14, 2000.
9. Gary Becker and Guity Nashat Becker, *The Economics of Life* (New York: McGraw-Hill, 1996).
10. Simeon Djankov, Rafael La Porta, Florencio Lopez-de-Silanes, and Andrei Shleifer, *The Regulation of Entry*, NBER Working Paper No. W7892 (National Bureau of Economic Research, September 2000).
11. Geeta Anand, "India's Colleges Battle a Thicket of Red Tape," *Wall Street Journal*, November 13, 2008.
12. Stephen Castle, "Europe Relaxes Rules on Sale of Ugly Fruits and Vegetables," *New York Times*, November 13, 2008.
13. Nicholas Lemann, "The Quiet Man: How Dick Cheney Rose to Power," *The New Yorker*, May 7, 2001.
14. Bruce Bartlett, "How Supply-Side Economics Trickled Down," *New York Times*, April 6, 2007.
15. Greg Mankiw's blog, March 11, 2007.
16. Rebecca M. Blank, "Fighting Poverty: Lessons from Recent U.S. History," *Journal of Economic Perspectives*, vol. 14, no. 2 (Spring 2000).
17. Jerry L. Jordan, "How to Keep Growing 'New Economies,'" *Economic Commentary*, Federal Reserve Bank of Cleveland, August 15, 2000.

CHAPTER 5. ECONOMICS OF INFORMATION

1. Gary Becker, *The Economics of Discrimination* (Chicago: University of Chicago Press, 1971).

2. Harry Holzer, Steven Raphael, and Michael Stoll, "Perceived Criminality, Criminal Background Checks, and the Racial Hiring Practices of Employers," *Journal of Law and Economics*, vol. XLIX (October 2006).
3. David Leonhardt, "In Health Reform, a Cancer Offers an Acid Test," *New York Times*, July 8, 2009.
4. "Testing Times," *The Economist*, October 19, 2000.
5. "Outsourcing: Separate and Lift," *The Economist*, September 20, 1997.
6. Geoffrey A. Fowler, "Kind of Blue: In Asia, Elite Offices Show Off with Icy Temperatures," *Wall Street Journal*, August 24, 2005.
7. Alan B. Krueger, "Children Smart Enough to Get into Elite Schools May Not Need to Bother," *New York Times*, April 27, 2000, p. C2.
8. All of the racial profiling examples come from a provocative article on the subject: Jeffrey Goldberg, "The Color of Suspicion," *New York Times Magazine*, June 20, 1999.

CHAPTER 6. PRODUCTIVITY AND HUMAN CAPITAL

1. Brier Dudley, "Gates Wants to Expand Mega-House," *Seattle Times*, February 28, 2001.
2. "The Rich Get Richer: A Survey of India's Economy," *The Economist*, June 2, 2001.
3. Evelyn Nieves, "Homeless Defy Cities' Drives to Move Them," *New York Times*, December 7, 1999.
4. "From Boots to Electronics: Shutting Military Bases," *The Economist*, June 21, 1997.
5. T. Paul Schultz, "Health and Schooling Investments in Africa," *Journal of Economic Perspectives*, vol. 13, no. 3 (Summer 1999), pp. 67–88.
6. Gary Becker, "Economic Evidence on the Value of Education," Remarks to executives of the Lotus Development Corporation, January 1999.
7. Gary S. Becker, Ryerson Lecture at the University of Chicago, as reprinted in Becker, *Human Capital* (Chicago: University of Chicago Press, 1993), p. 21.
8. Ibid., p. 23.
9. Roger Lowenstein, "The Inequality Conundrum," *New York Times Sunday Magazine*, June 10, 2007.
10. Dora Costa, "The Wage and the Length of the Work Day: From the 1890s to 1991," *Journal of Labor Economics*, January 2000.
11. All of the income inequality information, including the H. L. Mencken quotations, comes from Robert H. Frank, "Why Living in a Rich Society Makes Us Feel Poor," *New York Times Magazine*, October 15, 2000.

12. Philippe Aghion, Eve Caroli, and Cecilia Garcia-Penalosa, "Inequality and Economic Growth: The Perspective of the New Growth Theories," *Journal of Economic Literature*, vol. 37 (December 1999), pp. 1615–60.

13. Marvin Zonis, Remarks Presented at the University of Chicago Business Forecast Luncheon, December 6, 2000.

CHAPTER 7. FINANCIAL MARKETS

1. Johanna Berkman, "Harvard's Hoard," *New York Times Magazine*, June 24, 2001.

2. Richard Bradley, "Drew Gilpin Faust and the Incredible Shrinking Harvard," *Boston Magazine*, June 18, 2009.

3. "For Those in Peril," *The Economist*, April 22, 2006.

4. Darren Rovell, Sports Biz, CNBC, September 15, 2009.

5. Joseph Treaster, "Even Nature Can Be Turned into a Security; High Yield and Big Risk with Catastrophe Bonds," *New York Times*, August 6, 1997.

6. Simon Johnson, "The Quiet Coup," *The Atlantic*, May 2009.

7. Jane Spencer, "Lessons from the Brain-Damaged Investor," *Wall Street Journal*, July 21, 2005.

8. Peter Coy, "Can You Really Beat the Market?" *Business Week*, May 31, 1999.

9. Burton G. Malkiel, "The Price Is (Usually) Right," *Wall Street Journal*, June 10, 2009.

10. Jon E. Hilsenrath, "As Two Economists Debate Markets, the Tide Shifts," *Wall Street Journal*, October 18, 2004.

11. Ruth Simon, "Bonds Let You Sleep at Night but at a Price," *Wall Street Journal*, September 8, 1998.

12. Matthew Kaminski, "The Age of Diminishing Endowments," *Wall Street Journal*, June 6–7, 2009.

CHAPTER 8. THE POWER OF ORGANIZED INTERESTS

1. Robert Davis, "Museum Garage Is a Fine Cut; It May Be Pork, but City Hungry," *Chicago Tribune*, May 5, 1994.

2. Jason Hill, Erik Nelson, David Tilman, Stephen Polasky, and Douglas Tiffany, "Environmental, Economic, and Energetic Costs and Benefits of Biodiesel and Ethanol Biofuels," *Proceedings of the National Academy of Sciences*, vol. 103, no. 30 (July 25, 2006).

3. Nicholas Kristof, "Ethanol, for All Its Critics, Fuels Farmer Support and Iowa's Role in Presidential Races," *New York Times*, January 21, 2000.

4. Robert Gordon, Thomas Kane, and Douglas O. Staiger, "Identifying Effective Teachers Using Performance on the Job," The Hamilton Project Policy Brief No. 2006–01, April 2006.
5. Roger Ferguson, Jr., "Economic Policy for Our Era: The Ohio Experience," *Economic Commentary*, Federal Reserve Bank of Cleveland, May 15, 2000.
6. Joe Klein, "Eight Years: Bill Clinton Looks Back on His Presidency," *The New Yorker*, October 16, 2000, p. 201.
7. Elizabeth Kolbert, "Back to School," *The New Yorker*, March 5, 2001.

CHAPTER 9. KEEPING SCORE

1. Michael Cox and Richard Alm, *Time Well Spent: The Declining Real Cost of Living in America*, Federal Reserve Bank of Dallas, 1997 Annual Report.
2. Oded Galor and David N. Weil, "Population, Technology, and Growth: From Malthusian Stagnation to the Demographic Transition and Beyond," *American Economic Review*, vol. 20, no. 4 (September 2000).
3. Miriam Jordan, "Leprosy Remains a Foe in Country Winning the Fight Against AIDS," *Wall Street Journal*, August 20, 2001.
4. Jane Spencer, "Why Beijing Is Trying to Tally the Hidden Costs of Pollution as China's Economy Booms," *Wall Street Journal*, October 2, 2006.
5. David Leonhardt, "If Richer Isn't Happier, What Is?" *New York Times*, May 19, 2001.
6. Daniel Kahneman, Alan B. Krueger, David Schkade, Norbert Schwarz, and Arthur Stone, "Toward National Well-Being Accounts," *American Economic Review*, vol. 94, no. 2 (May 2004).
7. "Economics Discovers Its Feelings," *The Economist*, December 23, 2006.
8. Alexander Stille, "A Happiness Index with a Long Reach: Beyond GNP to Subtler Measures," *New York Times*, May 20, 2000, p. A17.
9. Edward Hadas and Richard Beales, "Sarkozy Imagines: No GDP," *Wall Street Journal*, January 10, 2008; David Jolly, "G.D.P. Seen as Inadequate Measure of Economic Health," *New York Times*, September 15, 2009.
10. David Gonzalez, "A Coffee Crisis' Devastating Domino Effect in Nicaragua," *New York Times*, August 29, 2001.
11. Christina D. Romer, "Back from the Brink," speech delivered at the Federal Reserve Bank of Chicago, September 24, 2009.
12. James B. Stewart, "Eight Days: The Battle to Save the American Financial System," *The New Yorker*, September 21, 2009.
13. Rebecca Kern, "Girl Scout Cookie Sales Crumble," *USA Today*, February 20, 2009.

14. "Hard Times," *The Economist*, September 10, 2009.
15. Christina D. Romer, "The Economic Crisis: Causes, Policies, and Outlook," testimony before the Joint Economic Committee, April 30, 2009.
16. Bruce Bartlett, "What Tax Cuts Can't Do," *New York Times*, December 20, 2000.
17. Romer, Chicago Federal Reserve speech.
18. Jagadeesh Gokhale, "Are We Saving Enough?" *Economic Commentary*, Federal Reserve Bank of Cleveland, July 2000.
19. "What a Peculiar Cycle," *The Economist*, March 10, 2001.
20. James W. Paulsen, *Economic and Market Perspective*, Wells Capital Management, October 1999.

CHAPTER 10. THE FEDERAL RESERVE

1. R. A. Mundell, "A Reconsideration of the Twentieth Century," *American Economic Review*, vol. 90, no. 3 (June 2000), pp. 327–40.
2. Justin Scheck, "Mackerel Economics in Prison Leads to Appreciation for Oily Filets," *Wall Street Journal*, October 2, 2008.
3. David Berreby, "All About Currency Printers: The Companies That Make Money from Making Money," *New York Times*, August 23, 1992.
4. Paul Krugman, "Fear Itself," *New York Times Magazine*, September 30, 2001.
5. Stephanie Strom, "Deflation Shackles Japan, Blocking Hope of Recovery," *New York Times*, March 12, 2001.
6. N. Gregory Mankiw, *Principles of Economics* (Fort Worth, Tex.: Dryden Press, 1998), p. 606.
7. Stephen G. Cecchetti, "Crisis and Responses: The Federal Reserve in the Early Stages of the Financial Crisis," *Journal of Economic Perspectives*, vol. 23, no. 1 (Winter 2009).
8. "The Very Model of a Central Banker," *The Economist*, August 27, 2009.

CHAPTER 11. INTERNATIONAL ECONOMICS

1. Thomas Jaffe and Dyan Machan, "How the Market Overwhelmed the Central Banks," *Forbes*, November 9, 1992.
2. Anatole Kaletsky, "How Mr. Soros Made a Billion by Betting Against the Pound," *The Times of London*, October 26, 1992
3. "Big Mac Currencies," *The Economist*, April 25, 2002.
4. Sylvia Nasar, "Weak Dollar Makes U.S. World's Bargain Bazaar," *New York Times*, September 28, 1992.
5. Ian Rowley, "Why Japan Hasn't Stopped the Yen's Rise," *Business Week* (online), January 15, 2009.

6. Paul Krugman, "Misguided Monetary Mentalities," *New York Times*, October 12, 2009.
7. Maurice Obstfeld and Kenneth Rogoff, "The Mirage of Fixed Exchange Rates," National Bureau of Economic Research Working Paper W5191, July 1995.
8. Anthony Ramirez, "Pepsi Will Be Bartered for Ships and Vodka in Deal With Soviets," *New York Times*, April 9, 1990.
9. Peter Gumble, "Iceland: The Country That Became a Hedge Fund," CNN Money.com, December 4, 2008.
10. "Cracks in the Crust," *The Economist*, December 11, 2008.
11. Associated Press, as reported by Yahoo! Finance. "Iceland Says Goodbye to the Big Mac," October 26, 2009.
12. "No Pain, No Gain," *The Economist*, December 13, 2003.
13. James Fallows, "The $1.4 Trillion Question," *The Atlantic*, January/February 2008.
14. Ibid.
15. "Reforming the Sisters," *The Economist*, February 17, 2001.
16. Ibid.

CHAPTER 12. TRADE AND GLOBALIZATION

1. Paul Krugman, "The Magic Mountain," *New York Times*, January 23, 2001.
2. Charles Wheelan, "Fast Food, Balinese Style," *Valley News*, January 25, 1989, p. 18.
3. "The Battle in Seattle," *The Economist*, November 27, 1999.
4. "Economic Nationalism: Bashing Foreigners in Iowa," *The Economist*, September 21, 1991.
5. Mary E. Burfisher, Sherman Robinson, and Karen Thierfelder, "The Impact of NAFTA on the United States," *Journal of Economic Perspectives*, vol. 15, no. 1 (Winter 2001).
6. Dan Barry, "A Mill Closes, and a Hamlet Fades to Black," *New York Times*, February 16, 2001.
7. Marvin Zonis, "Globalization," *National Strategy Forum Review: Strategic Outlook 2001*, National Strategy Forum, Spring 2001.
8. Kenneth F. Scheve and Matthew J. Slaughter, "A New Deal for Globalization," *Foreign Affairs*, July/August 2007.
9. David Cortright and George A. Lopez, eds., *The Sanctions Decade: Assessing UN Strategies in the 1990s* (Boulder, Colo.: Lynne Rienner, 2000).
10. Anthony DePalma and Simon Romero, "Orange Juice Tariff Hinders Trade Pact for U.S. and Brazil," *New York Times*, April 24, 2000, p. A1.

11. "UN Chief Blames Rich Nations for Failure of Trade Talks," *New York Times*, February 13, 2000, p. 12.
12. Thomas Friedman, "Protesting for Whom?" *New York Times*, April 24, 2001.
13. Nicholas D. Kristof and Sheryl WuDunn, "Two Cheers for Sweatshops," *New York Times Magazine*, September 24, 2000, pp. 70–71.
14. Thomas Friedman, "Parsing the Protests," *New York Times*, April 14, 2000, p. 31.
15. Zonis, "Globalization."
16. "Web Sites Provide Opportunity for Artisans Around the World to Sell Their Wares Thus Increasing Living Standards," National Public Radio, September 11, 2000.
17. Kristof and WuDunn, "Two Cheers for Sweatshops."
18. "A Survey of Globalization," *The Economist*, September 29, 2001.
19. Kristof and WuDunn, "Two Cheers for Sweatshops."
20. Paul Krugman, "Hearts and Heads," *New York Times*, April 22, 2001.
21. "Economic Man, Cleaner Planet," *The Economist*, September 29, 2001.
22. Krugman, "Hearts and Heads."
23. John Micklethwait and Adrian Wooldridge, "Why the Globalization Backlash Is Stupid," *Foreign Policy*, September/October 2001.

CHAPTER 13. DEVELOPMENT ECONOMICS

1. "No Title," *The Economist*, March 31, 2001.
2. *World Development Report 2008*, World Bank (New York: Oxford University Press, 2000).
3. William Easterly, *The Elusive Quest for Growth* (Cambridge, Mass.: MIT Press, 2001), p. 285.
4. *World Development Report 2002: Building Institutions for Markets*, World Bank, Oxford University Press, p. 3.
5. Thomas L. Friedman, "I Love D.C.," *New York Times*, November 7, 2000, p. A29.
6. Daron Acemoglu, Simon Johnson, and James Robinson, *The Colonial Origins of Comparative Development: An Empirical Investigation*, NBER Working Paper No. W7771 (National Bureau of Economic Research, June 2000).
7. Daniel Kaufmann, Aart Kraay, and Pablo Zoido-Lobatón, *Governance Matters* (Washington, D.C.: World Bank, October 1999).
8. "No Title," *The Economist*, March 31, 2001.
9. Erica Field, "Entitled to Work: Urban Property Rights and Labor Supply in Peru," undated manuscript.

10. "A Coke and a Frown," *The Economist*, October 7, 2000, p. 73.
11. "No Title," *The Economist*, March 31, 2001.
12. Gary S. Becker, *Human Capital*, p. 24.
13. Easterly, *The Elusive Quest for Growth*, p. 160.
14. "Fare Thee Well, Iowa," *The Economist*, August 18, 2001.
15. Jeffrey Sachs, *Tropical Underdevelopment*, NBER Working Paper No. W8119 (National Bureau of Economic Research, February 2001).
16. Donald G. McNeil, "Drug Companies and Third World: A Case Study in Neglect," *New York Times*, May 21, 2000.
17. Rachel Glennerster and Michael Kremer, "A Better Way to Spur Medical Research and Development," *Regulation*, vol. 23, no. 2.
18. Jeffrey Sachs, "Nature, Nurture, and Growth," *The Economist*, June 14, 1997.
19. Jeffrey Sachs, "Growth in Africa: It Can Be Done," *The Economist*, June 29, 1996.
20. Jeffrey A. Frankel and David Romer, "Does Trade Cause Growth?" *American Economic Review*, vol. 89, no. 3 (June 1999), pp. 379–99.
21. Sachs, "Growth in Africa."
22. Jeffrey D. Sachs and Andrew M. Warner, "The Big Push: Natural Resource Booms and Growth," *Journal of Development Economics*, June 1999, as cited in *Economic Intuition*, Montreal, Fall 1999.
23. "Tracking Angola's Oil Money," *The Economist*, January 15, 2000, p. 48.
24. Blaine Harden, "Angolan Paradox: Oil Wealth Only Adds to Misery," *New York Times*, April 9, 2000.
25. "Open to the Winds: A Nation of Traders," *The Economist*, September 12, 1987.
26. Norimitsu Onishi and Neela Banerjee, "Chad's Wait for Its Oil Riches May Be Long," *New York Times*, May 16, 2001.
27. Amartya Sen, *Development as Freedom* (New York: Alfred A. Knopf, 1999), p. 152.
28. Paul Collier, *The Bottom Billion: Why the Poorest Countries Are Failing and What Can Be Done About It* (New York: Oxford University Press), 2007.
29. "Coka and Al-Qaeda," *The Economist*, April 3, 2004.
30. Nicholas D. Kristof and Sheryl WuDunn, "The Women's Crusade," *New York Times Magazine*, August 23, 2009.
31. "Self-Doomed to Failure," *The Economist*, July 6, 2002.
32. Kristof and WuDunn, "The Women's Crusade."
33. Jeffrey Sachs, "The Best Possible Investment in Africa," *New York Times*, February 10, 2001.
34. "What's Good for the Poor Is Good for America," *The Economist*, July 14, 2001.

35. Jeffrey Sachs, "Growth in Africa: It Can Be Done," *The Economist*, June 29, 1996.

36. William Easterly, *The White Man's Burden* (New York: Penguin, 2007).

37. William Easterly, "Was Development Assistance a Mistake," *American Economic Review*, vol. 97, no. 2 (May 2007).

38. Craig Burnside and David Dollar, "Aid, Policies, and Growth," *American Economic Review*, vol. 90, no. 4 (September 2000), pp. 847–68.

39. Dani Rodrik, "Goodbye Washington Consensus, Hello Washington Confusion? A Review of the World Bank's *Economic Growth in the 1990s: Learning from a Decade of Reform*," *Journal of Economic Literature*, vol. XLIV (December 2006).

EPILOGUE. LIFE IN 2050

1. "Out of Sight, Out of Mind," *The Economist*, May 18, 2001.

2. Denise Grady, "In Quest to Cure Rare Diseases, Some Get Left Out," *New York Times*, November 16, 1999.

3. Anthony Lewis, "A Civilized Society," *New York Times*, September 8, 2001.

4. Phred Dvorak, "A Puzzle for Japan: Rock-Bottom Rates, but Few Borrowers," *Wall Street Journal*, October 25, 2001.

5. Simon Johnson, "The Quiet Coup," *The Atlantic*, May 2009.

Index